Water Security in the Middle East

ANTHEM WATER DIPLOMACY SERIES

More effective resolution of our increasingly complex, boundary-crossing water problems demands integration of scientific knowledge of water in both natural and human systems along with the politics of real-world problem solving. Water professionals struggle to translate ideas that emerge from science and technology into the messy context of the real world. We need to find more effective ways to bridge the divide between theory and practice and resolve complex water management problems when natural, societal and political elements cross multiple sectors and interact in unpredictable ways. The **Anthem Water Diplomacy Series** is a step in that direction. Contributions in this series diagnose water governance and management problems, identify intervention points and possible policy changes, and propose sustainable solutions that are sensitive to diverse viewpoints as well as conflicting values, ambiguities and uncertainties.

Series Editor

Shafiqul Islam – Tufts University, USA

Editorial Board

Water Security in the Middle East

Essays in Scientific and Social Cooperation

Edited by Jean Axelrad Cahan

ANTHEM PRESS

Anthem Press
An imprint of Wimbledon Publishing Company
www.anthempress.com

This edition first published in UK and USA 2020
by ANTHEM PRESS
75–76 Blackfriars Road, London SE1 8HA, UK
or PO Box 9779, London SW19 7ZG, UK
and
244 Madison Ave #116, New York, NY 10016, USA

First published in the UK and USA by Anthem Press 2017

© 2020 Jean Axelrad Cahan editorial matter and selection;
individual chapters © individual contributors

The moral right of the authors has been asserted.

British Library Cataloguing-in-Publication Data
A catalogue record for this book is available from the British Library.

Library of Congress Cataloging-in-Publication Data
Library of Congress Control Number: 2020930707

ISBN-13: 978-1-78527-254-7 (Pbk)
ISBN-10: 1-78527-254-3 (Pbk)

This title is also available as an e-book.

CONTENTS

ILLUSTRATIONS

Figures

Tables

ACKNOWLEDGMENTS

The Ruth Kroon Fund, under the auspices of the Norman and Bernice Harris Center for Judaic Studies, and the Robert B. Daugherty Water for Food Global Institute at the University of Nebraska provided generous support for the symposium associated with this volume. Dr. Adam R. Thompson, assistant director of the Kutak Center for Applied Ethics at University of Nebraska, contributed valuable research assistance.

ACKNOWLEDGMENTS

FOREWORD

The importance of water and food security in the Middle East, the most water-short region in the world and one where food supplies are often impacted by drought, cannot be overstated. A significant proportion of the population of this region is both food insecure and water insecure—without access to enough safe and nutritious food nor an acceptable quantity and quality of water to lead healthy and active lives—and exposed to frequent droughts. Ensuring sustainable food and water security for the people of this region in the face of rising population and income, a changing climate, and growing demands for scarce water resources amid falling groundwater tables and increasing water pollution and salinization is one of the region's most urgent challenges, with significant political, environmental, social and economic implications. Indeed, prospects for peace and security in the Middle East depend to a very significant degree on water and food security.

This water and food challenge is exacerbated by and intertwined with the civil war in Syria and related conflicts and civil unrest in many other countries in the area. While not everyone agrees that water shortages and inadequate responses to a severe and long-lasting drought were among the root causes of the outbreak of the civil war in Syria, there is little doubt that the large numbers of refugees in neighboring countries have strained limited water supplies. The water and food security situations of the various countries of the region are further linked because so many countries depend on surface and underground water resources that cross international borders. Few countries in the region can fully control their water resources without engaging in cooperative approaches with other countries, which is fraught with difficulties in a region wracked by war and unrest. A major question in the region is therefore whether the quest for water and food security going forward will advance efforts toward cooperation and peace building or lead to further competition and conflict. While some observers have talked gloomily about the prospects for "water wars," several scholars have argued persuasively that water is more often a mechanism for bringing people together to forge common solutions than a cause of war or violence.

This message is reinforced by *Water Security in the Middle East: Essays in Scientific and Social Cooperation*, and is one reason why it is exceptionally timely. The book arose out of a symposium on water in the Middle East jointly organized and sponsored by the University of Nebraska Norman and Bernice Harris Center for Judaic Studies and the Global Studies Program as well as the Robert B. Daugherty Water for Food Institute at the University of Nebraska in May 2014. The event brought together leading scholars and practitioners in water rights, conflict resolution and environmental studies in the region to discuss how water security in the Middle East will affect political and cultural discourse in the future. The event, organized by Jean Cahan, then director of the Harris Center, and Patrice C. McMahon, associate professor in University of Nebraska's Department of Political Science, aimed to raise awareness that water insecurity can exacerbate political and cultural tensions and to foster discussion on these issues among natural scientists and scholars from the humanities and social sciences.

Water Security in the Middle East is an important addition to the literature for at least three reasons. First, the book's contributors include some of the world's most knowledgeable scholars and practitioners on water in the Middle East, who know firsthand the scientific and technical dimensions of water security in the region as well as the broader issues of water diplomacy, public policy and politics. Second, the volume brings together in one place several thoughtful essays on a range of highly relevant subjects, including cooperation on transboundary systems in intractable conflicts, water demand management, climate change along transboundary basins and the role of adaptive management and technology, to name just a few. And third, the book explicitly seeks to incorporate a range of disciplinary perspectives from the physical and natural sciences as well as from philosophy, anthropology, religious studies, history, political science, sociology and economics. In so doing, the book provides a comprehensive understanding of the linkages between water and other social, political and philosophical issues.

By advancing understanding of water and food security issues in this critically important region from a multidisciplinary perspective, the book is also a significant contribution to the mission of the Water for Food Institute, where Jean Cahan and Patrice C. McMahon are faculty fellows. The institute was established in 2010 to bring the University of Nebraska's interdisciplinary expertise to address the challenges of improving water and food security across the globe. Working with and through faculty fellows like Cahan and McMahon and a global network of partners, the institute's mission is to have a lasting and significant impact on food and water security through research, engagement, communication and education programs.

Roberto L. Lenton
Founding Executive Director
Robert B. Daugherty Water for Food Global Institute at the University of Nebraska

Introduction

WATER SECURITY IN THE MIDDLE EAST: A ROLE FOR THE SOCIAL SCIENCES AND HUMANITIES

Jean Axelrad Cahan

This volume is based on papers presented at a small conference, "Water Security and Peacebuilding in the Middle East: Avenues for Cooperation," held at the University of Nebraska in May 2014. The meeting brought together leading researchers in the multidimensional problem of water security and related public policy issues. Since our focus was on the Middle East, the scholars invited were specialists in areas ranging from Ethiopia, to Israel and Palestine, to Iraq and the Gulf States. While generally aiming to underscore the efficacy of international water agreements, institutional mechanisms designed to implement them and scientific and technological advances that could be "game changers," the contributors nonetheless pointed to significant obstacles to cooperation and peace building. As the chapters that follow indicate, the authors are aware of the problems created by great inequalities of economic, political and military power throughout the region. And they share my view that a widened intellectual and disciplinary perspective is essential if wide and long-term shifts in attitudes toward water security are to be achieved.

The Need for a Broad Approach

In the famous opening to his work *Negative Dialectics* (1966), one of the foremost Western philosophers of the post–World War II era, Theodor Adorno, declared, "Philosophy, which once seemed obsolete, lives on, because the moment to realize it was missed" (Adorno, 2007, 3). By this statement he wanted to convey that, during the greatest political and human crises of the twentieth century, philosophers (among others) failed to concretize philosophy's most significant ideas regarding freedom and human possibility.

It may not be an exaggeration to say that philosophy and the humanities in general are faced with almost equally great challenges today. We are presently trapped in seemingly irreversible vectors of degradation of the planet's nonrenewable as well as renewable resources; vast economic and social inequalities; increasing urban populations and resultant economic and political pressures; and ideological and ethnic conflicts worldwide. Inadequacy and instability of water supplies worldwide must be numbered among these increasingly difficult circumstances, whether water insecurity is potentially a direct cause of armed conflict, as many have argued, or "merely" an exacerbating factor (Chellaney 2013; Wolf 1995; Abukhater 2013). And although some may hold that water security is mainly a matter for scientific experts and government leaders, I believe there is an urgent need for academics of all philosophical and political persuasions to engage with both the topic and the public. Fresh perspectives in hydrodiplomacy and hydropolitic are needed if there are to be changes in attitudes and preferences on the part of the public and civil society, to increase or even create cooperation and to lessen competition and conflict. In a matter of vital concern to every human being and every community, at the local as well as the national and international levels, the work of natural scientists, technologists, public policy makers and other experts should be understood and carried out within a larger civic and intellectual context. Not only philosophy but also the other humanities—anthropology, history, classical and religious studies—and the social sciences—political science, sociology and economics—should be brought to bear in academic discussions as well as public decision-making. This was one of the initial motivations of the present volume. Governments eventually respond to changing public attitudes, and scientists, too, are often concerned with identifying the public interest in and ramifications of their work. Ultimately, their research funding is affected by public attitudes, for better or for worse.

Progress toward Cooperation

In addition to the aim of broadening the horizon under which water-security issues are studied, a second aim of the conference was to explore further the possibilities for transboundary forms of cooperation on water security.

On the international level, political scientists, legal scholars and water-security experts of various kinds have examined some successes in managing transboundary water issues, notably the 1994 agreement between Israel and Jordan in regard to the Jordan River (though this success is also contested). The International Freshwater Treaties Database—which lists international freshwater agreements between 1820 and 2007—indicates that, whereas in earlier decades peace agreements did not usually contain provisions concerning water, more recently (between 2005 and 2010) most or all peace agreements do include sections relating to water (Troell and Weinthal 2013). Thus there has been real progress in what is known as integrated water-resource management, and the institutions and practices established to carry this out have endured even during full military conflicts between countries (Wolf 1995). Nonetheless, national ministries or agencies still engage in bureaucratic disputes, either with other agencies in their own governments or with their counterparts in other nations, often to the extent of allowing serious harm to continue to be done to water resources and water security. How such bureaucratic obstructionism is to be countered is a question for further study. But it will surely require understanding the particular culture, including the history and political structures and habits, of each nation or riparian. It is a task that greatly exceeds the range of hydrology or any related natural science, but it is not one that is always acknowledged. In part this may be due to academics in the humanities and social sciences themselves holding back from such topics out of reluctance to deal with the more technical aspects of water-related matters. But as the coeditor of another volume has suggested, it is worthwhile "to point out just how shaky the biophysical science foundation of water security is, and the extent to which social science is dismissed" (Zeitoun 2013, 11). If academic scholarship is to take account of "the historical specificity and embeddedness of water securities and rights in particular cultural ecological settings" (Boelens 2013, 242), studying local water values and meanings together with hydrological data, then a much wider segment of academic expertise will be needed.

Brief Summary of Water Insecurity in the Middle East

In 2009, the World Economic Forum Water Initiative prepared a draft report for discussion of the world's water problems titled "The Bubble is Close to Bursting: A Forecast of the Main Economic and Geopolitical Issues Likely to Arise in the World during the Next Two Decades" (World Economic Forum Initiative 2009). This was by no means the first such report relating to increasing water scarcity and insecurity, but it provided a useful overview. The draft dealt with thematic topics such as sectoral needs (agriculture, energy, trade) as well as regional problems in India, sub-Saharan Africa and the Middle East. It was already evident that "the Middle East Region is the most water scarce region in the world," and the authors of the report anticipated that the region will have "absolute water scarcity by 2025." Beyond the threats to basic nutrition and sanitation, water scarcity was also expected to threaten much-needed economic expansion and diversification in the Middle East and to exacerbate existing political and religious tensions and conflicts in the region.

The situation cannot be said to have improved significantly since then. Recent military and political conflicts—the present civil war in Syria; accompanying conflicts in Iraq and Kurdistan; civil unrest in Egypt, Libya, Lebanon and the Palestinian Authority (PA)—are compounding longstanding structural problems in the ecosystem. Current political and military problems are intertwined with dangerously low water tables; salination and pollution of groundwater; inadequate conservation efforts and treatment of wastewater; insufficient supplies of drinking water; water supplies for basic household and sanitation needs; and other water-related problems that have long been identified in the Middle East (Tal and Rabbo 2010; Allan 2002). Moreover, many or most Middle Eastern countries depend on transboundary water sources or imported water to obtain the water needed for domestic use and for their economies. These dynamics affect not only relationships among Arab countries but also between Arab and non-Arab states. The question thus arises whether, in this region as in others around the world, water needs (however defined) will be met through cooperation or aggressive competition and ultimately armed conflict. The Stimson Center of the Brookings Institution has concluded that "it is no exaggeration to say that water policy and water security are as central a determinant of the future well-being of the MENA [Middle East and North Africa] countries as is governance or ideology" (Michel et al. 2012, 1).

The problem of water supply and security is further complicated by climate change: droughts and declining rainfall, frequency and strength of storms and floods, and rising sea levels, to name only a few factors. Though climate has perhaps only an indirect connection to international conflict, insofar as it leads to extensive migration and related economic stresses, it may also exacerbate ethnic strife.

A considerable amount of work has been done in regard to preventive diplomacy, seeking to ensure a measure of cooperation before violent conflict erupts: the forward-leaning efforts of those engaged in water diplomacy (Shafiqul Islam and Lawrence E. Susskind; Aaron T. Wolf; and Jerome Delli Priscolli); scientific collaborations between Israel, Jordan and the West Bank (Alon Tal and Alfred Rabbo as well as members of the Arava Institute for Environmental Studies); the Arab Integrated Water Resources Management Network, the Arab Water Council, the joint commission between Israel and the Palestinian Water Authority; and various bilateral agreements. Hydrologists, geographers, humanitarian and nongovernmental organization (NGO) workers, and some political scientists have contributed to a considerable literature advocating for stable institutions to enable cooperative management of water issues prior to, during and following violent conflict. A consensus seems to exist that what is most needed are institutions that are responsible for basin-wide areas and that can sustain their activities during times of political or economic crisis (Lankford et al. 2013).

It is my belief, however, that all this work is not entirely sufficient. Though it has taken account of many stakeholders—that is, riparians represented through local and national governments, industrial, energy and agricultural sectors, households, public policy makers, NGOs and so on—more is needed to orient public attention to the long-term issues as opposed to immediate crises, such as one summer's drought. As Tony Allan has noted, there is wide-spread reluctance to confront the large-scale hydrological facts: "The Middle East as a region ran out of water in the 1970s. The news of this important economic fact has been little exposed. In political systems, facts, including those on water, which are judged to have costly political consequences, can easily be ignored or de-emphasized," and he suggested that this type of denial is particularly acute in the Middle East (2002, 5). Consequently, any proposed long-term solutions will have to be both philosophical and political in the broadest sense, recognizing that even when a technological solution is available, or when scientists and technical advisers are in agreement as to what needs to be done either in an immediate locality or an entire basin, political will and ideological conviction must support their recommendations. A rich understanding of diverse ways of life, and of political education and practice, is needed. It is here that universities can play an additional important role, beyond gathering empirical data and solving hydrological problems in a technical sense. To reiterate, philosophical, historical, anthropological and religious studies relating to water as well as social scientific studies should be encouraged and integrated into university education. If there is to be a large-scale transformation in public consciousness of water-security problems, and if citizens are to make informed choices and decisions, students across the globe will have to have a comprehensive understanding of, or at least an acquaintance with, linkages of water with other social, political and broadly philosophical issues

Potential Contributions from the Humanities and Social Sciences

Philosophy

Many writers on the topic of water security have noticed the undertheorized status of the concept of equity. It would be hard to overstate the importance of this concept in disputes over water worldwide. It appears in treaties, charters and legal documents relating to water sharing at both the national and international levels, often appearing in the phrase "equitable use." But what precisely this means in the context of water management (and how any given philosophical or legal theory about equity is to be actualized) remains relatively unexplored terrain. Recently, Ahmed Abukhater (2013, 15) has sought to draw the work of the distinguished American political philosopher John Rawls into discussion of the Israeli-Jordanian Peace Treaty of 1994 and its provisions concerning the Jordan River. But his treatment of Rawls's ideas about distributive justice is too abbreviated to be truly helpful in untying the tangled web of interpretations of this treaty. The points at issue concern not only what a fair distribution of water resources would look like but also what a just procedure would be for arriving at a distribution that all parties regard as fair. On this point Rawls may not in fact be the best source. His theory's bracketing of the vital role of cultural identity—which has a profound role in Middle Eastern and other conflicts—has been deeply criticized (Sandel 1982; MacIntyre 1981). There is a further problem in that most discussions of distributive justice originate in the West. This does nothing to alleviate intense suspicion of treaties and agreements that are the product, however indirect, of Western thought (Abukhater 2013).

Of course, there have been enormously influential attempts to break out of traditional Western epistemological framework and to develop political theories that are more sensitive to subaltern cultures. However, it would be difficult to name a specific theory of distributive justice arising out of this broad anti-colonialist endeavor. A more promising approach might be that of the Nobel Prize–winning Indian philosopher-economist Amartya Sen and the philosopher Martha Nussbaum, and the notion of a so-called capabilities approach to justice. In regard to existing approaches to equity and environmental sustainability, Sen has written,

> It must be asked whether the conception of human beings implicit in it [a utilitarian approach to sustainability] is sufficiently capacious. Certainly, people have "needs," but they also have values, and in particular they cherish their ability to reason, appraise, act and participate. Seeing people only in terms of their needs may give us a rather meager view of humanity. (2004, 1)

In addition to the concept of equity, there is a large philosophical literature on rights. Distinctions are drawn between positive and negative rights, rights of well-being and rights not to be harmed and many others. Rights are also related to and weighed against obligations (of varying degrees) to the least advantaged in any individual society or in other societies. For my purpose here, which is simply to expand the horizon of thinking about water security, there is no need to choose right now between theories of rights or of equality.

The point is rather to underscore that philosophy has much to offer in the way of conceptual clarification and enlarged perspectives in which to consider the problems of power, knowledge, rights and distributive justice, and what this might ultimately signify for water security.

Anthropology

The fact that Western-sponsored agreements are sometimes, perhaps often, viewed with suspicion indicates that not only deeper understandings of non-Western societies are needed but also more elaborate conceptions of the nature of dialogue between persons of different cultures. Beyond the studies of negotiation and communication already put forward, for example, by Lawrence E. Susskind (Islam and Susskind 2013), in this connection cultural anthropology and cultural linguistics will be highly relevant. For the Middle East, an excellent example is to be found in the work of Steven Caton on Yemen. In an essay titled "What Is an Authorizing Discourse?" Caton analyzes the origin and interpretation of Islamic prayers for rain and the role of such interpretations in a specific period of severe drought (Caton 2006). We may also note here an essay by Hussein Amery that (while not strictly anthropological) seeks to explicate Islamic ideas about water and the environment more generally. Amery shows the centrality of water in the Koran, where it is seen as a "unifying common medium among all species" and supports water management approaches that incorporate "culturally sensitive demand management strategies." He suggests that, by increased awareness of Islamic tradition relating to water and the environment, "policy-makers can tap into Muslims' religiosity and desire for salvation to design and implement an Islamically inspired water management strategy" (Amery 2001, 46). Others have carried out anthropological studies of Hindu religious rituals involving water and how these relate to a given landscape, customary architecture or waterscape (Hegewald 2002). The function of Islamic peace gardens has also received some, but by no means sufficient, attention.

Religious studies

Although I touched upon studies of religious thought, ritual and identity in the previous section, the way anthropologists approach this subject is different from that of religious studies scholars. Here the task is, with regard to the world's religions, to present concepts, theories, rituals, moral rules and many other aspects of religion through highly rigorous textual analysis and in historical perspective. Sometimes archaeological and anthropological evidence is brought in for support. The literature in this field is an enormous resource for anyone seeking a deeper understanding of any Middle Eastern society, either for the intrinsic value of such understanding or in the effort to address political, social and environmental needs. Numerous studies exist on Jewish, Christian and Islamic conceptions of the environment, and no doubt more are in the works.

History

Although historical perspective seems essential for understanding one's dialogue partner or opponent in a conflict, historical studies that integrate water and environmental issues into their main subject are not that common. The biologists and environmental activists Paul and Anne Ehrlich have on numerous occasions pointed out the role of water in the collapse of the Assyrian Empire, for example, but it is scarcely mentioned by most professional historians (Ehrlich and Ehrlich 2004).

The comparative lack of integrated historical studies is very noticeable in accounts of the 1967 Arab-Israeli war. Ophira Seliktar, for one, has pointed out that most historians and political analysts of this conflict have paid little or no attention to water as a factor, most likely because of the technical aspects of water-scarcity issues (2005). Some analysts—not professional historians— have concluded that there was a so-called hydrological imperative driving Israel's actions, while others have argued against this thesis. A great deal more research on this and related questions could be done in order to arrive at a fuller understanding of those events.

But the aim of informed historical discussion is not to arrive at a final decision as to the truth of the matter. History and historical narration are never finished. (Is there a definitive account of Europe's Thirty Years' War in the seventeenth century? Indeed, historians cannot even agree on whether or not it lasted 30 years.) This point is important because the notion that an agreed-upon historical narrative can or should be arrived at may be a hindrance rather than a help to political and social cooperation. While each side accuses the other of producing biased narratives and seeks to construct counternarratives, water insecurity is not alleviated. We cannot wait for a historical narrative that is somehow acceptable or convincing to all before engaging in constructive postconflict cooperation, whether in the Middle East, India and Pakistan, or anywhere else. Such a narrative will probably never materialize, and water problems are too urgent. However, neglect of nuanced histories is also not desirable. We need in-depth knowledge of the narratives of others in order to be able to understand or recognize the different parties and to initiate or carry on cooperation. Perhaps the best that can be hoped for is that, by a critical reading of one another's historical narratives, a gradual process of ideological adjustment can take place that leaves each side more open to cooperation and to seeking constructive solutions.

Social Sciences (Political Science, Sociology and Economics)

Sociology and economics

The need for an enlarged approach to water-security issues, in the Middle East as elsewhere, has been noted before. This is true in cases of both inter-state conflict and conflict within states. Regarding Israel, for example, Amnon Kartin and Eran Feitelson have, separately, described the economic as well as political incentives that block changes to current dangerous levels of groundwater extraction (Kartin 2000; Feitelson 2005). Regarding Lebanon, Karim Makdisi has pointed to a lack of political will, arising from complex circumstances beyond Israeli "de facto control" of the lower Litani and Hasbani Rivers, to provide an adequate minimum supply of water for its inhabitants. These circumstances include a political culture permeated by "clientalist and sectarian considerations in public policy" and a sort of general administrative ineffectiveness (Makdisi 2007). In the Middle East, where religious, cultural and ethnic attachments are ancient, diverse and intense, social, economic and political factors are perhaps a more evident "missing piece" than in other parts of the world. For other regions, such as South Asia, sociologists and culture theorists seem to have been more involved in integrating cultural, sociological and hydrological studies (cf. Anand 2007; Panda 2007). For example, they have placed more emphasis on the condition of women in relation to water needs for households and public sanitation and the social consequences of large amounts of time taken away from individual education and development as a result.

Political science

Connections between political systems and water policy are often treated in the context of national and military security, whether the system is an ancient oriental despotism or a modern nation-state (Lankford et al. 2013). More recently, a new conception of hybrid warfare has emerged, in which "a dangerous and complex combination of insurgency, civil conflict, terrorism, pervasive criminality and widespread civil disorder" are all present simultaneously. This in turn has led to critical changes in "the way threat assessments are being undertaken by national governments, regional organizations, and private sector analysts" (Zala 2013, 277). According to one analyst, Benjamin Zala, this has led to critical changes in the ways in which national defense analysts and policy makers assess water-security problems. Furthermore, the defense analysts' assessments are often quite different from those of academics, who tend to follow the so-called liberal institutionalist position that international judicial and conflict resolution institutions can contribute importantly to threat reduction. Academics, some defense analysts believe, overestimate the power of such institutions and rely on outdated historical data. Political power constellations shift too rapidly to be regulated by the international institutions already existing or envisioned. Work being done by Mark Zeitoun, Jan Selby and others in the "London School" of water-security studies suggests that there is a "potential for these [liberal institutional] dynamics to not only block cooperation but even to create conflict" (Zeitoun and Warner 2006, cited in Zala 2013, 278). Zeitoun and Selby further question the very meaning of the term "cooperation" in certain contexts, in particular that of the Israeli-Palestinian conflict. Relying on the Gramscian notion of cultural hegemony and Marxian conceptions of political economy they argue (separately) that cooperation merely serves as a discursive mask: real and very large inequalities of economic and political power are concealed by the apparent juridical equality of the PA and the State of Israel when they enter into negotiations over water or anything else. A relatively simple mechanism for coordination of water policy—the Joint Water Commission established by the 1995 Oslo II agreement—becomes redescribed as a model for political cooperation and a means of promoting peace building, which never materializes in fact:

> Much of what the Oslo II water accords directly achieved was discursive, insubstantial and altogether illusory. [...] "Cooperation," in this context, is above all an internationally pleasing and acceptable signifier which obscures rather than elucidates the nature of Israeli-Palestinian relations. (Selby 2003, 138)

This is not the place to review the plausibility—both theoretical and empirical—of these (Marxian) types of analysis of cooperation and liberal-institutional peace-building aspirations. However, even if we accept these assessments of the general academic contribution to solving international and transboundary water problems as at best too slow, and at worst as part of the problem of water security, it is safe to say that academic debate stimulates awareness and discussion in other fora such as think tanks, NGOs and perhaps even defense policy working groups. In addition, academic work—by all parties to a conflict, and in the social as well as natural sciences—can contribute to the legal adjudication of disputes and to processes of institutional cooperation involving governmental agencies, funding agencies and so on. There are profound questions lurking in the background as to the possibility of objective knowledge in any of these intellectual and political situations, but surely intersubjective discussion and debate are likely to produce at least some clarification, if not altered commitments.

Another categorization of theories well known to political scientists is that of the functionalist versus the realist approach to the study of international relations. Broadly, realists emphasize material interests, competition for power and influence, and national defense as the primary motivations for the behavior and interactions of nation-states. Functionalists are generally interested in processes that tend toward greater global integration, shared interests and common policies. But the history of functionalist theory also reveals important differences between the ideas of its earliest representatives, mainly David Mitrany (1888–1975), and some of its later proponents, such as Ernst B. Haas (1924–2003), who are known as neofunctionalists. For neofunctionalists it is *a testable hypothesis* that as states or parties to a conflict engage in relatively small-scale cooperative ventures in economics, science or technology, there will be an identifiable "spillover" effect into larger areas of economic and technical cooperation, and eventually a larger still political integration. A main example of such a pattern would be European integration, which began with coal and steel agreements as early as the 1950s and progressed toward fairly complex political integration in the form of the European Union. For Mitrany, generally regarded as the founder of functionalism, "joint functional arrangements" were important in a different way:

> I have watched carefully (so far) lest the functional idea likewise ossifies into another set dogma. All that one asks from political scientists who may be critical of the functional approach is that, on their part, they should in every instance watch closely for "the relation of things." That is indeed the hallmark of a student, in the philosophical sense of the term. [...] *I have tried to build bridges across doctrinal or institutional differences between groups so that they might join together for dealing with common problems.* (Mitrany, 1975, 45; emphasis added)

In other words, Mitrany was interested in confirmation of his functionalist approach in a very broad sense and did not regard any specific instance of a lack of "spillover" as a final refutation of his worldview. He sought, in thoughtful but ultimately quite pragmatic ways, to move beyond the oppressive, restrictive nationalisms of the Europe in the eras of World War I and World War II (while acknowledging the continuing relevance of "nationality") and to focus on "the real elements of whatever issue is at stake" (Mitrany 1975, 45). Perhaps what is needed now are further efforts to devise contemporary forms of this type of pragmatic cosmopolitanism, a type of internationalism that encourages "getting used to each other" (Appiah 2006) in uncomplicated ways. One example of such work is to be found in the Arava Institute for Environmental Studies. Its research is represented by chapter 4 below. It lends support to what is sometimes rather disparagingly referred to as the "peace school" in water-security studies (Chellaney 2013). This group of researchers maintains that "water is rarely the cause of war and large-scale violence," and that, even where armed conflict has occurred, water has "a powerful role in: building social community; generating wealth [...]; convening adversaries and providing common language for joint and creative dialogue" (Delli Priscoli 2012, 32).

Overview of the Volume

The chapters in this volume broadly argue that in the Middle East region, the most arid in the world, local as well as international cooperation on trans-boundary water issues is both possible and actual to some degree: with regard to data sharing; implementation of new technologies and techniques for waste-water treatment; conservation; desalination; and day-to-day management. Nonetheless, although each of the specific areas studied in this volume has some sort of international or joint commission to help alleviate water disputes, these are not nearly as effective as mechanisms in other regions, such as the Danube Commission in Europe. Strong forces operate to prevent both needed internal reforms within nations and the evolution of what may amount to no more than coordination into a firmer and warmer form of cooperation at the international level. Within nations, powerful agricultural and other interests, and popular patterns of consumption, often resist changes to water-pricing mechanisms, conservation and greater bureaucratic efficiency. Still, several of the authors urge that existing joint commissions be redesigned and given increased powers.

The first chapter, "Cooperation Rules: Insights on Water and Conflict from International Relations," by Patrice C. McMahon, provides an overview of international relations literature, roughly between 1945 and the present, on "water wars," or the thesis that water insecurity is linked to violent conflict. McMahon argues that the empirical evidence for this is limited. After briefly reviewing the history of security studies since the Cold War, she argues that even when international tensions—for example, over a transnational water-way—are very high, "states are likely to seek accommodation" rather than go to war, because of the associated military costs and uncertain benefits. Moreover, there are likely to be many other factors involved in militarized interstate disputes, and it is difficult to identify or quantify the weight of the water-security factor.

Chapter 2, "Water Security in Transboundary Systems: Cooperation in Intractable Conflicts and The Nile System," by Jenny R. Kehl, provides a detailed analysis of the calculations that can lie behind decisions either to escalate to violence or to pursue a negotiated settlement in water disputes within the Nile River system. According to Kehl, the Nile system "perennially tests the commitment to cooperation": it is a system under extreme water stress, food insecurity and population growth, while at the same time embodying very sharp asymmetries in political and military power. Although the mechanisms of cooperation laid out in the Nile Basin Initiative have worked to some degree, the aforementioned factors constantly undermine its efficacy, and it needs to be strengthened both by institutional changes such as increased legal codification, and socioeconomic development that reduces economic and trade inequalities. Using cross-sectional regression analysis, Kehl seeks to assess the influence of several types of factors—including geographic, military, political and economic—on water conflict resolution in the Nile system, and then goes on to compare that with seven other systems worldwide. She concludes that weak and strong riparians may exert different types of power, and whether violence or cooperation is the final result depends on very complex—but measurable—dynamics between societies and their neighbors.

Chapter 3, Hussein Amery's essay, "Water-Demand Management in the Arab Gulf States: Implications for Political Stability," is both descriptive and normative. It gives an overview of the Gulf economies and their increasing globalization, while arguing that the concept and the practice of sustainability have been too weak. Inappropriate pricing mechanisms and conservation measures as well as a general "culture of excessive consumption" and various political interests have been the main causes of this inadequate attention to real sustainability, despite the widespread availability of public awareness programs.

Chapter 4, "A Watershed-Based Approach to Mitigating Transboundary Wastewater Conflicts between Israel and the Palestinian Authority," by Clive Lipchin and Tamee Albrecht, recounts efforts at scientific and technological cooperation through implementation of new, highly sophisticated mapping techniques. These in principle enable better understanding of all sorts of problems relating to groundwater, wastewater, basin management and so on. However, the wider political context, and the asymmetries of power, between Israelis and Palestinians are constantly in the background. Nonetheless, the authors argue, the temptation to fall back on unilateral solutions should be resisted, since adequate solutions often depend on managing or treating water both at its source and far beyond that, that is, across boundaries: "[W]e believe that collaboration is key in minimizing the impact [of pollution] on the environment throughout the watershed." Similarly, in chapter 5, "The Evolution of

Israeli Water Management: The Elusive Search for Environmental Security," Alon Tal sees Israel's hard-won, relative water security as potentially having an important influence on Israel's relationships with her neighbors. Desalination, a key element of this security, however, brings its own problems, perhaps not all that different from those facing the Arab Gulf States: it may undermine the ethos of conservation that was critical to Israel's development, and it requires its own very large consumption of energy. A further potential harm lies in the increasing privatization of water production and management-related activities. While perhaps not in itself a bad thing, it tends to undercut Israel's historical commitment to social equity and may widen already existing socioeconomic gaps.

Neda A. Zawahri's essay, "Adapting to Climatic Variability along International River Basins in the Middle East," chapter 6, seeks to assess the likely effects of climate change on the already very insecure water-distribution patterns throughout the Middle East. As she points out, "any decrease or variability in supplies is likely to intensify an already stressful crisis" and may reduce "states' ability to comply with existing treaties or protocols governing the region's inter-national rivers." She argues that improving the region's capacity to adapt to climate change should include adjusting or putting in place interstate institutions such as river basin commissions. Zawahri thus favors the neoliberal institutional approach to international relations generally, seeing it as the one with the great-est potential to reduce tensions and threats to water security in the Middle East. Her chapter is based on research in Jordan, Israel, Turkey, Syria and Palestine.

Chapter 7, "Water and Politics in the Tigris–Euphrates Basin—Hope for Negative Learning?", by David Forsythe, is more skeptical than most of the other essays in this volume as to the prospects of cooperation on water secu-rity. Focusing principally on relations among Turkey, Syria and Iraq, Forsythe notes that the concept of safe water as a fundamental, international human right receives no meaningful recognition in that general region. All three states have historically used access to water—rivers and dams—as instruments of their foreign policies and as pretexts for escalating violence and militarization of disputes. The situation may eventually deteriorate to a point at which the only option for survival is to seek improved water management, but no one seems to be there yet, especially in the current crisis created by the takeover of large swaths of territory by the terrorist organization Islamic State in Iraq and Syria (ISIS).

The concluding chapter, "The Political and Cultural Dimensions of Water Diplomacy in the Middle East," is written by Lawrence E. Susskind, a leader in water conflict resolution, both in theory and in practice. In the present essay, Susskind argues that the well-known and relatively traditional approach to transboundary water management—integrated water-resource management—does not ensure that the needs of *all* water users are met in a sustainable way. It should give way to an approach called the water-diplomacy framework, developed by Susskind himself together with Shafiqul Islam. This approach places greater emphasis on nonstate rather than state actors, on trust rather than economic efficiencies and on "value creation," that is, multiple usages of the same water plus water trades that are advantageous to all. It seeks to understand the wider political contexts (often transboundary and transnational) in which water allocations are made, and advocates negotiation processes in which civil society has a much bigger voice "at the table."

It is my hope that philosophers, anthropologists and other "cultural workers" will soon join the authors of this volume in both research and teaching about water security. Through learning about the usages of water in different cultures and different historical periods, learning about specific water disputes or conflicts in particular regions of the world and learning about local needs and attitudes, students can gradually—as they move into the labor force and into official positions of various kinds—help change the preferences of the societies they live in. Thus they may in the long run help in alleviating water-security problems.

References

Abukhater, Ahmed. 2013. *Water as a Catalyst for Peace: Transboundary Water Management and Conflict Resolution.* London: Routledge.

Adorno, Theodor W. *Negative Dialectics.* Translated by B. Ashton. New York: Continuum, 2007.

Allan, Tony. 2002. *The Middle East Water Question: Hydropolitics and the Global Economy.* London: I. B. Tauris Publishers.

Amery, Hussein A. 2001. "Islam and the Environment." In *Water Management in Islam*, edited by Naser Faruqui, Asit K. Biswas, and Murad J. Bino. Tokyo: United Nations University Press, 39–48.

Anand, P. B. 2007. "Capability, Sustainability and Collective Action: An Examination of a River Water Dispute." *Journal of Human Development* 8 (1): 109–132.

Appiah, K. Anthony. 2006. *Cosmopolitanism: Ethics in a World of Strangers.* New York: W. W. Norton.

Berry, Kate A., and Eric Mollard. 2010. *Social Participation in Water Governance and Management: Global Perspectives.* London: Earthscan from Routledge.

Boelens, Rutgerd. 2013. "The Shotgun Marriage: Water Security, Cultural Politics, and Forced Engagements between Official and Local Rights Frameworks." In *Water Security: Principles, Perspectives and Practices*, edited by Bruce Lankford, Karen Bakker, Mark Zeitoun and Declan Conway. London: Routledge, 239–255.

Caton, S. C. 2006. "What Is an Authorizing Discourse?" In *Powers of the Secular Modern: Talal Asad and His Interlocutors*, edited by D. Scott and C. Hirschkind. Stanford, CA: Stanford University Press, 31–56.

Chellaney, Brahma 2013. *Water, Peace and War: Confronting the Global Water Crisis.* Lanham, MD: Rowman & Littlefield.

Delli Priscoli, Jerome. 2012. "Introduction." *Water Policy* 14: 3–8.

Delli Priscoli, Jerome, and Aaron T. Wolf. 2009. *Managing and Transforming Water Conflicts*. Cambridge: Cambridge University Press.

Ehrlich, Paul R., and Anne H. Ehrlich. 2004. *One with Nineveh: Politics, Consumption and the Human Future*. Washington, DC: Island Press.

Faruqui, Naser I., Asit K. Biswas and Murad J. Bino, eds. *Water Management in Islam*. Tokyo: United Nations University Press.

Feitelson, Eran. 2005. "Political Economy of Groundwater Exploitation: The Israeli Case." *International Journal of Water Resources Development* 21 (3): 413–423.

Feldman, David Lewis. 2012. *Water*. Malden, MA: Polity Press.

Hegewald, Julia A. B. *Water Architecture in South Asia: A Study of Types, Development and Meanings*. Leiden: Brill, 2002.

Hillel, Daniel. 1994. *Rivers of Eden: The Struggle for Water and the Quest for Peace in the Middle East*. Oxford: Oxford University Press.

Islam, Shafiqul, and Lawrence E. Susskind. 2013. *Water Diplomacy: A Negotiated Approach to Managing Complex Water Networks*. London: Routledge.

Kartin, Amnon. 2000. "Factors Inhibiting Structural Changes in Israel's Water Policy." *Political Geography* 19: 97–115.

Lankford, Bruce, Karen Bakker, Mark Zeitoun and Declan Conway, eds. 2013. *Water Security: Principles, Perspectives and Practices*. London: Routledge.

MacIntyre, Alasdair. 1981. *After Virtue*. Notre Dame, IN: University of Notre Dame Press.

Makdisi, Karim. 2007. "Towards a Human Rights Approach to Water in Lebanon: Implementation Beyond 'Reform.'" *Water Resources Development* 23 (2): 369–390.

Megdal, Sharon B., Robert G. Varady and Susanna Eden, eds. 2013. *Shared Borders, Shared Waters: Israeli-Palestinian and Colorado River Basin Water Challenges*. Boca Raton, FL: CRC Press.

Michel, David, Amit Pandya, Syed Iqbal Hasnain, Russell Stickler and Sreya Panuganti. 2012. *Water Challenges and Cooperative Response in the Middle East and North Africa*. Report prepared for the Brookings Project on U.S. Relations with the Islamic World. *U.S.-Islamic World Papers*, November.

Mitrany, David. 1975. *The Functional Theory of Politics*. London: Martin Robertson & Company.

Nussbaum, Martha. 2003. "Capabilities as Fundamental Entitlements: Sen and Social Justice." *Feminist Economics* 9 (2–3): 33–59.

Orlove, Ben, and Steven Caton. 2010. "Water Sustainability: Anthropological Approaches and Prospects." *Annual Review of Anthropology* 39: 401–415.

Panda, Smita Risha. "Women's Collective Action and Sustainable Water Management: Case of SEWA's Water Campaign in Gujarat, India." Washington, DC: Capri Working paper No. 61, 2007.

Sandel, Michael. 1982. *Liberalism and the Limits of Justice*. Cambridge, UK: Cambridge University Press.

Selby, Jan. 2003. "Dressing Up Domination as 'Cooperation': The Case of Israeli-Palestinian Water Relations." *Review of International Studies* 29 (1): 121–138.

Seliktar, Ophira. 2005. "Turning Water into Fire: The Jordan River as the Hidden Factor in the Six-Day War." *Middle East Review of International Affairs* 9 (2): 57–69.

Sen, Amartya. 1999. *Reason before Identity*. New York: Oxford University Press.

———. 2004. "Why We Should Preserve the Spotted Owl." *London Review of Books*, 26 (3): 10–11.

Sufian, Sandy, and Mark LeVine, eds. 2007. *Reapproaching Borders: New Perspectives on the Study of Israel-Palestine*. Lanham, MD: Rowman & Littlefield Publishers.

Tal, Alon, and Alfred Abed Rabbo, eds. 2010. *Water Wisdom: Preparing the Groundwork for Cooperative and Sustainable Water Management in the Middle East*. New Brunswick, NJ: Rutgers University Press.

Teclaff, Ludwik A. 1967. *The River Basin in History and Law*. The Hague: Martinus Nijhoff.

Troell, Jessica and Erika Weinthal. "Harnessing Water Management for more effective peacebuilding: Lessons Learned." In *Water and Post-Conflict Peacebuilding*, edited by Erika Weinthal, Jessica Troell and Mikiyasu gNakayama. London: Routledge, 2013.

Weinthal, Erika, and A. Marci. 2002. "One Resource, Two Visions: The Prospects for Israeli-Palestinian Water Cooperation." *Water International* 27 (4): 460–467.

Weinthal, Erika, Jessica Troell and Mikiyasu Nakayama, eds. 2013. *Water and Post-Conflict Peacebuilding*. London: Routledge.

Wolf, Aaron T. 1995. *Hydropolitics along the Jordan River: Scarce Water and Its Impact on the Arab-Israeli Conflict*. Tokyo: United Nations University Press.

Wolf, Aaron T., Kerstin Stahl and Marcia F. Macomber. 2003. "Conflict and Cooperation within International River Basins: The Importance of Institutional Capacity," www.transboundarywaters.orst.edu/publications/abst…Wolf_2003.pdf.

World Economic Forum Water Initiative. 2009. "The Bubble Is Close to Bursting: A Forecast of the Main Economic and Geopolitical Water Issues Likely to Arise in the World during the Next Two Decades," www.weforum.org.

Zala, Benjamin. 2013. "The Strategic Dimensions of Water: From National Security to Sustainable Security." In *Water Security: Principles, Perspectives and Practices*, edited by Bruce Lankford, Karen Bakker, Mark Zeitoun and Declan Conway. London: Routledge.

Zeitoun, Mark. 2008. *Power and Water in the Middle East: The Hidden Politics of the Palestinian-Israeli Water Conflict*. London: I. B. Tauris.

Zeitoun, Mark, 2013. "The Web of Sustainable Water Security," in *Water Security: Principles, Perspectives and Practices*, edited by Bruce Lankford, Karen Bakker, Mark Zeitoun and Declan Conway. London: Routledge, 2013.

Zeitoun, M., and J. Warner. 2006. "Hydro-hegemony: A Framework for Analysis of Trans-boundary Water Conflicts," *Water Policy* 8 (5): 435–460.

Chapter 1

COOPERATION RULES: INSIGHTS ON WATER AND CONFLICT FROM INTERNATIONAL RELATIONS

Patrice C. McMahon

At least implicitly, many disciplines recognize that a changing climate with higher temperatures and altered precipitation patterns will require adaptive water- management strategies. Climate change necessitates a collective and coordinated response to water shortage, and states must yield to this reality. If these processes are not carefully calibrated to respond both to physical characteristics and to cultural norms, the path ahead will have grave implications for future generations who will experience human suffering, social and political discord and an impoverished environment. An important question for political scientists is this: will water insecurity—whether it is caused by access, allocation, degradation or scarcity—necessarily result in violent conflict between states?

The answer may depend on whom you ask and the region in question. Although research on water politics and international conflict has led to separate substantial literatures, this chapter considers them together and presents a tentative answer. I argue that, although literature in international relations (IR) is historically predisposed to focusing on war and interstate violent conflict, when it comes to arguments and research on water there is a decisive, if largely overlooked, consensus that it is cooperation rather than violent conflict that dictates interstate water relationships. The past is not always the best predictor of the future, but research on war and conflict thus far indicates that water insecurity is unlikely to result in violent conflict between states. As Aaron Wolf puts it, water may be a tool, target or victim of warfare, but up until this point it has not been the cause (2007, 4).

Nonetheless, a significant amount of scholarship in IR assumes, and sometimes asserts, that problems with access to freshwater and water insecurity will not only lead to violence within states but also result in interstate war (Setter et al. 2011). Especially for scholars who focus on certain regions where water scarcity is severe, where political tensions are significant and where there are no international institutions in place to promote cooperation, violent conflict is overdetermined. The Middle East is usually considered one of the likely hot zones where the quest for water is seen as a catalyst for future conflict either within states or between states (Dinar 2002). This volume's focus on the Middle East and peace building demonstrates clearly that conflict over water is not inevitable and that many institutions, mechanisms and ideas exist to encourage states, local authorities and members of civil society to use water as a conduit for cooperation and peaceful interactions. Employing literature from IR and security studies, this chapter provides several explanations for cooperation and many examples of cooperative water management, even in the Middle East.

I begin the next section with an overview of water's role in IR literature, specifically in research that deals with war and interstate conflict, known as security studies. This section argues that, while the politics of water has long been a concern in IR literature, it is relatively new to discussions about security and conflict. The section on how water is framed presents a summary of water-related research, highlighting distinct differences in the framing of global water issues. This section provides a sampling of the literature written in English from 1990 to 2015 found in the *International Political Science Abstracts* (*IPSA*), which contains articles from more than one thousand journals worldwide.[1] To be sure, this sample is neither comprehensive nor conclusive, but this analysis does highlight important trends in how global water politics is studied. This literature is complemented with books and other articles on shared waters and water security written largely by scholars from other disciplines. This section suggests that water's potential role in violent conflict not only depends on the region studied but is also shaped by an author's discipline and methodological approach and thus the frame for water issues.

In light of this literature, I then examine different mechanisms of cooperation identified in the IR literature. Most IR literature, and security studies in particular, focuses on the state as the level and unit of analysis. This is problematic when thinking about water cooperation because water transcends many levels and the unit of analysis is not always—in fact is not often—the state. Although much of the literature on transboundary water treats political entities as homogeneous monoliths, claiming that "Canada feels" or "Jordan wants," the reality is far more complex (Wolf 2007, 13). Literature on water

---

1   I thank Sarah Michaels for her contribution to this aspect of the research. We conducted these searches together on April 1, and revised searches were done on April 5, 2015.

management is an interdisciplinary endeavor that examines various levels and actors with great sensitivity to scale. Given the wealth of factors and mechanisms associated with water cooperation, but also IR's tradition of levels of analysis, section 3 highlights macro-, meso- and microlevel factors that shape water cooperation. I maintain that, while potential violent conflicts over water indeed demand our attention, there are good theoretical and empirical reasons why water is not likely to be the primary factor in future interstate conflicts. This is exactly why an interdisciplinary book on water and peace in the Middle East is so important.

Water and Conflict in International Relations

An overview of IR assumptions and theories provides significant insight into why water insecurity and tensions between states are not likely to result in militarized conflict between states. IR as a field of political science has traditionally focused more on the possibilities of war than the reasons for peace. Such a statement is most closely identified with realist theories that assume that international anarchy, state interests and national security animate the most important dynamics in international politics (Waltz 1979). Anarchy and the absence of a world government mean that conflicts between states are inevitable and wars always loom in the background. This is a position that is often adopted by water scholars intent on justifying the water wars thesis. As Hussein Amery's article titled "Water Wars in the Middle East: A Looming Threat" warns, while many cooperative solutions to resource conflicts will emerge in the Middle East, violent confrontations over vital resources such as water are still highly probable in the next few decades (2002, 322).

IR scholarship reminds us that, although international anarchy is a powerful permissive condition, states only go to war to advance their interests when they can, and this is, in turn, determined largely by their power capabilities. Power—and by this realists mean military might—is considered the best indicator for why and when wars occur. Interpretations vary, but balance of power theory argues that although their interests diverge, states are rational actors and will only risk war when they have the power to do so. War happens only when states calculate that the gains will be greater than the losses, and unless power differences are small and the potential rewards great, states generally do not go to war (Gilpin 1981). In many places in the world, including the Middle East, power differentials and military capability are so significant that even when tensions over water are great, states are likely to seek accommodation and compromise. It is simply rational to do so and thus, in the post–Cold War period in particular, interstate war is quite rare.

During the Cold War, IR theories and security studies specifically focused on great power wars and national security and how military power shaped the likelihood of interstate war. Threats and security were construed narrowly in terms of weapons and capabilities, and rarely were other factors considered in research on international war. Defending its narrow, military focus, Stephen Walt explains that "security studies is principally about the phenomenon of war; it assumes that conflict between states is always a possibility, and that the use of military force has far-reaching effects on states and societies" (Walt 1991, 212). In the 1980s, as tensions between the United States and the Soviet Union declined, some IR scholars called for a broadening of security studies and for research to look to for new or previously overlooked threats (Lowi 1999, 376). As Richard Ullman explained, portraying security in "excessively narrow and excessively military terms" not only misrepresents reality but also means that we are ignoring what is really happening in the world (1983, 129–130).

By the beginning of the 1990s, it was impossible to ignore the new issues that were contributing to violence all over the world. Ethnicity, religion and even the natural environment were suddenly cast as crucial contributing factors to instability and interstate violence. As Robert Kaplan (1994) dramatically put it, worldwide demographic, environmental and societal stress, in which criminal anarchy emerges, is the real strategic danger, eroding the integrity of states and creating internal anarchy rather than great power interstate wars. This sudden interest in so-called new security issues or nonmilitary threats produced various terms, including "environmental security" and "environmental scarcity." It also spawned multidisciplinary research on the relationship between the natural environment and security, with an emphasis on whether and to what degree environmental issues affect the likelihood of war. The US government in particular wants to understand how new threats might impact national security and the security of its allies around the world.

One US government intelligence report concluded that "there were at least ten places in the world where war could break out over dwindling shared water," the majority in of which were in the Middle East (Dolatyar and Gray 2000, 67). At least for a while, environmental concerns pushed the US government to shift its focus accordingly, creating new institutions and offices to address and respond to looming environmental threats. Events of the 1990s only accelerated the intellectual move to redefine and broaden security studies and to reassess the causal relationship between water and conflict. Two research programs in particular, the Toronto Group and the the Swiss-based Environmental Conflict Project (ENCOP), engaged in high-profile studies that tested so-called Malthusian claims or environment–conflict linkages. In the United States, Tad Homer-Dixon's research in Toronto was "initially greeted enthusiastically by the defense establishment, this time in the setting of the post–Cold War redefinition of relevance" (Wolf 2007, 4). Homer-Dixon's research evolved significantly, implicating water initially in interstate conflicts, while later his research recognized that war between states over water is likely only under limited circumstances. His research thus focused more on the intervening variables and factors that contribute to intrastate violence (Environmental Change & Security Report 2000).

Much of the early research on environmental security relied on historical cases and qualitative methods, examining how the quality or quantity of resources such as water leads to competition between individuals and groups and thus increases the likelihood of intrastate violence. Although environment–conflict linkages were found in many of the historical cases, other researchers, specifically Nils Petter Gleditsch from the International Peace Research Institute, Oslo (PRIO), argued that the environmental security literature lacked clarity, important variables were overlooked and, in general, the arguments were so complex that they were "virtually untestable" (Environmental Change & Security Report 2000, 78). In other words, it was too difficult to assess the independent contribution of the natural environment to violence (Meierding 2013, 188). Quantitative researchers were often the most vocal critics of this research, but during the 1990s only two large N-analyses were attempted, and they presented inconsistent findings on the environment-conflict linkage. Unfortunately, by the time quantitative studies were completed, interest in environmental security was overshadowed by other concerns, namely, international terrorism because of the September 11 attacks on the United States.

Only in the last decade has interest in the natural environment—and specifically water—returned, because of the unique aspects of water and concern over climate change. Much of this research has been quantitative in nature and focuses on the role of geography in affecting the likelihood of war. Among the explanations for the robust relationship between neighboring states and war is territory, because it is a vital resource with military and economic importance. In addition, territory harbors important natural resources, including water, making it an even more important resource. To a great extent, this research has examined "the role of territory as either a cause or a facilitating factor in conflicts between neighboring states, with water and competition for shared water resources featured prominently in these studies" (Brochmann and Gleditsch 2012, 518). Research on shared rivers, for example, tries to discern the independent effects that sharing a river might have on the probability of interstate conflict.

These studies have been done in various ways and they sometimes involve the same authors, but they have produced inconsistent findings when it comes to the linkages between water and conflict (Gleditsch et al. 2006; Brochmann and Gleditsch 2012). However, the most recent findings indicate that, since almost all neighboring states share at least one river, it is "impossible to disentangle the effect of sharing a river from the effect of being neighbors" (Brochmann and Gleditsch 2012, 519). Territory and proximity may indeed increase the likelihood of interstate militarized disputes, but future research needs to do a better job conceptualizing and measuring the issues under contention (Hensel 2000). Thus, while neo-Malthusians predict water wars in the future, such a conclusion is considered largely premature by IR scholars, because there is little evidence that water in and of itself has created a war or even a credible threat of one.

Liberal assumptions and theories in international relations recognize that while war is possible between states, it does not always occur because of the range of institutions that exist to encourage states to address conflicts peacefully. Liberals also assume that states are often interested in their individual absolute gains rather than in the gains of others, which means they are more likely to seek out cooperation (Powell 1991). Moreover, as international politics becomes more globalized and states become more interdependent, war and violent conflict in general will be less likely to help states advance their interests. Liberal assumptions and theories are often founded in research on water, because "shared interests along a waterway seem to consistently outweigh water's conflict-inducing characteristics" (Wolf 2007, 7). This means that under certain circumstances, and especially as they become more interdependent, states are even more likely to think about absolute gains and peaceful solutions to conflicts.

Globalization will inevitably make states more interdependent, and non-state actors including international and regional organizations will help facilitate cooperation. Simply put, in the twenty-first century, war is less cost effective than pursuing the same goal through cooperation and trade. Liberal authors thus maintain that if interdependence is peace promoting in general, then this will be true for resource-based conflicts as well (cited in Barnett 2000, 273). Water scarcity by its nature creates zero-sum or positive-sum dynamics, because water links states' fates in a unique way. Cooperation means that everyone benefits, while the failure to cooperate leaves both states worse off. According to this perspective, "water is too vital a resource to be put at risk by war; increasing water scarcity generally pushes decision-makers to find substitution by coordinated, cooperative and conciliatory arrangements" (Dolatyar and Gray 2000, 67).

Regardless of whether realist or liberal assumptions about international politics and states are correct, important and surprising developments in the 1990s prompted more changes in terms of the threats that security scholars examined, the actors they focused on and the events they studied. The good news that IR scholars have had to accept but also respond to is that interstate war has been declining since World War II. As the forum on "The Decline of War" proclaimed, "war appears to be in decline," and this is particularly true of the great powers and developed states (Gleditsch et al. 2013, 396). Civil or intrastate wars, while increasing in number from the 1960s through the 1990s, have also declined in number, and the worldwide rate of death from interstate and civil war combined has fallen significantly. In the twenty-first century, as new forms of violence surface and nonstate violence proliferate, security studies has again needed to assess whether and to what degree the discipline will redefine and broaden its understanding of threats, the unit of analysis and the focus of research. Security scholars have reacted in different ways, with some returning to a focus on how security has or ought to be redefined to include a variety of nonmilitary factors that threaten states' values and way of life. Other IR scholars have consciously shifted away from international processes and interstate war to the study of intrastate conflict and subnational violence (Koubi et al. 2014). For both of these reasons, but also because of changing environmental conditions and specifically the attention that is given to climate change and its effects, the politics of water will undoubtedly remain an issue of utmost importance to IR scholars, particularly those interested in war and conflict. As President Barack Obama proclaimed in 2009, the "urgent dangers to our national and economic security are compounded by the long-term threat of climate change which if left unchecked could result in violent conflict" (Meierding 2013, 185).

How Water Is Framed

In an effort to understand how the politics of water is discussed in international politics, the following provides a preliminary analysis of results from a comprehensive search of articles written in English indexed in the *International Political Science Abstracts* (IPSA) from 1990 to 2015. Two basic searches were conducted, and only articles written in English that were not based on US water issues (unless there was an international component or some comparative component) were considered. The first search was limited to articles that contained "water" and "war(s)" in the subject to better understand *who* frames and presents these new security issues and *how* they do so. Since "water wars" articles do not encompass all the water-related research in international politics, a more general inclusive search was done to capture other dynamics. The broader search included a number of terms associated with international water (including river, water basin and transboundary) and conflict (such as hydropolitics, hydrosolidarity, security, management, violence, cooperation and peace). The goal of this broader search was to analyze "water-related" articles in English that capture a range of relationships between water and conflict internationally but that do not include war as a subject.

Three motivations inspired our bibliographic searches. Our primary interest was gauging the degree to which the politics of water internationally is framed. Given the international changes, we were interested in seeing how the evolution of security studies had impacted research on water since the Cold War's end. Does research on water politics see it as a security issue, or what other issues are addressed? Second, although we are still engaged in other bibliographic searches, we were interested in potential disciplinary differences in terms of how the politics of water is framed, researched and discussed. In this regard, we assumed that water-related research would cover many geographic regions. Finally, if research focused on water wars or interstate violence, what regions or countries were addressed? After presenting some preliminary observations of these searches, this section analyzes "water wars articles" in more depth, while the next section addresses how the articles take a broader perspective on the politics of water internationally, identifying different mechanisms that promote cooperation—even in unlikely places.

From the academic literature indexed in IPSA from 1990 to 2015, the following observations can be made: first, research on water politics in international relations thrived in the 1990s and in the early 2000s but decreased after 2005. Second, although research that uses the term "water war(s)" decreased significantly after 2005, other kinds of water-related research increased during this same period (see figure 1). Third, literature that emphasized water wars, violence and conflict disproportionately focused on the Middle East, a finding that Jon Barnett (2000) also observed. Finally, literature written after 2000 often highlighted and discussed what some claim is an emerging consensus among water experts, particularly among those scholars who rely on quantitative methods: interstate wars over water are unlikely if nonexistent. "Existing event datasets on international river basin conflict and cooperation indicate that international disputes over water issues are quite common. But none of these disputes have thus far escalated into a militarized interstate dispute in a form that would, according to common definitions, qualify as a war" (Bernauer and Siegried 2012, 237). Although policy makers and politicians often argue to the contrary, academic research—whether it is written by geographers, environmental management scientists or political scientists—tends to conclude that water waters simply do not exist (Dolatyar and Gray 2000; Barnett 2007; Wolf 2007; Priscoli and Wolf 2009; Katz 2011; Brochmann and Gleditsch 2012; Meierding 2013).

Revealingly, the bulk of the articles published in English between 1990 and 2015 on "water wars" focused predominantly on the Middle East, particularly on Israel and the Jordan basin. These articles were often written by public policy scholars, areas studies experts or political scientists, though it is sometimes difficult to discern an author's discipline. However, the water wars articles were overwhelmingly qualitative and historical in nature; in fact, out of 26 articles in English that used water war(s) in the subject, only 2 were empirically based, while the others were a mix of literature reviews, historical analyses or comparative qualitative studies. Often water-war articles incorporated some theories about wars and conflicts, providing background information on likely cases and invoking realist theories as a rationale for thinking about water in terms of resource wars (Barnett 2000). As J. A. Allen confidently puts it, since the Middle East is the most water-challenged region in the world (and as realist theory and popular intuition suggest), "the scarcity of water in the region will lead to water wars" (2002, 255–256).

Even though most scholars are careful to emphasize the increased risk of interstate war, policy makers often pay attention to and exaggerate the inevitability of violence in relationships between states over water. Again this is often the case in research that focuses on the Middle East. Summarizing and destabilizing the environment-conflict thesis, Jon Barnett explains that there is a typical pattern to this water-wars literature: the geographical misfit between water and national boundaries is explored; then a healthy dose of "practical geopolitical reasons is applied"; then, having made much of the prospect of water wars, there is usually a brief discussion of remedial measures, which tends to be an afterthought (2000, 276). The region most frequently mentioned is the Middle East, because it is already rife with religious, ethnic and political tensions. For many authors, "water scarcity will be the proverbial spark that starts the metaphorical Middle East bonfire, which in turn is seen to threaten international security" (2000, 276).

Occasional and well-chosen statements by politicians from the region only reinforce water-war thinking. It was Boutros Boutros-Ghali, when he was Egypt's foreign minister, who observed that "the next war in the region will be over the waters of the Nile, not politics" (Gleick 1991, 22). And in 1998 a member of the Egyptian parliament said that his country's national security should not only be viewed in military terms but also in terms of wars over water (Amery 2002, 314). Much of the water-wars literature glosses over or ignores completely the many examples of cooperation throughout the region, including but not limited to the peace treaty of 1994 between Israel and Jordan. This treaty not only addresses water-related matters but also water is regarded as a resource that is crucial for inspiring and sustaining cooperation. According to Ahmed Abukhater, "the demise of the Jordan River was the catalyst for peace and cooperation between Israel and Jordan," and water issues to this day encourage peaceful interactions (2013, 67).

IR scholars are accustomed to such gloom-and-doom discussions about international politics. All that changed in the 1990s is that water was identified separately or as part of a bundle of environmental issues. Regardless, into the 1990s, IR scholars subscribed to the assumption of a causal link between changes in the availability of natural resources, such as water, and violent conflict. The logic was simple if not simplistic: "a high level of resource consumption causes a deterioration of water resources; this increases water scarcity, leading to intense competition, thereby increasing the risk of violence" (Setter et al. 2011, 443). However, since much of this research could not prove this causal link, especially when it came to interstate war, scholars interested in testing water-wars claims shifted their focus to the factors that underpin the relations between water resources and conflict to see whether environmental change and water scarcity should actually be included among the potential threats to a specific state's security (Lowi 1999, 380). Thus, instead of thinking about water and interstate conflict in all international river basins, it was more important to consider the degree to which certain riparian states perceive water to be a national security concern and states' dependence on water and geography.

Miriam Lowi uses the case of Egypt to highlight complexity and the importance of contextual features to clarify whether and how the depletion or degradation of water supply should be construed as a national security issue. These features depend on (1) the quantity and quality of the resource relative to the present and future consumption demand; (2) the nature of the resource dependence; and (3) in the case of transboundary rivers, the number of riparian states involved, the nature of relations and geographic location (Lowi 1999, 382). Scholarship on this very point emphasizes how and when water is securitized, the discursive construction of scarcity and threats, and conflict-internal dynamics. In other words, the meanings that conflict actors and mediators ascribe to water, as well as the legitimacy of their claims as actors in these conflicts, is inextricably linked to culture and discourse (Setter 2011, 443).

Although water-wars research has declined in the 2000s, it has also become more nuanced, shifting the unit of analysis from the state to groups and sub-state actors and from interstate wars to intrastate violence and to state failure. Thus, some research addresses the complex relationships between the environment and human (rather than national) security, examining the dynamics between multiple environmental and social factors across a range of spatial and temporary scales. There is still a tendency to establish cause-effect relationships between water as a contested issue and conflict, but the outcome is no longer assumed. In fact, "it is no longer assumed that the outcome of environmental degradation needs to be conflict, but that cooperation is as likely to occur and is, empirically, the more usual option" (Setter et al. 2011, 444). Qualitative studies of pastoral groups in Kenya, as well as much of the quantitative work, emphasize this precise point that even in times of disaster people pull together and cooperate rather than compete (Theisen 2001).

Articles on water cooperation and water management in international relations have become popular in the academic literature on water politics, pushing some scholars even to argue that "the popular myth of water wars […] be dispelled once and for all" (Setter et al. 2011, 444). In different ways and often without referencing any theoretical perspectives directly, the water cooperation research uses both realist and liberal arguments to explain why states cooperate over water. In line with realist arguments, water conflict is not efficient or rational for most states that share water basins. Resource scarcity along with differing levels of military power means that cooperation has been common, and even a number of recent climate change-conflict analyses have observed that even in times of scarcity, conflict behavior declines, as groups cooperate in order to survive (Meierding 2013,196). Discussing some of the good news in the area of postconflict peace building, scholars argue that shared water has in fact proven to be the natural resource with the most potential for interstate cooperation and local confidence building (Troell, Weinthal and Nakayama 2013).

A 2012 report entitled *Global Water Security*, prepared by the US National Intelligence Council (NIC) of the Office of the Director of National Intelligence, reflects what may be the newest thinking in water-wars research in the United States. It is decidedly tentative, highlighting the risks of instability, state failure and increases in regional tensions due to water insecurity rather than interstate violence or war. It explains that, while wars over water are unlikely within the next 10 years, water challenges—shortages, poor water quality, floods—will likely increase the risk of instability and state failure, exacerbate regional tensions and distract countries from working with the United States on important policy objectives (*Global Water Security* 2012, 3). A 2014 climate assessment, entitled *National Security and the Accelerating Risks of Climate Change*, which is a follow-up to a 2007 landmark study on climate and national security, reexamines the impact of climate change on US national security in the context of a more informed but more complex and integrated world. As with the 2012 reports on global water security, this report highlights the effects of water as "threat multipliers that will aggravate stressors abroad such as poverty, environmental degradation, political instability and social tensions," but it does not focus on interstate war. Instead it underscores how climate change and certain conditions can enable terrorist activity and other forms of violence. Moreover, this report emphasizes that the potential security ramifications of global climate change should serve as a catalyst for cooperation and

change and that the United States must be more assertive and expand cooperation with our international allies to bring about change and build resilience
(*National Security and the Accelerating Risks of Climate Change* 2014, 2).

Avenues to Water Cooperation

Traditionally security scholars have focused narrowly on water, viewing it
largely as a potential threat and a cause or potential contributor to violent
conflict between or within states. The vast and interdisciplinary literature on
global water politics is far more complex, and water-related research includes
scholars from numerous disciplines, including geography, natural resources,
ecology, fisheries science, urban planning, public health and environmental
sciences, to name a few. This literature also engages a whole host of subject
areas that are affected by water (Cook and Bakker 2013, 51). Unlike the water
wars articles, broader water-related scholarship addresses several regions and
countries, and of the 32 articles written in English, only 6 focused on the
Middle East. Of these articles, 4 discussed the possibilities or specific details
of cooperation. As Itay Fischhendler explains in his article on the Israeli-
Jordanian peace agreement, "a long-term broad perspective shows that water
conflicts have, to date, been successfully addressed in general. Historically,
over 3,600 treaties pertaining to different aspects of international water exist,
most of which were signed since 1948" (2008, 91).

While not attempting to provide a comprehensive overview of the mechanisms and institutions promoting water cooperation throughout history, the
following discusses some of the prominent avenues to water cooperation recognized in international politics. IR scholarship organizes theories in terms
of levels to simplify the complex causes of international outcomes. Outcomes
are thus due to international-, state-, or individual-level factors. These three
levels of analysis, but also the centrality of sovereignty as an institution and
practice in IR research, do not coincide perfectly with the mechanisms and
actors involved in water cooperation or water management. "Water is used in
all facets of society, from biology to economics to aesthetics to spiritual practice" and "all water management is multi-objective and based on navigating
competing interests. Within a nation these interests include domestic users,
agriculturalists, hydropower generators, recreation enthusiasts and environmentalists" (Wolf 2007, 5). And like other natural resources, water regularly
defies sovereignty, affecting and being affected by multiples levels and various
stakeholders.

As Anton Earle explains, most research on transboundary water management has focused on the state level, investigating how sovereign states
cooperate or compete over transboundary water issues. Yet, the state is an

abstraction, and this monolithic view of "the state" as the prime actor in water cooperation needs to be challenged because of the range of subnational actors that influence the position taken by a state (Earle 2013, 103). While acknowledging the differences and importance of scale in water management, this section identifies macro-, meso- and microlevel mechanisms that are discussed in the articles indexed in the *IPSA* between 1990 and 2015 as well as other articles and books on water cooperation in international politics. Although I discuss these mechanisms separately, much of research and case studies of water cooperation remind that these strategies operate in an overlapping and synergistic way.

In international relations, macrolevel explanations explore the role of global or international factors that are above that of the state to explain an international outcome, decision, or event. Although there is no world government in place to help states arbitrate water conflicts, there are a growing number of international institutions and mechanisms in place to help countries address and manage water resources. Research on states' cooperation explores the role that international organizations can play in promoting water cooperation between states. For example, despite problems for many years, India and Pakistan eventually cooperated concerning the Sutlej River, signing an international water treaty in 1960. Although some analyses of this cooperation state that it was water rationality that prompted the states to sign an agreement, the question is, who or what actors encouraged Indian and Pakistani leaders to think along these lines? A critical actor in this water dispute was the World Bank and the good offices that it established. Equally important was the trust the World Bank tried to cultivate among leaders in the two countries as well as the financial support both countries received through the Indus Basin Development Fund (IBDF) (Alam 2002). Cooperation between Pakistan and India was rational because both countries "needed water urgently to maintain existing works, and tap the irrigation potential in the Indus basin to develop socioeconomically, but it was the involvement and strategies of the World Bank that encouraged this kind of rational thinking (Alam 2002, 347). By cooperating with each other, both countries were able to safeguard their long-term water supplies from the Indus basin.

Much of the macrolevel literature on water cooperation focuses on the important role of international law. International environmental law as a separate area of public international law did not officially begin until the 1970s with the Stockholm Conference on the Environment. Water law principles, however, have a long history with roots in the Middle East and the Mediterranean, "as regions where major legal ideas about water law and rights arose and spread to the rest of the world" (Elver 2006, 887). As in the natural sciences, legal scholarship recognizes water as an essential resource, but it focuses on the rights of users and the use of legal institutions to make just allocations for users while respecting state sovereignty over natural resources. Legal scholars examine and seek resolution of interstate water conflicts through the rule of law and the acceptance of law by all parties. The body of international law regarded as international water law addresses water availability, access and conflicts-of-use management based on the principals of equitable and reasonable utilization, the due diligence obligation not to cause significant harm and the duty to cooperate.

Modern international water law is built upon the assumption that all states whose territories contribute to an international drainage basin have a right to an equitable share of the waters and an equal right to develop their available resources. By promoting fair access to a common resource, international water law ideally aims at restraining unilateral water-resources development. The principles of equity and reasonable use are reaffirmed in several non-binding declarations, conventions and treaties, all of which aim to establish the utilization, development, conservation, management and protection of international watercourses. The general principles enshrined in international water law are repeated in various international and regional instruments and organizations all over the world, including the United Nations (UN) and the Council of the European Union and various transgovernmental commissions that focus on specific bodies of water. For example, the UN Charter contains the fundamental tenets of the "law of nations," promoting regional peace and security and advancing the fundamental freedoms for all, but only more recent UN resolutions have reinforced the law of nations and the duty to cooperate in the peaceful management of freshwaters across national borders (Lab and Wouters 2013, 29–30).

International laws and principles are reinforced by a number of multilateral environmental agreements (MEAs) that may not have water as their primary objective but that affect water access and quality. Over the past four decades, there has also been a tremendous evolution and proliferation of water law because of human rights law, which has provided "a helping hand" with the UN General Assembly (GA) and Human Rights Council (HRC) in respective resolutions recognizing the human right to water and sanitation in 2010 (Leb and Wouters 2013, 38–39). In addition, universal and regional human rights conventions related to women, the rights of indigenous peoples and the rights of children have all reinforced and advanced new normative principles related to the right to water (Elver 2006, 891). Despite positive developments, international water law has not necessarily achieved equity, adaptation or sustainable development because, as IR scholars are quick to remind, relations between states are driven by the anarchic structure of international relations, power politics and state interests.

International organizations, international law, or other structures that exist "above the state" are sometimes helpful in promoting cooperation and water management, but as with much of international politics, it is states and the behavior of states that are recognized as the main drivers of water policies and international cooperation. Given IR's fixation with the state as the main repository of authority and decision-making, a lot of the water-related research emphasizes and details the history of bilateral agreements, the importance of institutional design and state-to-state dynamics. In particular it explains how general agreements and principles in certain areas encourage new legal instruments and institutions that adapt to a specific basin and country conditions. In Central Asia, for example, the Syr Darya river basin is seen as potentially one of the most problematic cases in the world because of the riparian states' history, their level of economic development and their political differences. Yet, multilateral negotiations and the creation of the Interstate Commission for Water Coordination (ICWC) allowed numerous multilateral and bilateral agreements to be signed after 1995 (Bernauer and Siegfried 2012, 233).

States are crucial not only to making bilateral agreements but also to providing the bureaucracies and institutions necessary to implement agreements. Multilateral and bilateral agreements and institutions have not solved the water issues in the Syr Darya basin, but militarized conflict—which was highly anticipated—has not occurred, and, as in other places in the world, state-to-state negotiations and relationships were crucial to addressing water disputes and transforming conflict into cooperation. During the Cold War, some thirty-seven hundred water agreements were concluded, though there was an imbalance in the distribution among regions and states. Developed countries concluded many of these agreements. while developing countries either did not make water agreements at all or did not efficiently implement these bilateral or multilateral agreements. According to a UN study, 72 percent of all major international river basins are in developing countries located in Africa, Asia and Latin America, but fewer than 33 percent of the relevant agreements signed worldwide between 1948 and 1972 covered the rivers in these countries (Elver 2006, 890).

There are many reasons and actors that influence how states "get to cooperation," but invariably an important factor in determining the way states acquire and use water are states' motives and perceptions rather than realities about water and water scarcity (Abukhater 2013, 9). In other words, whether water is a catalyst for cooperation or an important variable in conflicts between states depends on what IR scholars call "high politics," or the priorities of states and how domestic politics interprets states' relationships with their neighbors and adversaries. Thus, as much of the research on water management details, the role of water often depends on perceptions of water and the other, and how water and the politics of war are framed by elites. As Shimon Peres declared in 1993, "The water shortage proves the objective necessity of establishing a regional system [...] like all wars in the political and strategic reality of our times, wars fought over water do not solve anything" (Dolatyar and Gray 2000, 76).

Many studies of water cooperation try to open up the black box, examining the role of subnational actors and many microlevel factors that shape states' behavior, making agreements more likely to move discussions from rights to needs to benefits. Rather than assume states' interests, Fischhendler's 2008 research on the Israel–Jordan water agreement emphasizes the role of ambiguity in shaping the agreement and helping defuse domestic opposition, while other ambiguities incorporated into the treaty provided leeway to adjust resource allocation during a future crisis without the need to renegotiate the treaty. Water has several attributes that turn its appropriation and management into a potential source of conflict such as nonexcludability, rivalry, transboundary factors and the erratic nature of the availability and demand of the resource. By addressing these in the Jordanian-Israeli case, "the extensive use of ambiguities seems to have defused these attributes and led the way to ratification of the treaty between Israel and Jordan" (104).

Most of the literature on international water management dates from the mid-1960s, and while there are many similarities in the actors and variables affecting water cooperation, much has also changed. In the twenty-first century, new actors are emerging that are both above and below the nation-state but that influence water relations, including transnational actors, epistemic communities and networks of public and private actors. For example, Joseph DiMento's research on the Black Sea acknowledges the role of institutions and law in promoting cooperation around the Black Sea, but he contends that international law and other international-level factors exist alongside and often serve as an enabler of the work of epistemic communities and international nongovernmental organizations (NGOs) that work with governmental actors to create an environmental regime (DiMento 2001, 240–245). Similarly, others have acknowledged how the multifaceted effects of globalization have created intensive communications and global networks of public and private actors focused specifically on water issues. The "awakening effect" of global communications has allowed international NGOs and civil society groups to work together to address water issues (Elver 2006).

Like transnational actors, regimes and networks, there are other mechanisms of cooperation that do not clearly fit easily on any level but are invoked by water optimists that relate to both the supply and demand for water, specifically technological improvements and pricing policies (Dolatyar and

Gray 2000). Although technology does not fit comfortably in any of the levels described here, technological innovations are certainly discussed a great deal in the context of water management in the Middle East. Virtual water theory and practice emphasizes how the importation of water and/ or agricultural produce eliminates the need for the irrigation of domestic production. Virtual water and water trade is not necessarily a solution in every context; however, as the chapter in this volume by Hussein Amery confirms, this policy represents clearly a way of addressing and managing water scarcity. As other chapters on Israel detail, the process of desalinization to increase the productive use of water has been important, as has water pricing, to manage the demand for water and curb wasteful use of water. Although technology will continue to have an important impact on freshwater supply and demand in the future, we must remember that these changes will be evolutionary and take time.

Conclusion

It may be difficult to be optimistic when it comes to water, particularly in the Middle East, not only because of the numerous long-standing problems between many countries in this region but also because several states are in the process of imploding and disintegrating. Current realities in Syria, Iraq, Libya and Yemen, for example, demonstrate the profound fragility of this region as nation-states give way to a variety of substate actors. Yet, as this chapter has suggested, it is important not to exaggerate the uniqueness of any region in the severity of global water politics. Weak and failing states exist alongside more and stronger international laws and organizations, and all of this reflects broader global trends as new structures and relationships augment and complement states.

Scholars use the word "glocalization" to describe these divergent transformational trends, as subnational units become unbounded or disembedded from nation-states (Blatter, Ingram and Doughman 2001, 5). Sometimes these processes cause the complete unraveling of states, violence and human suffering, but often they do not. The explosion of interterritorial linkages and communication is happening in various ways all over the world, creating a proliferation of actors and institutions that are above the state but also below the state. A post-Westphalian system, where sovereignty is replaced with overlapping spheres of authority, will undoubtedly cause many challenges for water management and cooperation. Yet, international politics and global governance in the twenty-first century create many new opportunities as subnational bodies, cities, international organizations, nonprofit organizations and specific individuals assume more responsibility for managing water problems and facilitating state cooperation.

IR scholars have certainly identified ways in which water management will become the next global crisis. The search was not completely in vain, but what was unearthed, to the surprise of many, including this author, is that there are an equal number of examples where water problems have pushed new norms, created new institutions and facilitated cooperation and compromise. As Emily Meierding (2013) concludes, "Even if the proposed theoretical developments do not result in the discovery of future climate change connections, they will move the research program forward by offering more compelling evidence that such a relationship does not exist" (200). Water pessimists maintain that, even if water has not played an important role in generating war or significant violence up to this point, the past is not always the best predictor of the future. Yet this review of IR research and many interdisciplinary studies indicates that this is true for both conflict and cooperation. The hope is that this chapter's findings will encourage future IR scholarship to think more about water's potential for cooperation and peace building.

References

Abukhater, Ahmed 2013. *Water as a Catalyst for Peace: Transboundary Water Management and Conflict Resolution*. London: Routledge.

Alam, U. Z. 2002. "Questioning the Water Wars Rationale: A Case Study of the Indus Waters Treaty." *Geographical Journal* 168 (4): 341–353.

Allan, J. A. 2002. "Hydro-Peace in the Middle East: Why No Water Wars? A Case Study of the Jordan River Basin." *SAIS Review* 33 (2): 255–272.

———. 2005. "Water in the Environment/Socio-economic Development Discourse: Sustainability, Changing Management Paradigms and Policy Responses in a Global System." *Government and Opposition* 40 (2): 181–199.

Amery, H. A., 2002. "Water Wars in the Middle East: A Looming Threat," *Geographical Journal*, 168(4): 313–323.

Barnett, J. 2000. "Destabilizing the Environment-Conflict Thesis." *Review of International Studies* 26 (2): 271–288.

Bernauer, T., and T. Siegfried. 2012. "Climate Change and International Water Conflict in Central Asia." *Journal of Peace Research* 49 (1): 227–239.

Blatter, J., and H. Ingram, eds. 2001. *Reflections on Water: New Approaches to Transboundary Conflicts and Cooperation*. Cambridge, MA: MIT Press

Brochmann, N., and N. P. Gleditsch. 2012. "Shared Rivers and Conflict—a Reconsideration." *Political Geography* 32: 519–527.

Clayton, M. 2008. "Is Water Becoming the New Oil?" *Christian Science Monitor*, May 29. Accessed April 22, 2015. http://www.csmonitor.com/Environment/Global-Warming/2008/0529/is-water-becoming-the-new-oil.

Crossette, B. 1995. "Severe Water Crisis Ahead for Poorest Nations in Next 2 Decades." *New York Times*, August 10. Accessed April 22, 2015. http://www.nytimes.com/1995/08/10/world/severe-water-crisis-ahead-for-poorest-nations-in-next-2-decades.html.

Dadwal, S. R. "The Politics of Water in West Asia." *Strategic Analysis* 19 (3): 467–482.

Davenport, C. 2014. "Climate Change Deemed Growing Security Threat by Military Researchers." *New York Times* May 20.

Deudney, D. 1990. "The Case against Linking Environmental Degradation and National Security." *Millennium: Journal of International Studies*, 19: 3461–476.

DiMento, J. D. 2001. "Black Sea Environmental Management: Prospects for New Paradigms in Transitional Context." In *Reflections on Water*, edited by Blatter and Ingram. 239–266.

Dolatyar, Mostafa, and T. S. Gray. 2000. "The Politics of Water Scarcity in the Middle East." *Environmental Politics* 9 (3): 65–87.

Elver, H. 2006. "International Environmental Law, Water and the Future." *Third World Quarterly* 27 (5): 885–901.

Gilpin, R., 1981. *War and Change in the International System*. Princeton: Princeton University Press.

Gizelis, T., and A. E. Wooden. 2010. "Water Resources, Institutions, and Intrastate Conflict." *Political Geography* 29 (8): 444–453.

Gleditsch, N. P., and K. Furlong et al. 2006. "Conflicts over Shared Rivers: Resource Scarcity or Fuzzy Boundaries." *Political Geography* 25: 361–382.

Gleditsch, N. P., Pinker, S., Thayer, B. A., Levy, J. S., and Thompson, W. R. 2013. "The Forum: The Decline of War," *International Studies Review* 15 (3): 396–419.

Gleick, P. 1993. "Water and Conflict: Fresh Water Resources and International Security." *International Security* 18 (1): 79–112.

"Global Water Security 2012," Intelligence Community Assessment ICA 2012-08, 2 February 2012. US Department of State.

Harris, S. 2014. "Water Wars: Forget the Islamic State. The New Conflicts of the Future Could Be Sparked by Climate Change." *Foreign Policy* September 18. Accessed April 22, 2015. http://foreignpolicy.com/2014/09/18/water-wars/.

Hensel, P. R., 2000. "Territory: Theory and Evidence in Geography and Conflict." In *What Do We Know about War* edited by John A. Vasquez (Boulder, CO: Rowman and Littlefield, 2000), 57–84.

Kaplan, R. D., 1994. *The Coming Anarchy: Globalization and the Challenges of a New Century: A Reader.* Bloomington: Indiana University Press, 2000, 34–60.

Kolodziej, A. 1992. "The Renaissance of Security Studies? Caveat Lector!" *International Studies Quarterly* 34 (2): 421–438.

Koubi, V., G. Spilker, T. Böhmelt and T. Bernauer. 2014. "Do Natural Resources Matter for Interstate and Intrastate Armed Conflict?" *Journal of Peace Research*, 51(2): 227–243.

Lankford, B., K. Bakker, M. Zeitoun and D. Conway, eds. 2013. *Water Security: Principles, Perspectives and Practices.* New York: Routledge.

Lietzmann, K. M., G. D Vest, A. Carius, M. Kemper, S. Oberthur, D. Sprinz, C. Rudolph, A. Najam and R. A. Matthew, 1999. "Environment and Security in an International Context. Executive Summary Report," *WW Environmental Change and Security Project Report* 97(5): 34–48.

Lowi, M. R. 1999. "Water and Conflict in the Middle East and South Asia: Are Environmental Issues and Security Issues Linked?" *Journal of Environment and Development* 8 (4): 376–396.

Matthews, P., and D. St. Germain. 2007. "Boundaries and Transboundary Water Conflict." *Journal of Water Resources Planning and Management* 133 (5): 386–396.

Meierding, E. 2013. "Climate Change and Conflict: Avoiding Small Talk about the Weather." *International Studies Review* 15: 185–203.

National Security and the Accelerating Risks of Climate Change. 2014. Report by the CNA Military Advisory Board. Accessed April 5, 2015. http://www.cna.org/sites/default/files/MAB_2014.pdf.

Neack, L. 2007. *Elusive Security States First, People Last.* Lanham, MD: Rowman & Littlefield.

Pathak, M. 1999. "Water Wars over Litani River." *Asian Profile* 27 (2): 181–186.

Postel S. L., and A. T. Wolf. 2001. "Dehydrating Conflict." *Foreign Policy* 126 (September–October).

Powell, R., 1991. "Absolute and Relative Gains in International Relations Theory," *American Political Science Review* 85(4): 1303–1320.

Ramachandran, S. 2015. "Water Wars: China, India and the Great Dam Rush." *The Diplomat*, April 3. Accessed April 22, 2015. http://thediplomat.com/2015/04/water-wars-china-india-and-the-great-dam-rush/.

Rousseau, R. 2015. "The Growing Potential for Water Wars." *International Policy Digest*, April 12. Accessed April 22, 2015. http://www.internationalpolicydigest.org/2015/04/12/the-growing-potential-for-water-wars/.

Selby, J. 2005. "Oil and Water: The Contrasting Anatomies of Resource Conflicts." *Government and Opposition* 40 (2): 200–224.

Shaheen, M. 2000. "Questioning the Water-War Phenomenon in the Jordan Basin." *Middle East Policy* 7 (3): 137–150.

Starr, J. R. 1991. "Water Wars." *Foreign Policy* 82 (Spring): 17–36.

Stetter, S. et al. 2011. "Conflicts about Water: Securitizations in a Global Context." *Cooperation and Conflict* 46 (4): 441–459.

Ullman, R. 1983. "Redefining Security." *International Security* 8 (1): 129–153.

Walt, S. 1991. "The Renaissance of Security Studies." *International Studies Quarterly* 35 (2): 211–239.

Waltz, K., 1979. *Theory of International Relations.* Reading: Addison-Wesley.

Wolf, A., S. Yoffe and M. Giordano. 2003. "International Waters: Identifying Basins at Risk." *Water Policy* 5 (2): 29–60.

Wolf, A. T. "Shared Waters: Conflict and Cooperation 2007." *Annual Review Environmental Resources* 32 (3): 2–3:22.

Chapter 2

WATER SECURITY IN TRANSBOUNDARY SYSTEMS: COOPERATION IN INTRACTABLE CONFLICTS AND THE NILE SYSTEM

Jenny R. Kehl

Transboundary water-governance systems are emerging to negotiate water-sharing policies to promote security, stability and sustainability. Yet transboundary water disputes occur within most major shared water systems, and weak riparians are often coerced to agree to water-sharing policies that adversely affect them. This chapter examines strategies to promote cooperation in seemingly intractable water conflicts. For example, the chapter analyzes power asymmetry and the complex relations between strong and weak riparians in the Nile River system, in which water stress perennially tests the commitment to cooperation. The larger quantitative analysis examines the strategies weak riparians use to assert leverage in the international river basin, and the success of those strategies in achieving cooperation versus conflict.

The decision to resolve water disputes through negotiated settlements or to escalate the disputes into violent conflict is a complicated and contentious calculation. Water-based explanations of conflict and cooperation need to incorporate economy, ecology, technology, security, politics and policy. The multiple conflicting uses and competing users makes hydropolitics "one of the most urgent, complex, and contentious issues that the developing countries and the international community will have to face and resolve in the next century," as Arun Elhance articulates (1999, 4). Although there are successful water-sharing arrangements and more instances of cooperation than violent conflict (Wolf 1998), the institutionalized cooperative management of international water basins is still extremely rare (Elhance 2000). One substantive impediment to cooperative management is power asymmetry in hydropolitical complexes, which affects the legitimacy, complexity and feasibility of international water-sharing arrangements.

Yet despite the complexity and intensity of water stress in transboundary river systems, there are many examples of cooperation in seemingly intractable water conflicts. The case of the Nile system is compelling because the level of water stress seems insurmountable in the context of extreme food insecurity, burgeoning populations and climate change, while riparians continue to move between times of military threats and military mobilizations on the borders near the river to times of cooperative agreements and collaborative efforts to govern the river system in the interests of political and economic stability.

The transboundary governance structure of the Nile Basin Initiative is newly being tested by the construction of the Grand Ethiopian Renaissance Dam (GERD) on the Blue Nile in Ethiopia, which will be the largest dam in Africa. The diplomatic dispute this caused between Egypt and Ethiopia peaked with two contentious actions and demonstrations of force: Egypt's military collaborated with Sudan to begin building an airstrip for the overtly stated potential of bombing the dam if necessary (Carlson 2013) and a declaration by Egyptian president Mohamed Morsi stated that "if our share of the Nile water decreases by a single drop, our blood will be the alternative" (El-Behairy 2013). Yet in this context of high-stakes Nile politics, the presidential transitions and Egypt's ongoing regeneration of itself after the Arab Spring have possibly ushered in a new era of cooperation in the Nile region.

In a historic de-escalation of conflict, Egyptian President Abdel-Fattah al-Sisi signed a cooperative agreement on a new Declaration of Principles to conditionally support the GERD in Ethiopia. He stated publicly that the agreement represents a new chapter in the history of Egyptian-Ethiopian and Nile relations, he raised the ring of friendship (arms interlocked and elevated overhead) with Sudanese President Omar al-Bashir and Ethiopian Prime Minister Hailemariam Desalegn, and he was quoted as saying, "Ethiopia, Sudan and Egypt are inaugurating a new era of trust which will secure life, future and prosperity of the peoples of the three nations" (*Sudan Tribune*, March 23, 2015). The cooperative agreement remains highly contingent on diplomatic assurances and empirical evidence that GERD will not affect the flow of Nile water into Egypt. The importance of this contingency should not be underestimated. It will provide a true test of the choice between cooperation and conflict in the water-stressed region, and it will be a case of great consequence in the dynamics of hydropolitics and transboundary governance of the mighty Nile River.

The purpose of this study is to examine the dynamics of hydropolitical complexes—international organizations of states that share a river system—and the strategies weak riparians use to promote cooperation in international river systems with asymmetrical power. Riparians have a land bank adjacent to a natural watercourse or body of water, and they have a right to reasonable use of the water, albeit undefined. International river systems have multiple riparians, which are sovereign but interdependent. There are approximately 145 countries worldwide with shared river systems and 261 water basins that cross international boundaries, all of which have geographic, political and economic dimensions that affect most of the world's food security and political stability.

This chapter analyzes the effects of geographic, military, political, economic, technological and external influence on water governance in eight international river systems. The results demonstrate that weak riparians mobilize the assets and capacities of external actors, such as donor countries and international organizations, to increase their leverage within hydropolitical complexes. Based on the theoretical framework of power asymmetry and hard and soft power, the study finds that strategies to balance hard power are largely ineffective. They fail to achieve cooperative water-sharing arrangements and often exacerbate conflict. In contrast, strategies to balance economic power and soft power, such as market access and political legitimacy, are more successful in promoting cooperation and preventing conflict in transboundary water systems.

Strong riparians with a disproportionately high amount of political, economic and military leverage can often coerce weaker riparians into agreeing to water-sharing policies that adversely affect them. Weak riparians do not have sufficient resources to balance asymmetrical power, so they frequently appeal to international actors outside the hydropolitical complex. The cross-sectional analysis in the present research provides empirical evidence to support the importance of external international influence on asymmetrical power relations, negotiations and cooperation within hydropolitical complexes. The research also offers additional insights to support previous work that has illustrated the complexity and necessity, in many cases, of international involvement in river system management. Three important examples stand out. First, the research of Ariel Dinar and Senai Alemu on the impasse in the negotiations over the Nile water-sharing policies in 1997 resulted in the Nile riparians requesting the involvement of the World Bank to provide financial incentives to promote cooperation (Dinar and Alemu 2000). Second, Greg Browder's research on the Mekong Agreement emphasizes the role of donor assistance to overcome the mistrust that tainted negotiations in the past (Browder 2000).

Finally, Dinar's and Elhance's critical work on hydropolitics concludes that "during the long and often frustrating process of negotiating water-sharing agreements many formidable obstacles have to be overcome. Sustained support by third parties is often critical in creating and maintaining the momentum for such negotiations" (Dinar 2000, 220; Elhance 2000). In the interest of understanding the role of third parties and the strategies of weak riparians to promote cooperation in international river systems with asymmetrical power, the guiding questions of this analysis are the following: How do weak states encourage strong states to establish equitable water-sharing agreements? How do weak states gain leverage in negotiations? How do weak states renegotiate water-sharing policies that adversely affect them in the long run? To what degree do weak riparians turn to external forces, resources and allies to balance power within the hydropolitical complex?

The theoretical framework of hard and soft power (Nye 2004) holds considerable explanatory value for addressing these questions, particularly regarding the hard power of geographical riparian location, military capacity and the "sticky power" (Mead 2004) of economic influence. Hydropolitical complexes differ from traditional security complexes in several ways. The most important distinction is that traditional security complexes are organized to balance the power of external actors or adversarial security alliances, while hydropolitical complexes are organized to address conflict between the riparians within the hydrological basin or international river system. In the Nile River system, for example, Egypt has the greatest military capacity, economic dominance and political power in comparison to other riparians such as Ethiopia, Sudan, Rwanda and Tanzania. This power translates into a disproportionately high amount of water use for Egypt, even though Egypt does not control the headwaters of the Nile and depends on the deference of other riparians (Klare 2001). The weaker riparians can leverage their geographic advantage of controlling the headwaters of the Nile, but this provokes volatile conflict with Egypt, which threatens to use military force if necessary to protect its disproportionately high access to the water from the Nile. To avoid conflict with Egypt, the weaker riparians are coerced by Egypt's hard power to agree to inequitable water-sharing policies that may adversely affect them in the long run.

To complete the story, however, the Nile Basin Initiative demonstrates that the hydrohegemonic power (Zeitoun and Warner 2006) of Egypt is not total, and cooperative frameworks for water sharing continue to develop. The hard power of geographic riparian location, in addition to the external influence of the World Bank and United Nations Development Program, have left room for the otherwise weak riparians to negotiation water-sharing arrangements. The Nile Basin Initiative has achieved a remarkable amount of credible commitment and cooperation "given Egypt's regional dominance and historical disregard for other riparian states" (Posthumus 2000), but faces substantial obstacles to sustain the agreements. Most of these obstacles are related to hard and soft power asymmetry within the hydropolitical complex: the ongoing conflict of interests between upstream and downstream riparians, the lack of legal codification and institutionalization, economic inequality, trade dependence and persistent armed conflicts between the riparians and throughout the region.

Discussion of the Nile River system provides a context in which to link theory and practice, provides insights into the complexity of relationships between strong and weak riparians and presents possibilities for cooperation in seemingly intractable water disputes. More quantitatively, this research augments regional insights and anecdotal evidence from the case of the Nile and previous studies by developing a database and conducting a systematic empirical analysis of power dynamics within several hydropolitical complexes. Cross-sectional regression analysis is used to test the effects of geographic, military, political, economic and external factors on water conflict resolution in eight major international river systems. The results expose the asymmetrical power dynamics within hydropolitical complexes and suggest internal and international adjustments to make weaker riparians less easily exploitable in water-sharing policies. In sum, this analysis specifies the political, economic and international conditions in which weak riparians and dominant riparians assert distinct types of power and the success or failure of those strategies in promoting cooperation versus conflict.

Analytical Framework

One of the difficulties in analyzing cooperation in international river systems is that the same factors, such as water scarcity or economic development, can trigger conflict or cooperation. Hydropolitical complexes are evolving as transnational institutions to facilitate cooperation by providing incentives and imposing constraints as well as disseminating information about the costs and benefits of cooperation versus conflict. It is generally accepted that transnational institutions have boundaries, structures, rules, coherence and agency (Wallerstein 1974), but it is often forgotten that the refinement of the transnational institutional framework was influenced by research on geoecological regions that cross state boundaries (Braudel 1979). This legitimation of geoecological regions as units of analysis is important for the study of water basins that cross political boundaries. Hydropolitical complexes negotiate policies and treaties for geoecological regions identified by a shared international water resource. Transnational complexes can increase the benefits of cooperation and increase the costs of conflict for member states. This study examines the internal power asymmetries and power dynamics of hydropolitical complexes as well as the ongoing dependence of the weakest riparians on external actors and the foreign interference effect.

Relative inequality—natural and historical—and power asymmetry between the member states in a hydropolitical complex can distort the costs and benefits of conflict versus cooperation. An influential study by Bertram Spector concludes that one of the crucial variables in facilitating conflict or cooperation is the relative inequality between parties (2000). The inequalities in hydropolitical basins are long-standing. The most fundamental inequality stems from nature's unequal distribution of natural resources. Natural geographic and environmental inequalities have been exacerbated by population growth in developing countries and unprecedented levels of human consumption in wealthy and newly industrializing countries. Historical and structural inequalities such as the legacy of colonization, primary commodity dependence and global trade practices perpetuate core–periphery inequalities. In the context of this global system, hydropolitical complexes function as "mini world systems" (Wallerstein 1974) in which weak states have structural disadvantages that cause them to develop in a way that reproduces their subordinate status (Chase-Dunn and Grimes 1995). Structural, political, economic and environmental inequalities are exacerbated by power asymmetry in hydropolitical complexes and affect the type of leverage riparian states use to negotiate water-sharing arrangements.

In hydropolitical complexes with relative inequality and asymmetrical power, leverage is asserted through the geographical location of riparians, financial resources, commerce, access to information, technology transfer, military capacity and mobilization and other sources of power that vary widely between riparians. A parsimonious framework for understanding these dynamics is the asymmetry of four types of hard and soft power: structural power, sticky power, political power and ideational power. Hard power includes military might, geographic location and hydrohegemony (Zeitoun and Warner 2006), in which the hydrohegemon, such as Egypt on the Nile, asserts structural power over other riparians in the hydrological basin. The indicators of hard and structural power for this analysis are domestic military capacity, international military support, military mobilization, hydrohegemony and geographic riparian position at or near the headwaters of the river system. The substantive discussion of these factors is narrowed for the statistical analysis, which uses the variable of military mobilization to indicate leveraging of hard power and the variable of proximity to the headwaters to determine the level of control over the headwaters. Sticky power (Mead 2004) is economic power. It is the capacity to leverage trade and aid over other riparians that may be economically dependent. For this analysis, sticky power and economic dependence are measured as economic capacity (gross domestic product; GDP), amount of trade plus aid from other riparians, amount of trade plus aid from external actors, international financial aid as percentage of GDP and level of market access. For the statistical analysis, the leveraging of economic power is measured as the amount of bilateral trade plus aid from another riparian in the hydropolitical complex. Trade plus aid from an external source (external to the hydropolitical complex) is considered in the section on external influence on hydropolitical conflict and cooperation. Soft power, as articulated by Joseph Nye, comes in the form of political power and diffusion of ideas (2004). Political power is the capacity to control political decisions and secure compliance. This capacity is indicated by political legitimacy, preexisting legal agreements and political leverage. Political legitimacy in the form of democratic accountability is considered to be one of the strongest predictors of the sustainability of water-sharing policies (Elhance 2000) and is used as a regressor for the statistical analysis. Ideational power is generally defined as the ability to diffuse ideas, technology, culture and values (Lukes 1997). The current study uses the variable technology transfer, which is quantifiable and reliable, to indicate ideational soft power. It is difficult and subjective to quantify the variables of ideational power. For example, it is difficult to measure culture and to further measure cultural diffusion, and it is often erroneous to quantify culture. Some would say it is unethical and would recommend qualitative analysis over quantitative analysis of culture and other ideational variables. As this is a quantitative regression analysis, it is limited to a narrow construal of ideational power, which is measured by technology diffusion because it is identifiable and quantifiable despite its limitations in comparison to qualitative analysis for ideational variables. The variable specification is discussed in the Methodology and Elements of Analysis section.

The internal power asymmetries in hydropolitical complexes hold substantial explanatory value for understanding cooperation and conflict in international river basins and for identifying the reasons weak riparians often comply with disadvantageous policies. Yet internal power dynamics alone do not capture the consequential relationship between hydropolitical complexes and the global system. The analytical framework would be incomplete and the model would be misspecified if it did not consider the foreign interference effect. Weak states may not have the resources or power to offer incentives for cooperation and impose constraints on stronger riparians, but they frequently turn to foreign states to provide the necessary incentives and constraints. Foreign states play a crucial role in levying resources and leveraging power in international water systems, and this role may become increasingly important as water resources become increasingly scarce and international water-sharing practices become increasingly contentious. As articulated by

Elhance, "sustained international initiatives and support are often needed to overcome the many barriers to interstate cooperation in hydropolitics and to persuade and enable the respective riparian states to see cooperation as a 'win-win' situation for all concerned" (1999, 7). Strong riparians have the power to compel weak riparians to comply with water-sharing arrangements that may adversely affect them, but if the weak riparians gain the support of external actors to provide incentives and impose constraints, the strong states may not be able to "win" unless they participate in a cooperative negotiation process and a more equitable water-sharing policy.

A Test Case

Cooperation and seemingly intractable water stress in the Nile River system

The Nile basin hydropolitical complex illustrates the link between theory and practice and exhibits all the major elements of the analytical framework outlined in the preceding section: the internal power dynamics of the riparians in the hydropolitical complex as well as the dependence of weaker states on appeals to external sources of power. The strongest riparians have superior military capacity, can assert political pressure over weak riparians, have strong economies upon which other riparians may be dependent for trade or aid, or have access to advanced water-extraction and water-use technologies. Hydrohegemons and other strong riparians have several overlapping advantages. For example, Egypt has clear economic, political and military dominance over weaker Nile riparians such as Sudan and Kenya, even though Egypt does not control the headwaters. Egypt uses that leverage to control decisions about water sharing, and to coerce weak riparians to agree to policies that may adversely affect them in the long run.

Past leadership in Egypt has asserted its military power by threatening that Egypt will go to war, if necessary, over water. Former president Anwar Sadat declared, "The only matter that could take Egypt to war again is water" (1979, qtd. in *Aljazeera* 2013), and the former minister of foreign affairs of Egypt and later secretary general of the United Nations (UN) Boutros Ghali stated, "The next war in our region will be over the waters of the Nile" (1980, qtd. in Hillel, *Rivers of* Eden, 1994). Yet this contentious historical context has been changing with executive leadership turnover and the ongoing transition from the Arab Spring as well as renewed international attention to the Nile riparian relations as they are being tested by the construction of the GERD. Egyptian president Abdel-Fattah al-Sisi recently agreed to a new declaration of principles to support the GERD, contingent on the dam having no negative impact on the water flow into Egypt. This new cooperative agreement is seen as a continuation of the regional stability of the Nile Basin Initiative. However, the critical contingency—no negative impact on the water flow—is unlikely to be met from an engineering or environmental perspective, and thus the dam will pose an important test to the cooperative agreement, the durability of regional stability and the assertion of asymmetrical power by the hydrohegemon to protect their access to vital water resources.

One of the most promising characteristics of the Nile hydropolitical system is the relative stability in the region, which is facilitated in part thorough the Nile Basin Initiative. This is a general agreement to solve water disputes through cooperation. Yet the potential for conflict resurges perennially because of worsening droughts, lack of equity in the water-sharing policies, control of dams and food insecurity. Recent disruptions in the relatively stable riparian relations under the Nile Basin Initiative have been threefold: increasing food insecurity due to population growth and environmental degradation including extreme water scarcity, decreasing perception of legitimacy of the colonial arrangements under which the Nile waters were divided and ongoing construction of the GERD.

Food insecurity in the region has been worsening for a decade. It became more noticeable with the food riots during and after the Arab Spring. The Nile countries have been plagued with food insecurity, water scarcity, poverty and environmental degradation and insecurity as well exploding populations, climate change, out-of-date irrigation methods and pollution, all of which erupted in food and water riots from 2007–2012. The messages of the food and water riots were eventually translated into demands on the respective governments to increase their capacity to prevent and address food and water shortages. In Egypt, increasing food and water security has meant increasing the use of the Nile water. Of the Nile riparians, Egypt has the highest level of dependence on the Nile water. Approximately 95 percent of Egypt's water comes from the Nile River. Egypt has very little precipitation and no other substantial sources of surface water or ground water. It is Egypt's high level of dependence on the single source of the Nile River that makes the stakes so high for Egypt. A small decrease in the amount of water in the Nile has a large impact on Egypt's economic and political stability. Thus, Egypt asserts its asymmetrical power in other areas such as political power, economic capacity and military might in order to protect its access to this vital water resource.

The high level of dependence on the Nile is one of the arguments Egypt uses to provide justification for its disproportionate share of the water allocations. The Nile Treaty of 1929 allocates 75 percent of the Nile water to Egypt and 25 percent of the Nile water to be shared between the other nine riparians. The asymmetry in the allocation is clear. The legitimacy of this arrangement is currently being challenged by the other riparians. The primary challenge is made on the basis of postcolonial rights of sovereign nations. They claim sovereign nations should no longer be beholden to laws or treaties that were made while they were under colonial rule. The 1929 treaty is used as an example of weak riparians being coerced to agree to water-sharing policies that adversely affect them in the long run. If the treaty is deemed to be illegitimate because it was made under colonial rule and does not account for the needs or rights of sovereign nations, and if food insecurity and economic recession continue to erode the perception of legitimacy of governments and regional security complexes, then the challenges to stability in the Nile region will intensify. The most obvious contemporary test of regional stability and riparian cooperation will likely be the GERD.

The weaker riparians in the Nile system, particularly Ethiopia, Sudan, South Sudan, Uganda and Kenya, have appealed to the external influence of wealthy foreign governments as investors, private foreign investment firms, sovereign wealth funds and other financial institutions, including the World Bank, to provide exogenous incentives to construct large-scale projects independent of Egypt or absent Egypt's approval, as in the case of the GERD, or to incentivize Egypt to cooperate. The World Bank historically financed most of the world's major hydroelectric projects but no longer directly funds projects that do not have the cooperation and compliance of all riparians in the international river system. Therefore, Ethiopia, Egypt and other riparians will not generally receive direct World Bank funds for large-scale hydroelectric dams in Ethiopia, Egypt or elsewhere on the Nile unless all riparians give their consent for the project. It is important to recognize that this power dynamic can be utilized by both weak and strong riparians, depending on the preferences of the World Bank or other external forces. This dynamic alone merits an independent study, but for present purposes it illustrates one of the ways weak riparians may be able to identify less traditional sources of leverage or appeal to external forces to compensate for their lack of capacity and resources to influence water-sharing arrangements. In the case of Ethiopia's GERD, the government turned to domestic and international bonds, substantial Chinese foreign investments and other sources to fund the project.

The case of the GERD presents a new test of the riparian relations and whether Egypt will assert itself as a hydrohegemon. The claims of newfound cooperation under new executive leadership are promising but highly conditional. Egypt's new leader signed a potentially historic cooperative agreement promising cooperation if water supplies to Egypt are not adversely affected, but this is highly unlikely. The Nile case represents the variety, complexity and intensity of the factors tested in this analysis and, again, illustrates the relevance of the characteristics of hydrohegemony including political asymmetry, economic leverage and the importance of external influences. These variables are not just theoretical constructs or hypothetical influences but they are also concrete and consequential factors in the future of governing the Nile waters. In addition to the insights and illustrations of these realities in the case of the Nile, there is explanatory value in regressing these variables to provide further evidence that the relationships are statistically significant in the outcomes of conflict versus cooperation.

Cross-National Analysis

Cross-Sectional Time Series (CSTS) regression is used to test statistical correlations in this analysis because it can illustrate spatial relations and temporal dynamics of the strategies that promote cooperation versus conflict. It identifies distinct patterns in the use of geographic, military, political, economic, technological and external-appeals strategies by both weak and strong riparians as well as the outcomes of those strategies in achieving cooperation and preventing conflict. The analysis also tests the effects of contributing factors such as ethnic conflict, economic inequality and the level of dependence on the shared water source. The data consist of 52 country cases in eight major international river basins from 1950–2007: the Nile, Zambezi, Parana–La Plata, Amazon, Jordan, Ganges–Brahmaputra–Barak, Indus and Tigris–Euphrates basins. If cooperation is achieved and a water-sharing agreement is established in an international river system, the study assesses the sustainability of the negotiated settlement by testing a lag to verify whether the agreement was maintained or broken within a year.

The cross-sectional analysis addresses four basic statistical considerations common to CSTS in the interest of correctly establishing correlations: time order, heteroskedasticity, autocorrelation and spuriousness. Time order is assumed for this study. The data are structured in time-series panels, chronologically by year, so the assumption of time order is not problematic. However, time-series analysis can produce heteroskedasticity, which results in biased and inconsistent results. Heteroskedasticity occurs when the variance in the terms or parameters differs across observations, and it can cause bias in the results. This study uses panel-corrected standard errors to correct for heteroskedasticity and provide better coefficient estimates. Another common problem in CSTS regression is autocorrelation, the correlation of the variables beyond the boundaries of the dataset and the time constraints. Panel-corrected standard errors are used to make minor statistical corrections, although autocorrelation is not shown to be highly problematic in this particular study. Cross-section analysis can also suffer from spuriousness, which

Amazon Basin
Bolivia
Brazil
Colombia
Ecuador
French Guyana
Guyana
Peru
Suriname
Venezuela

Parana–La Plata Basin
Argentina
Bolivia
Brazil
Paraguay
Uruguay

Indus Basin
India
Pakistan
China
Kashmir-
disputed
territory

Zambezi Basin
Angola
Botswana
Congo-Kinshasa
Malawi
Mozambique
Namibia
Tanzania
Zambia
Zimbabwe

Nile Basin
Egypt
Ethiopia
Sudan
Kenya
Uganda
Rwanda
Burundi
Congo-Zaire
Tanzania

Tigris–Euphrates Basin
Iran
Iraq
Syria
Turkey

Jordan Basin
Israel
Jordan
Lebanon
Syria
Palestinian-
disputed
territory

Ganges Brahmaputra Barak Basin
Bangladesh
Bhutan
China
India
Myanmar
Nepal
Tibet-disputed territory

Figure 2.1 International river basins, country cases in eight hydropolitical complexes
Source: Jenny R. Kehl.

exposes the possibility that the statistical relationship is caused or distorted by variables not specified in the model. Spuriousness is avoided by controlling for the three most plausible sources of spuriousness in the analysis of hydropolitical complexes: economic inequality, ethnic conflict and the level of dependence on the shared river.

The 52 country cases are standard and designated by the official UN definitions of the countries and territories in each international river basin. It is important to note that the country-case total includes large country cases such as India and China that are riparians in two different hydrological basins. For example, India is a country case in the Indus hydrological basin and the Ganges–Brahmaputra–Barak hydrological basin, and India is a member state of each hydropolitical complex. The distinct cases are referred to as India–Indus and India–Ganges.

The international river systems are selected based on wide variation in the power distribution within the hydropolitical complex and the types of strategies used to assert influence, which translates into maximum variation in the independent variables for the statistical analysis. The second essential consideration in the case selection is the availability of data that are double documented. The eight international basins selected for this analysis have data that can be measured and documented, whereas other basins require additional data collection in the field before the variables can be quantified and verified. Substantive examples from the Nile basin are used to illustrate the central points of this quantitative analysis, which will be followed by a qualitative comparative case study of hard and soft power dynamics in the eight hydropolitical complexes, a seven-year fieldwork study nearing completion in 2009.

Dependent Variable

Conflict and cooperation

The dependent variable, cooperation versus conflict, is specified on a spectrum developed by the North Atlantic Trade Organization (NATO): (1) negotiated settlement, (2) qualified negotiated settlement, (3) unresolved dispute and (4) violent conflict (NATO 2014). At the turn of the century, NATO rearticulated its definition of security alliances with a stronger emphasis on the relationship between energy security, resources security and economic security. Applied to international water management, NATO describes a *negotiated settlement* as the result of cooperation to achieve a water-sharing policy or to resolve a water dispute. A *qualified negotiated settlement* is cooperation that is preceded by any form of military action or perceived threat. An *unresolved dispute* is a failure to achieve a negotiated settlement, and *violent conflict* is a failure to avoid the use of violence in addition to a failure to achieve a negotiated settlement (NATO 2014). Hydropolitical complexes are not always in a state of negotiating settlements or experiencing conflict, and the absence of conflict does not necessarily indicate the presence of cooperation. Thus, for the purpose of the present study, the dependent variable measures a change in the status quo of conflict or cooperation, or the lack of either. The NATO designation of the dependent variables is widely accepted and internationally recognized as a measure of cooperation and conflict and, despite its limitations, holds considerable explanatory value for understanding the levels of conflict and cooperation in hydropolitical complexes.

Independent Variables

The independent variables represent conceptual categories of power. The variables are indicators of military, geographic, economic, political, techno-logical and third-party sources of leverage. The conceptual category of hard power, or structural power, includes military and geographic variables.

Military mobilization

The leveraging of military power is indicated by the change in the level of military mobilization at the border of other riparian countries. The level of military mobilization is measured as troop levels and documented by the Correlates of War project. The variable is calculated as the change in the level of military mobilization. Change is measured and standardized on an interval scale, meaning the difference between the levels of an attribute that are posi-tive (affine) and linear, which is appropriate for regression analysis.

Control of headwaters

Geographic location is the most intuitive type of leverage in hydropolitical complexes and the most static, and it is measured as proximity in kilometers to the headwaters. The countries that control the headwaters or the points of contention can assert leverage by threatening to alter the water supply to countries downriver. Although the proximity to the headwaters can be found in many data sources, this study uses UN-Water data, managed through UNESCO, because it is consistent and uses the geographic identification of the water source, rather than localized or politicized identifications of the water source.

Economic power is a conceptual category, often referred to as sticky power, which encompasses production, consumption, market size, market access, trade and aid rules and practices. Most of these variables covary, which gener-ates statistical problems, so this study selects the type of economic power that is leveraged most often in negotiations over water-sharing agreements: trade and aid.

Trade and aid

Trade and aid can be easily leveraged. Riparians can promise to increase trade and aid as an incentive to promote cooperation, and they can threaten to reduce trade and aid to enforce cooperation. It is important to note that economic leverage can also be used to compel dependent riparians to agree to water-sharing policies that adversely affect them in the long run, for fear of losing trade and aid from wealthier riparians. The variable *trade and aid* is measured as the bilateral trade plus aid between dyads of riparians as a percentage of GDP. The total amount of trade plus aid is important in transnational negotiations, and the percentage of GDP can infer a level of dependence on trade and aid, which might affect the outcome of asserting economic power.

The conceptual category of soft power refers to political power and ideational power. Soft power is asserted to exert pressure toward or to compel agreement and enforce compliance, and often takes the form of legitimation and diffusion.

Political accountability

Political power is the capacity to offer political gains or threaten political condemnation, which affects economic relations, diplomatic relations, military relations and inclusion in the decision-making structure of the hydropolitical complex. The efficacy of offering political gains or levying political threats is largely determined by the credibility of the regime that leverages the gains and losses. Illegitimate regimes that have high levels of corruption or are unable to fulfil their basic governance roles do not have the political credibility or accountability to assert political power, especially at the international level, although they often compensate by using other forms such as structural, economic or military power. Political credibility, in the form of political accountability, is also salient for hydropolitical complexes because accountability is a strong indicator of the willingness of states to enter into water-sharing agreements with other states. Political accountability increases trust and decreases risk for riparian states. It has been stated that "democratic polities are also often the best guarantors of the acceptability and longevity of international water accords" (Elhance 2000, 215), but this variable posits that it is the broader concept of political accountability, which may or may not manifest as democratic polities, that increases credibility and political power.

Technology transfer

Another source of soft power that can be leveraged is ideational power: access to and diffusion of information and advanced technologies. Accurate information, reliable data, energy, infrastructure and access to technologies that improve water-use efficiency in industry or agriculture are highly valuable in water-scarce regions. Access to information and technology can be transferred or withheld in order to affect the outcome of negotiations over water-sharing policies. Technology transfer has only recently been quantified and recorded as data, and is not available for most of the 57-year time span of this study. Thus, technology transfer is measured as a change in the level of technological capacity, documented by the World Bank, which can be indicative of diffusion.

External power

If riparians do not have the resources or domestic capacity to assert leverage in negotiating water agreements, they can appeal to external international actors for support. Hydropolitical complexes are intended to offer incentives to cooperate and impose constraints on conflict over shared water. However, weak riparians often do not have the resources or power to offer incentives and levy constraints, and may appeal to external international actors to do so. Foreign governments, nongovernmental organizations and international financial institutions may assert economic, political or military leverage on the member states of hydropolitical complexes if it is in their interests to promote cooperation versus conflict. Although external power has many dimensions, magnitudes and measures, this study uses the change in total trade plus aid from sources external to the hydropolitical complex to indicate the foreign interference effect.

Additional contributing factors include economic inequality, ethnic conflict and the level of dependence on the shared water source (what percentage of a country's water comes from that water source alone).

Economic inequality

The level of economic inequality between the riparians within a hydropolitical complex affects the utility of different types of leverage. For example, if there is a high level of economic inequality, measured as the disparity in GDP per capita between states, economic leverage such as trade and aid might be more effective.

Ethnic conflict

Ethnic conflict may disrupt or distort the negotiation process of establishing water-sharing agreements. Ethnic conflict also destroys infrastructure, absorbs resources and generates opportunity costs that affect the possibilities for cooperation in water-sharing policies. Ethnic conflict is measured as the events of ethnic conflicts that report human injuries, as documented by the Correlates of War database.

Dependence on the shared river

The level of dependence on the shared river also affects conflict and coopera-tion. Some riparians may be more dependent on one water source, whereas other riparians may have access to alternative water resources. For example, Egypt is almost entirely dependent on the Nile for its water. Therefore, Egypt may be more likely to heighten the intensity of conflict in order to main-tain its dominance in the hydropolitical complex and its control over water-sharing policies. The level of dependence on the shared river is measured as the amount of water extracted from the river as a percentage of total water use, which is documented as data by UNESCO and UN-Water.

It is important to reiterate that the measurements of the variables are inter-val data, which are appropriate for regression analysis. Most of the variables measure change to indicate the leveraging of types of power rather than the static levels of power, except for geographic power. More information about the indicators, measurements and data sources can be found in the variable chart in Appendix 1. The temporal dynamics of the variables in the CSTS analysis are also informative, as the correlations alone do not demonstrate the direction of causality. For example, an increase in economic leverage, such as market access, may be correlated with an increase in cooperation between riparians in the hydropolitical complex, but the correlation does not determine whether the increase in market access promoted hydropolitical cooperation or whether the hydropolitical cooperation facilitated an increase in market access. The ele-ment of time in the CSTS and the original data must be reviewed to determine whether change in the independent variable precedes change in the dependent variable. We should recall time order is assumed for this analysis because the data are structured in chronological time-series panels with panel-corrected standard errors. This study focuses on factors that contribute to cooperation in hydropolitical complexes and in negotiating water-sharing policies, thus it analyzes the correlations in which changes in the use of political, structural, geographical, ideational and economic leverage precede changes in the level of conflict or cooperation in international river systems.

Results

Weak riparians in hydropolitical complexes are often coerced to agree to water-sharing policies that adversely affect them. The primary contribu-tion of this research is to provide systematic analysis and statistical evidence to demonstrate that weak riparians can assert economic and soft power in water-sharing negotiations by appealing to and utilizing the capacities of external actors, and that economic and soft power are the most successful

Table 2.1 The effects of specific types of leverage on cooperation versus conflict in hydropolitical complexes

Regressor	Type of leverage used by weakest riparian				EQ$_3$	Type of leverage used by strongest riparian		
	EQ$_1$	Outcome	EQ$_2$	Sustained		Outcome	EQ$_4$	Sustained
Geographic	0.81*	Conflict			0.68*	Conflict		
Military	0.27*	Qualified negotiation	0.09	No	0.43*	Qualified negotiation	0.02	No
Political	0.04				0.19*	Qualified negotiation	0.01	No
Economic	0.11*	Negotiation	0.01	Yes	0.17*	Negotiation	0.09	Yes
Technological	0.08*	Negotiation	0.01	Yes	0.09*	Negotiation	0.01	Yes
External	0.73*	Negotiation	0.28*	Yes	0.01			
Incentive	0.39*	Negotiation	0.07*	Yes	0.33*	Negotiation	0.01	No
Constraint	0.07				0.09			
Economic inequality	0.19*	Qualified negotiation	0.09	No	0.08*	Qualified negotiation	0.01	No
Ethnic conflict	0.22*	Conflict					0.21*	Conflict
Basin dependence	0.40*	Conflict					0.23*	Conflict
Number	102		31		102		18	
R-Square	0.57		0.38		0.49		0.21	

Central tendency and dispersion for x<-(number=102, mean=0, standard=1): minimum -1.12, mean 0.17, maximum 1.41.

* Statistically significant at the 0.05 level, two-tailed test.

** Statistically significant at the 0.01 level, two-tailed test.

Test Equations*

Equation One: How do the types of leverage used by the weakest riparian affect the outcome of cooperation versus conflict?

EQ_1: cooperative, negotiated settlement versus conflict = $b_1 + b_2$(geographic) + b_3(military) + b_4(political) + b_5(economic) + b_6(technological) + b_7(external) + b_8(incentive) + b_9(constraint) + b_{10}(inequality) + b_{11}(ethnic) + b_{12}(dependence) + e

Equation Two: If a cooperative, negotiated settlement is achieved, is it sustainable for at least a one-year lag?

EQ_2: cooperative, negotiated settlement = $b_1 + b_2$ (military) + b_3(economic) + b_4(technological) + b_5(external) + b_6(incentive) + b_7(inequality) at $t_{+1} + e$

Equation Three: How do the types of leverage used by the strongest riparian affect the outcome of cooperation versus conflict?

EQ_3: cooperative, negotiated settlement versus conflict = $b_1 + b_2$(geographic) + b_3(military) + b_4(political) + b_5(economic) + b_6(technological) + b_7(external) + b_8(incentive) + b_9(constraint) +b_{10}(inequality) + b_{11}(ethnic) + b_{12}(dependence) + e

Equation Four: If a cooperative, negotiated settlement is achieved, is it sustainable for at least a one-year lag?

EQ_4: cooperative, negotiated settlement = $b_1 + b_2$(military) + b_3(political) + b_4(economic) + b_5(technological) + b_6(external) + b_7(incentive) +b_8(inequality) at $t_{+1} + e$

Source: Jenny R. Kehl.

in achieving cooperative agreements in hydropolitical complexes. In other words, weak riparians may turn to external third parties such as foreign governments or international financial institutions to assert influence on the strong riparians within the hydropolitical complex, because the external forces have the resources to compensate for the disproportionately low influence of weak riparians. The international community should be knowledgeable about this dynamic because, as water scarcity increases and water-sharing policies become more contentious, the role of international actors will become more consequential. International influence will be a significant factor in promoting cooperation or provoking conflict in hydropolitical complexes, which affects regional stability and international security.

The results indicate the leverages and strategies used by weak and strong riparians, the outcomes of conflict or negotiated settlements and the sustainability of the negotiated settlements.

Structural and Hard Power

Geographic leverage

In all cases in the study, the country with the geographic advantage asserted it. This is not surprising. If a country controls the headwaters or the upriver point of contention, it uses the geographic advantage as leverage over other countries that may have an advantage in political power, military might or economic dominance. Ethiopia, for example, is no match for the political, military and economic prowess of Egypt, but Ethiopia controls the water upriver from Egypt on the Nile. Thus, Ethiopia has at least one powerful bargaining chip and uses it in times of extreme scarcity, although this test of Egypt's resolve has not been pushed to the point of escalating conflict. The future power plays of Ethiopia and Sudan with Egypt, as well as plausible riparian alliances, is receiving an increasing amount of scholarly attention (Klare 2001) but has yet to produce a source of hard power that trumps the military hard power or economic sticky power of Egypt.

The problem verified in this study, however, is that asserting geographic leverage results in conflict in almost all cases. In the case of the Nile, when Ethiopia asserts its geographic advantage, Egypt responds by increasing its political pressure, military threats and economic leverage, which often exacerbates conflict rather than promoting cooperation. In sum, geographic leverage is statistically significant because the riparians that have the geographic advantage use it, but the use of geographic leverage is highly correlated with conflict, not cooperation.

Military Strategy

Countries will mobilize their militaries to protect access to vital water resources. Part of the objective of hydropolitical security complexes is to minimize the need for military mobilization around contentious water issues and to promote cooperation between interdependent states in international river systems. The results of this research demonstrate that many negotiations over water-sharing policies are qualified negotiated settlements, which indicates that a form of military leverage such as threats or mobilization preceded negotiations. This suggests that the application of military leverage can bring both sides to the negotiation table because military threats, mobilization and use of force are not generally ignored, especially if the military power of the weaker riparian is asserted through terrorist attacks or backed by external military capacity. Other types of leverage such as economic constraints can be neglected while time passes, even if the initial water-sharing dispute is not resolved. The problem with bringing riparians to the negotiating table by threatening or mobilizing military options is that the subsequent settlements are not sustainable.

Sticky Power

Economic leverage

Weak riparians use economic leverage to achieve negotiated settlements on water-sharing policies, and the negotiated settlements are sustainable for at least a year. This can be explained in part by the reality that market access is highly coveted. The promise to increase market access can serve as an incentive to promote cooperation. Leveraging market access can alter the cost-benefit analysis by making cooperation more beneficial: cooperation will result in gaining access to markets, and conflict will be more "costly" because it will result in sanctions or the loss of access to markets. The difference between strong and weak riparians in this regard is that the strong riparians can assert economic leverage based on their own markets and assets, while weak riparians often have to turn to external actors such as the World Bank to provide economic incentives and constraints on their behalf to promote cooperation in the region.

External Influence

To avoid being coerced to accept water-sharing policies that adversely affect them, weak riparians often appeal to external forces to assert power and leverage in the negotiations of hydropolitical security complexes. The use of external influence is statistically significant in promoting cooperation in hydropolitical complexes,

and the negotiated settlements are sustainable. As concluded by Elhance, international financial institutions can offer "powerful economic leverages to persuade
reluctant states to cooperate," and the cooperative arrangements tend to endure
at least as long as the aid keeps flowing (2000, 216). The promise of international
aid can serve as an incentive to resolve resource disputes through cooperation.
Donor organizations can design aid programs to alter the cost-benefit analysis
of resolving disputes through negotiated settlements as opposed to violent conflict. Recipient countries can use international financial aid to promote economic
growth, build infrastructure, increase government capacity to provide public services and other development projects to advance economic and political stability.
Financial aid operates through mechanisms governing how the money can be
used and what degree of accountability must be achieved. In addition to general
development goals, "aid conditionality can help strengthen incentives for ending
conflict and discourage a return to war" (Boyce 2002). For example, the World
Bank will give financial aid to help develop large regional water supply systems
for potable water, irrigation and hydroelectric projects. However, the loans are
contingent on the agreement and cooperation of all riparians. If one riparian
does not agree with the proposed water-development project, the World Bank
will withhold financial aid until a negotiated settlement can be reached.

Soft, Political and Ideational Power

Political leverage

Political leverage is not a statistically significant factor in the capacity of weak
riparians to promote cooperation, but it does correlate with the ability of
strong riparians to achieve negotiated settlements. This is interesting for two
main reasons. First, political legitimacy is significant for strong riparians but
not for weak riparians, presumably because strong riparians meet a threshold
of legitimacy that allows them to offer credible political gains and to allocate
political losses, whereas weak riparians do not generally have the capacity to
do so. Second, it exposes a probable source of multicollinearity, which was
tested and verified, between military power, political legitimacy and economic
resources. Political leverage is only effective in cases where the riparian has
overlapping advantages in military capacity and economic assets that can be
leveraged. In addition, the settlements are qualified negotiated settlements,
which means that the negotiations were preceded by military actions such
as threats or mobilization and that the settlements are not sustainable. The
weaker riparian may have succumbed to political pressure to conform to policies that adversely affect them, but these policies may not be sustainable if the
political pressure lets up for any reason in the future.

Diffusion of technology

The capacity to leverage access to valuable technologies can bring riparians to the negotiating table. Both strong and weak riparians can offer to provide or use technologies that increase water-use efficiency or produce hydroelectric power, which may have distinct benefits or consequences for different riparians. The primary issue with leveraging technology, however, is that most countries will turn to external sources to gain access to new technologies or the money to finance them. International financial institutions such as the World Bank typically get involved in large infrastructure development projects and technology transfers. The definitive work of Spector demonstrates that cooperation often depends on external "facilitating elements" such as technology, which can be engineered to promote cooperation and prevent conflict (Spector 2000, 224).

Contextual factors

There is a complicated relationship between economic inequality and regional conflict. Economic inequality can provoke violent conflict within and between countries. Regarding resource disputes, however, economic tensions have a dual effect: inequality can exacerbate conflict or bring countries to the bargaining table. The statistical results of this study show that economic inequality results in qualified negotiated settlements that follow volatile disputes, which indicates that contradictory forces are in play; disputes many be settled in a way that temporarily decreases the likelihood of an outbreak of violence but increases long term economic inequality, thus increasing the likelihood of instability and violence in the future. In contrast, the effects of ethnic conflict are clear and consequential. Ethnic conflict disrupts the negotiation process and distracts the attention and resources of the participants. It is not surprising that ethnic conflict has a statistically significant correlation with the continuation of conflict. Another complicating factor is the level of dependence on the shared river system. A high level of dependence means a high likelihood of conflict. However, the implications of this finding are more substantial. As demand increases and water scarcity increases, the level of competition to control the resource will also increase. Strategies for conflict prevention and resolution will need to address this increase in the intensity of competition to control the water source.

Conclusion

The complexity and intensity of transboundary water governance will increase as water stress increases, food insecurity is exacerbated and demands are heightened on water resources that are shared between competing users and riparian countries. Transboundary waters cross political boundaries and economic interests and are an important challenge in global environmental governance and regional security. The emerging hydropolitical complexes are generally successful in promoting cooperation through water-sharing policies and through resolving water disputes, even in seemingly intractable disputes. Yet almost every transboundary water system and hydropolitical complex is being newly tested due to worsening water scarcity and asymmetrical power, in which weak riparians are often subject to water-sharing policies that adversely affect their prosperity and regional stability.

To counteract asymmetrical power, weak riparians are most successful at influencing water-sharing policies when they utilize the resources of external actors to augment their economic and technological capacity. With external support, weak riparians can assert economic leverage and soft power, which this study shows to be the most effective in achieving cooperation in hydropolitical complexes. However, these exogenous sources of influence are used the least often. The types of power that are asserted most frequently are geographic location and military capacity, which are shown in this study to be the least successful in achieving consistent cooperation and sustainable settlements. The general conclusion is highly problematic for the cooperative management of international river systems: the strategies that are the most successful at promoting cooperation are used the least often. This is, in part, because hydropolitical complexes are intended to be regional security organizations that promote regional stability and prosperity concerning shared water resources. However, if weak riparians find that they are being coerced to accept water-sharing policies that adversely affect them owing to power asymmetry in the regional complex, they may turn to external actors to gain the leverage necessary to negotiate better arrangements. A positive spin on this finding is that the external actors tend to augment economic and soft power as opposed to promoting hard power. There are known strategies for asserting economic power—such as altering the amount of trade and aid—and for leveraging soft power—such as technology transfers—that can be used to increase cooperation. This serves the objectives of hydropolitical complexes, albeit indirectly, which are to increase regional cooperation and achieve negotiated settlements for water-sharing policies in shared river systems.

The weakest riparians do not have the economic resources, political capacity or nonviolent leverage to balance asymmetrical power in hydropolitical complexes, so they often appeal to external actors to augment their power. The cross-sectional analysis provides empirical evidence to support the importance of external international influence on asymmetrical power relations and cooperation within hydropolitical complexes. The role of external actors will become increasingly important in the internal power dynamics of hydropolitical complexes as competition between riparians intensifies. The decision to promote cooperation or provoke conflict will become more consequential as water use and water scarcity increase. International actors that choose to get involved in international water disputes and regional hydropolitical complexes will need to keep pace with these changes.

One of the most compelling recent dynamics in hydropolitical complexes is the augmentation of cooperation in the Nile River system in response the construction of the GERD on the Blue Nile in Ethiopia. A historic de-escalation of conflict was initiated by Egyptian president al-Sisi when he signed a new cooperative agreement to tentatively support the construction of the dam if it upholds the declared ten principles of water sharing and does not affect the flow of water into Egypt. Historically, the Egyptian government has asserted its military dominance to threaten any incursion on the Nile's flow, as illustrated in former President Hosni Mubarak's strong statement that if Egypt's waters are diminished, "our response will be beyond anything they can imagine" (Klare 2001). In a reality check around the turn of the twenty-first century, Michael Klare's work *Resource Wars* reminded us that "the Egyptians have never agreed to any water-sharing scheme that was not under their direct control" (2001). Egypt has rejected cooperative Nile water-sharing policies in the recent past if they decreased Egypt's 75 percent allocation of Nile water. It rejected the Cooperative Framework Agreement 2009 signed in Democratic Republic of the Congo by regional riparians; the Cooperative Framework Agreement 2010 signed in Uganda by Rwanda, Ethiopia, Uganda and Tanzania; and the Cooperative Framework Agreement 2011 signed by Burundi, Uganda, Rwanda, Tanzania, Ethiopia and Kenya. Yet President al-Sisi's recent ushering of a new era of cooperation has changed the rhetoric, if not the reality. The president's promise of cooperation is highly conditional on the GERD not affecting the flow of water into Egypt, which is highly unlikely from the view of engineering and environmental dynamics. The true test of the commitment to cooperation will come when Egypt's share of the Nile waters are jeopardized by the GERD. It could alter Egypt's calculations of the benefits of cooperation versus conflict, and Egypt may reassert its asymmetrical power and its position as hydrohegemon in the region.

Future research on transboundary governance, hydrohegemony and asymmetrical power needs to disaggregate the findings of this study, and others, as well as analyze the motives behind unilateral actions and international involvement in hydropolitical complexes. We cannot ignore the temptation of external actors to manipulate water disputes in order to increase or maintain their own access to vital resources. New research also needs to be conducted on the effects of multinational corporations as external international actors, asserting leverage in hydropolitical complexes. A systematic comparative analysis of variation in the strategies and outcomes of foreign influence by multinational corporations, foreign governments and international financial institutions would be informative. As water becomes increasingly scarce, the capacity of governments to address food and water insecurity comes under challenge, the legitimacy of "politics as usual" is questioned in transboundary water-sharing systems and corporations consolidate their control over vital natural resources, it is useful to anticipate the impact on international river systems so that the international community can offer alternative forms of economic and soft power to promote cooperation and prevent conflict.

APPENDIX: Variable Specification

Category	Indicator	Variable	Measure	Data Source
Hard Power	Military	Level of military mobilization	Change in troop levels on the border of riparian states	Correlates of War
Hard Power	Geographic	Control of headwaters	Proximity to headwaters	UNESCO: UN-Water
Sticky Power	Economic	Total trade plus aid from a riparian state	Total trade plus aid from riparian state, as percentage of GDP	World Bank, Bilateral Trade and Aid
Soft Power	Political	Political accountability	Change in level of democratic accountability	Governance Indicators, World Bank
Soft Power	Ideational diffusion	Technology transfer	Change in amount of technological capacity	World Bank
External Power	Involvement of a third party	Total trade plus aid from an external actor	Change in the level of total trade plus aid from external source	World Bank
Incentive	Perceived positive character of leverage	Incentive	Dummy variable, 1 = incentive, 0 = no incentive	Inter-coder reliability over 98%

Category	Indicator	Variable	Measure	Data Source
Constraint	Perceived negative character of leverage	Constraint	Dummy variable, 1 = constraint, 0 = no constraint	Inter-coder reliability over 98%
Contextual	Economic inequality	Economic inequality between riparians	Economic disparity in GDP pc between riparians	UNDP
Contextual	Ethnic conflict	Ethnic conflict	Change in the number of ethnic events reporting human injuries	Correlates of War
Contextual	Dependence on shared river	Dependence on shared river	River water extraction as percentage of total water use	UNESCO: UN-Water

References

Aljazeera. 2013. "Next on Egypt's to-do; Ethiopia and the Nile." December 3, 2013. http://www.aljazeera.com/indepth/features/2013/12/next-egypt-do-ethiopia-nile-201312872410501805.html

Boyce, James. 2002. *Investing in Peace: Aid and Conditionality after Civil Wars*. Adelphi Paper 351. Oxford: Oxford University Press for the International Institute for Strategic Studies.

Braudel, Fernand. 1979. *Civilisation matérielle, économie et capitalisme, XVe–XVIIIe siècle, le temps du monde vol. 3*. Paris: LGF Publishers (1979) and Berkeley: University of California Press (English translation 1992).

Browder, Greg. 2000. "An Analysis of the Negotiations for the 1995 Mekong Agreement." *International Negotiation* 5: 237–261.

Carlson, Andrew. 2013. "Who Owns the Nile?" *Origins: Current Events in Historical Perspective*, origins.osu.edu, The Goldberg Center, The Ohio State University, 6 (6): 0–1.

Chase-Dunn, Christopher, and Peter Grimes. 1995. "World-Systems Analysis." *Annual Review of Sociology* 21: 387–417.

Dinar, Ariel, and Senai Alemu. 2000. "The Process of Negotiation Over International Water Disputes: The Case of the Nile Basin." *International Negotiation* 5: 331–356.

Dinar, Shlomi. 2000. "Negotiations and International Relations: A Framework for Hydropolitics." *International Negotiation* 5: 375–407.

Elhance, Arun P. 1999. *Hydropolitics in the Third World: Conflict and Cooperation in International River Basins*. Washington DC: United States Institute of Peace Press.

———. 2000. "Hydropolitics: Grounds for Despair, Reasons for Hope." *International Negotiation* 5: 201–222.

El-Behairy, N. 2013. "If Our Share of the Nile Water Decreases, Our Blood Will Be the Alternative." *Daily News Egypt*, June 12. http://www.dailynewsegypt.com/2013/06/11/morsi-if-our-share-of-nile-water-decreases-our-blood-will-be-the-alternative.

Hillel, D. 1994. *Rivers of Eden: The Struggle for Water and the Quest for Peace in the Middle East.* New York: Oxford University Press, 66.

Klare, Michael. 2001. *Resource Wars: The New Landscape of Global Conflict.* New York: Henry Holt and Company, 158.

Lukes, S. 1997. *Power: A Radical View.* Basingstoke: Palgrave Macmillan.

Mead, W.R. 2004. "America's Sticky Power." *Foreign Policy* 141: 46–53.

NATO. 2014. NATO Glossary of Terms and Definitions, document number AAP-06(2014). http://www.cimic-coe.org/wp-content/uploads/2014/06/NATO-EU-UN-glossary-on-DCB-and-CP.pdf.

Nye, J. 2004. *Soft Power: The Means to Success in World Politics.* New York: Perseus.

Posthumus, B. 2000. "Nile Basin Nations Move Towards Cooperation." European Platform for Conflict Prevention and Transformation. *Conflict Prevention Newsletter Special on Water and Conflict, One World* 3: 4–7, 13–20.

Spector, Bertram. 2000. "Motivating Water Diplomacy: Finding the Situational Incentives to Negotiate." *International Negotiation* 5: 223–236.

Sudan Tribune, 2015. "Nile Water Countries Sign Framework Deal on Renaissance Dam," March 23, http://www.sudantribune.com/spip.php?article54369.

Wallerstein, Immanuel. 1974. *The Modern World-System, vol. 1: Capitalist Agriculture and the Origins of the European World-Economy in the Sixteenth Century.* New York and London: Academic Press.

Wolf, Aaron. 1998. "Conflict and Cooperation along International Waterways." *Water Policy* 1 (2): 251–265.

Zeitoun, M. and J. Warner. 2006. "Hydro-hegemony: A Framework for Analysis of Trans-boundary Water Conflicts" *Water Policy* 8 (5): 435–460.

Chapter 3

WATER-DEMAND MANAGEMENT IN THE ARAB GULF STATES: IMPLICATIONS FOR POLITICAL STABILITY

Hussein A. Amery

The Arabian Peninsula is one region where the terrain, climate and available natural resources have all played an important role in shaping human–environment relations, economic development and population size. Its harsh climatic conditions have historically deterred colonial powers from attempting to control the peninsula, save for the Ottomans, who controlled a coastal strip, a route to Mecca and Medina, and the British, who captured a few port cities. In addition to the Persian Gulf, the Indian Ocean and the Red Sea, the vast and harsh desert that covers much of the interior of the peninsula—extending all the way to the Euphrates River—was a virtual barrier to transportation, making much of the area feel like an island (*jazeera* in Arabic) to its inhabitants.

While this popular image of the past still lingers, the active exploitation of the hydrocarbon wealth that started in the 1950s has been instrumental in transforming the human–environment relations as well as the socioeconomic base and political organization of the area. For instance, up until the modern development of the 1960s, the water needs of the people of Abu Dhabi were met solely from springs and shallow wells that tap groundwater resources. Water extraction and delivery methods were traditional and labor intensive. "The traditional jazra system, which uses animals to pull water from deep wells, was still in use until a few decades ago" (EAD 2014). Politically, the Gulf states formed the Gulf Cooperation Council (GCC) in 1981, a political institution that is made up of Saudi Arabia, United Arab Emirates (UAE), Qatar, Oman, Bahrain and Kuwait. This political alliance allows the mostly small countries to align many of their energy and foreign policies. In recent years, they have initiated cooperative efforts on water issues. One such effort is the

2013 agreement to jointly build a massive $7 billion desalination plant on the Arabian Sea (the Indian Ocean side), which would avoid potential contamination from either a radioactive spill from Iran's nuclear facilities or an oil spill in the Persian Gulf shipping lanes. Due to the abundance of oil and natural gas, within a few short decades the Gulf states went from pervasive poverty and from being an inconsequential region in the world to having rapidly growing, globally integrated economies that boast world-class infrastructure, and to providing the native population a high standard of living. This massive, comprehensive state building led to policies that catered to native residents whose incomes are not taxed and who have reliable provisions of water and electrical power at heavily subsidized prices or free of charge. The hot and dry environment, the newly found high quality of life, and social contracts that rely on heavy subsidies of services and utilities have helped in creating a culture of high water consumption. These largely water-deficient countries have come to rely on the energy-intensive desalination technology to provide water for their people. In addition to building bigger desalination plants, they have been mining more water from their mostly fossil, nonrenewable aquifers. Current utilization of groundwater reservoirs in the emirate of Abu Dhabi is about 15 times faster than the natural recharge rates (EAD 2013). Overabstraction from aquifer lowers their water tables, making aquifers susceptible to saltwater intrusion. In addition, water pollution from agricultural, industrial and household sources have led one author to conclude that "water is most definitely a finite resource in this regard" (WEF 2007).

The young Gulf states that gained independence some forty-five years ago are now politically and economically sophisticated actors.[1] They are at the cusp of a shift from long-practiced water-supply management toward water-demand management. The literature on water management under conditions of scarcity argues that as development expands over time, management of water projects becomes more a means of allocating and reallocating supplies among different sectors and hence a form of demand management (Frederick 1993, 69–72). This chapter outlines the intricate relationship between the social contracts that set the rapport between the native ("local") population and ruling families in the Arab Gulf states, and how the resulting political climate affects decision makers' ability to implement comprehensive and effective water-demand management policies. It argues that, while the governance system in the GCC countries is constrained by the social contract, decision makers have been promoting water-conservation policies that are socially viable, that is, ones that do not risk political stability and national security.

---

1   Saudi Arabia was formed 90 years ago.

Water-Demand Management

Water-demand management and sustainable water development are related in that both advocate water conservation by curtailing water demand through water-use efficiency. Water managers must be mindful of the medium- and long-term needs and of potential supply interruptions. As countries develop and grow, their water development, supply and management evolve accordingly along the following phases:

1. Manual supply phase: Hand-to-mouth, meager and intermittent water supply that is fetched manually from a well or stream; its quality is variable.
2. Mechanical supply phase: Providing freshwater resources by installing or expanding infrastructure and by improving the efficiency of existing water supply systems. Here water supply is more stable and predictable and water quality is consistent.
3. Early conservation phase: Boosting the efficiency of available freshwater by collecting, treating and reusing wastewater.
4. Intermediate conservation phase: Prohibiting certain wasteful practices such as flood irrigation, and phasing out the cultivation of low-value, water-intensive crops.
5. Advanced conservation phase: Disallowing most types of traditional, outdoor farming.

The amount of time that it takes a society to move from one phase to the next will vary. Some may linger in a particular one or get stuck in it. The third and fourth phases are approximately where most Gulf states are today. They have active programs that seek to raise residents' awareness of wasteful water practices, and some have removed subsidies from water used to irrigate thirsty landscape grasses and certain low-value crops.

Water conservation can also be achieved through infrastructural improvements such as maintenance of the distribution network so as to minimize breakdowns and leakages. Nonstructural approaches to water conservation may include a legal approach where, for example, policies would impose a quota for water use or require new (and existing?) residences to install water-efficient technologies. Social measures usually include sensitization campaigns that raise consumer knowledge and awareness about water stress. Finally, economic approaches may include a system of progressive pricing or subsidizing consumers' investments in water-saving steps or technologies in their homes and businesses. Gradual policy measures that are targeted tend to garner greater public support and acceptance than policies that include price increase or merely limit water supply (Millock and Nauges

2010; Randolph and Troy 2008; Aljamal, Bagnied, and Speece 2015). In the cultural sphere, Gulf governments routinely use pulpits of mosques where imams in Friday sermons propagate messages of environmental protection and water conservation by linking these practices to Islamic history and theology (Amery 2006; Amery 2001). For the softer, voluntary approach to water savings to be effective, consumers would need regular reminding and encouragement to act on their knowledge (Ferraro and Price 2013).

Water-demand management can help societies achieve numerous social and equity objectives such as providing sustainable water-supply services that are reliable and available to all social classes in society. The latter is an especially important objective in developing countries where equity is often lopsided. Another goal is to reduce the vulnerability of water infrastructure through timely maintenance, updating and overall upkeep of the production and distribution system, hence minimizing supply disruptions. This, as well as the decentralization of desalination plants and the diversification of energy sources that are used to operate them, would collectively enhance water security at the community and national levels. Small local plants that rely on a renewable energy source will significantly reduce the distance water is pumped to reach the consumer and therefore cut the cost. It will also improve the sustainability of the plant by decreasing social as well as environmental costs that are associated with mega desalination plants.

Hamoda argues that water-scarce countries should consider alternative solutions that range from "developing any underdeveloped water resource," to water desalination, to water conservation and reuse of treated wastewater, to greater efficiency in water distribution and use, to "importing water from neighbouring countries" (2001, 391). Because society affixes low economic value to water and it happens to be a heavy liquid, it is very inefficient to transport over long distances, which explains why countries usually import "virtual water," the embedded volumes of water that were required to produce food crops and other water-intensive goods. However, it is worth noting that economic considerations are not always the primary reason for avoiding water imports (Amery 2013; Amery 2015). For example, Qatar and Kuwait had formally considered importing water from Iran. Despite their geographical proximity to their Persian neighbor, the Arab states feared the hydrohegemonic influence of Iran and decided not to develop an external dependency for such a critical resource (Amery 2012).

Population Pressure on Resources in the GCC

There are different degrees of freshwater scarcities. Societies that have less than 500 cubic meters per capita are classified as being in a state of "absolute scarcity" (Falkenmark 1989). The average water availability in the Arab States was 3,300 cubic meters per person per year in 1960. It is forecast to drop by 85 percent to reach 500 cubic meters per person per year in 2025 (IFAD 2009). The pressure on water resources is a lot more acute in the Arab Gulf states where water demand is currently 170 percent of available sustainable water sources (EAD 2013).

A few decades ago, the once-distant backwater region had a very small population size that was consistent with its then-limited natural resource endowments. Oil and gas discoveries and the wealth that followed have greatly increased the population size and demand on water. For example, the total population of Qatar grew from 25,000 people in 1950 to over 111,000 in 1970. Similarly, the UAE's population went from 70,000 in 1950 to 558,000 in 1974. At around the time they became independent in the early 1970s, both countries had more foreigners than natives (see table 3.1). These realities point to the significant economic expansion that was taking off in these countries, their long-standing need for foreign workers and the pressure that these activities apply on their meager freshwater resources. Kuwait also had a comparable demographic trajectory. It was the first Gulf state to develop its oil resources and to utilize them in developing infrastructure and improving the people's quality of life. Some five decades ago, the government of Kuwait was spending more than $140 per person to provide freshwater and electricity, and "every tree and shrub that decorates her [Kuwait's] thoroughfares and public squares costs an average of some $250 a year." During the preceding two decades, "the whole face of Kuwait has changed beyond recognition" (Shehab 1964). The population explosion and the rapid improvement in the quality of life put significant pressure on the limited water supplies, so much so that between 1970 and 2000, per capita freshwater availability in the Gulf states went from 680 cubic meters to 180 cubic meters (IMF 2015).

Since shortly after World War II, governments of the Middle East have been considering different methods of increasing the water supply and of improving the management of this limited resource in order to make it more sustainable. Increasing water efficiency has been part of the public debate since at least 1947 when UNESCO created the Middle East Science Cooperation Office in Cairo and one of its scientific research and policy objectives was "water conservation and the development of arable land" (PBS, n.d.). As oil prices surged in the period since the mid-1970s, the Gulf states began launching various ambitious development projects that prompted a major influx of guest workers. Between 1975 and 1980, the population of the region was growing at an astronomical rate (see Table 3.1). Had the growth stayed at that rate, it would have doubled in size about every 11 years. Some three decades later, the population growth slowed down somewhat, reducing doubling time to more

Table 3.1 Total population size and total fertility in select countries

	Population (thousands)			Total fertility (average number of children per woman)					
	1950	2013	2025	1975–1980	2000–2005	2005–2010	2010–2015	2015–2020	2020–2025
Bahrain	116	1300	1600	5.23	2.67	2.23	2.10	1.98	1.88
Kuwait	150	3400	4400	5.89	2.58	2.71	2.60	2.51	2.43
Oman	460	3600	4800	8.10	3.21	2.89	2.91	2.54	2.28
Qatar	25	2200	2700	6.11	2.95	2.21	2.05	1.92	1.83
Saudi Arabia	3100	29 000	34000	7.28	3.54	3.03	2.68	2.43	2.24
United Arab Emirates	70	9400	11500	5.66	2.40	1.97	1.82	1.73	1.66
Jordan	450	7300	8700	7.38	3.85	3.64	3.27	2.98	2.75
Iran	17100	77500	88000	6.28	1.97	1.89	1.93	1.89	1.86
USA	157800	320000	350600	1.77	2.04	2.06	1.97	1.98	1.98

Source: UN 2013 and Gulf Research Center, n.d.

than 20 years for the period 2005 and 2010. Qatar offers an extreme example of growth, where its population tripled in size between 2006 and 2013.
Population growth, especially at such high rates, has implications for building
water infrastructure that is capable of meeting the needs of residents in terms
of providing reliable freshwater supply and collecting and treating wastewater.

Anemic Water Reforms

The history of water management at the Emirates Golf Club illustrates the
early thinking of urban planners about how water could be deployed to bolster Dubai's elitist image in order to help in attracting foreign investment
and how attitudes have changed in recent years. In 1988, the city built the
Emirates Golf Club, the first all-grass course in the Middle East. It did not pay
for the potable water that it used to keep the fairways and greens lush. While
building such amenities has helped in attracting wealthy tourists to this emerging globalized city, it also meant that, by 2007, the 69 hectares of grass were
using 2.68 billion liters of water annually. Since then, however, new management of the club has introduced salt-resistant grass, an innovative and more
efficient irrigation system with over 2,200 sprinklers and started using treated
sewage effluent given to it from the city of Dubai. By 2013, annual water use
in the course had dropped to 1.36 billion liters (Todorova 2015). Today, many
golf courses in the GCC countries use treated wastewater, including Oman's
Almouj course.

   In recent years, the Gulf states have started paying closer attention to
the potential economic and environmental benefits of treating and reusing
wastewater. In 2008, Abu Dhabi built the Strategic Tunnel Enhancement
Programme to transport the city's wastewater to treatment plants, which
streamlined the previous system by replacing the main collector system and
eliminating the need for many of the aging pumping stations (EAD 2014).
Annually, the emirate of Abu Dhabi produces about 450 million cubic
meters of treated wastewater, which amounts to 7.2 percent of the principal-
ity's total water production. Only about 60 percent of this water is reused
in nonfood-producing activities or in aquifer recharge.[2] This limited use is
"due to the capacity of distribution system after treatment" (Dawoud, Sallam
and Abdelfattah 2012). While there are many obvious benefits to treating and
reusing wastewater, there are some not-so-obvious concerns and risks (see
Table 3.2).

---

2   The Environment Agency Abu Dhabi plans to expand the use of treated wastewater
    but "for non-drinking purposes" only (EAD 2014).

Table 3.2 Advantages, disadvantages and possible risks of wastewater reuse

Advantages	Disadvantages	Risks
Improvement of the economic efficiency of investments in wastewater disposal and irrigation – Conservation of freshwater sources – Recharge of aquifers through infiltration water (natural treatment)	Wastewater is normally produced continuously throughout the year, whereas wastewater irrigation is mostly limited to the growing season. – Wet seasons that are long and intense may result in seasonal discharge of untreated wastewater.	Potential harm to groundwater due to heavy metal, nitrate and organic matter
Use of the nutrients of the wastewater (e.g., nitrogen and phosphate) – Reduction of the use of synthetic fertilizer – Improvement of soil properties (soil fertility, higher yields)	Some substances that can be present in wastewater in such concentrations that they are toxic for plants or lead to environmental damage	Potential harm to human health by spreading pathogenic germs Gases such as sulfuric acid produced during the treatment process can result in chronic health problems.
Reduction of treatment costs: – Soil treatment of the pretreated wastewater via irrigation (no tertiary treatment necessary, highly dependent on the source of wastewater)	If implemented on a large scale, revenues to water supply and wastewater utilities may fall as the demand for potable water for nonpotable uses and the discharge of wastewater is reduced.	Potential harm to the soil due to heavy metal accumulation and acidification

Beneficial influence of a small natural water cycle

Reduction of environmental impacts by limiting pollution of seawater, rivers and groundwater.

– Capital costs are low to medium for most systems and are recoverable in a very short time (this excludes systems designed for direct reuse of sewage water)

– Operation and maintenance are relatively simple (except in direct reuse systems)

– Provision of nutrient-rich wastewaters can increase agricultural production in water-poor areas.

Source: Adapted from Dawoud et al. 2012; OAS, n.d.; and Drechsel et al. 2010.

Decision makers in the Gulf region have become aware of the fact that their freshwater resources are finite and must be managed sustainably. A report by the Environment Agency Abu Dhabi (EAD 2014) highlighted a statement by Sheikh Mohammed bin Zayed, the crown prince of Abu Dhabi and deputy supreme commander of the armed forces, in which he says that "water is more important than oil for the UAE. We are preoccupied by this major issue." He added that desalination plants provide the people's water needs but that within a few decades "the situation will be different" because the technology needed "to help meet the region's demand on fresh water" is not yet available (EAD 2014). The crown prince appears to be acknowledging that the energy-intensive desalination technology is unsustainable. Saudi minister of water and electricity Abdullah Al-Hussayen described water-consumption data that exceeded eight million cubic meters per day nationally, or 265 liters per person, as "frightening," and said that desalination is "expensive and unsustainable since it costs about $1 per cubic meter to produce and consumes eight times more energy than groundwater projects" (Relox 2013).

Estimated prices vary significantly because they are affected by the technology that is being used, the price of energy at any given point in time, the distance that produced water has to be pumped to reach customers and so on. It costs up to $3 to produce one cubic meter of freshwater using desalinated technology; this is twice as expensive as treating wastewater or surface water (Johnston 2015). Others find the cost to be $1 per cubic meter or less, which is a far cry from $5.50, which was the 1979 price (Fayad, Batri and Ayoub 2011). The desalination production costs of the Qatar General Electricity and Water Corporation (also known as Kahramaa) stands at $1.64 per cubic meter, while distribution costs $1.10 per cubic meter for a total of $2.74 per cubic meter (Saif 2012). While the cost of producing desalinated water has been declining (see Table 3.3), water demand has been rising, sometimes rapidly, due to improvements in the overall quality of life, population growth rates and massive transnational migration. In 2009, desalination water tariffs in the UAE were set at $0.06 per cubic meter, while the actual cost of the produced water was $1.75 per cubic meter (excluding capital and fuel).

Table 3.3 Cost of desalinated water over time (in US dollars per cubic meter)

1980	between $4.50 and $1.50
2005	between $2.0 and $0.50
2012	between $1 and $0.50

Source: Abazza (2012).

Oil and gas, the economic backbone of Gulf states, are offered to citizens at a subsidized price and make up the single largest operational expense of desalination plants. Recent dramatic fluctuations in oil price, where the price of Brent crude went from its peak of around $115 in midsummer 2014 to about half that a few months later, created added pressure on Gulf governments to consider tapping into new sources of revenue to meet budget shortfalls. In the past few decades, when oil and gas prices would decline, officials start talking about "subsidy reforms," a topic that has never resulted in significant lifting of subsidies. More commonly, the reform rhetoric loses steam and is dropped. Subsidy reform usually mean "raising retail gasoline and diesel prices (in 2011 and 2014), which are still way below international market levels (by about 50 percent compared to the US prices)" (IMF 2015).

Hydrocarbon wealth is the economic foundation of the GCC countries, whose respective ruling families have comparable social contracts with their native local populations. The latter receive many goods and services, like freshwater supplies, at heavily subsidized prices, if not free of charge (Amery 2015; Aljamal, Bagnied, and Speece 2015) (see Table 3.4). In return, the local populations tend not to challenge the political authorities. Fuadi Pitsuwan (2014) asserts that "governments of developing, oil-exporting countries" implicitly subsidize petroleum consumption by selling fossil fuels to their citizens "at levels significantly lower than the free-market prices." For example, the people of Saudi Arabia "enjoy the second lowest domestic fossil fuel prices in the world, behind only Venezuela." He adds that "studies have shown that fossil fuel subsidies [...] lead to economic inefficiency, adverse impacts on social equity, and high fiscal cost for these governments." Fossil fuel subsidies cost the Saudi monarchy a total of $32.5 billion in 2009, $43.6 billion in 2010 and $60.9 billion in 2011. "Of its total subsidy spending in 2011, 76 percent went to subsidizing oil, while 24 percent went to electricity, which is also derived from oil" (Pitsuwan 2014) (see Table 3.5). Similarly, despite its small economic base, Kuwait spends over $1.2 billion per year to provide freshwater. "The government estimates that by the year 2050, given current consumption patterns, the majority of the country's revenue that is generated by oil will be required to fund the increased production of desalinated water" (Fattouh and Mahadeva 2014, 6). Energy subsidies increase carbon dioxide emissions and skew the cost of pumping groundwater. This underpricing of water provides an unintended incentive for farmers to use water wastefully and to cultivate profitable, water-intensive nonfood crops, all of which aggravate the depletion of groundwater. This depletion "represents an estimated wealth loss of as much as 1–2 percent of GDP for some countries" in the Middle East and North Africa (Sdralevich et al. 2014).

Table 3.4 Water tariffs in the GCC countries

Country	Type of user/Customer	Consumption or other criteria	Tariffs in US dollars
Bahrain	Residential compound	25 mm (1") service connection size	397.86 US
		50 mm (2") service connection size	2387.15 US
	Nondomestic 2013	Over 1,000 cubic meters/monthly	1.33 US
	Nondomestic 2015	consumption	1.86 US
Kuwait 2015	Consumers, state facilities & companies	<10,000 gallons/month	.8 KD = 2.65 US/1000 gal
	Supported industrial companies		.25 KD = .83 US/1000 gal
UAE			
Dubai 2015	Residential, industrial & commercial	0–6000 IG or greater consumption/ month	.035–.04 AED/IG = .01 US
Abu Dhabi 2015	Residential nationals	Average daily consumption	new 2015 Tariff/1000 liters
	Flat or villa	<700 liters/day to over 700 liters/day	1.7 AED–1.89 = .46–.51 US
	Residential expats		
	Flat or villa or embassy residence	<700 liters/day	5.95 AED = 1.62 US
		over 700 liters/day	9.90 AED = 2.70 US
	Social card holders/assistance		
	National	<9804 liters/day	free
		>9804 liters/day	1.7 AED = .46 US
	Expat	<2801	free
		>2801	5.95 AED = 1.62 US
		Property type	new 2015 Tariff

Government	all	9.90 AED = 2.70 US
Commercial, fisheries, livestock, embassy buildings	all	4 AED = 1.09 US
Agriculture	all	2.2AED = .60 US
Premises without meters	per month (Flat rate)	90 AED/month= 24.51 US
Oman 2015	Type of customer	Monthly consumption/gal	Tariff/gal
	Domestic (residence), commercial (business) and government	1 to 5,000 to over 5000	.0002–.00025 OMR = 0 US
Qatar 2015	Sector type		Tariff M3
	Residential flat or villa; industrial		4.4 QAR = 1.21 US
	Commercial, hotels, productive farms		5.2 QAR = 1.43 US
	Government		7 QAR = 1.92 US
Saudi Arabia 2013	Segment	m3/month	price US$ m3/month
	1–3	1 to 200	0.027–0.53
	4–5	201 and over	1.07–1.6

Sources: Various web pages of relevant ministries in the GCC countries.

Table 3.5 Costs of low energy and water prices in the GCC countries

	In percent of GDP	Recent reforms
Bahrain	12.5	Industrial tariffs for gas in Bahrain were increased by 50 percent on January 1, 2012. Tariffs for electricity and water for nondomestic use were also raised (in October 2013).
Kuwait	7.0	A study on the impact of a differentiated electricity and water tariff structure was completed in 2014. Subsidies on diesel have been discontinued.
Oman	6.2	Plans to double the feedstock gas prices by 2015. An energy sector study is ongoing, with a view to gradually reduce the overall fuel subsidy.
Qatar	3.5	Qatar raised the pump prices of gasoline by 25 percent and of diesel by 30 percent in January 2011. Diesel prices were again raised in May 2014, by 50 percent. Efforts are underway to improve desalination technologies and promote public awareness of sustainable use of energy.
Saudi Arabia	9.9	Saudi Arabia increased the average price of electricity sold to nonindividual users by 9.6 percent on July 1, 2010. Currently, to curb the rapid growth in energy consumption, the authorities are strengthening building and appliance energy efficiency standards, including in industry. Tighter vehicle emission standards and public transportation networks are planned over the medium term.
United Arab Emirates	5.7	UAE increased gasoline prices in 2010 to the highest level in the GCC, but still below international prices. Abu Dhabi is developing a comprehensive electricity and water consumption strategy, which led to an increase in tariffs from January 2015. Dubai raised water and electricity tariffs by 15 percent in early 2011.

Note: For Kuwait and Oman, official budget amounts are shown. For Bahrain, the number includes on-budget and off-budget subsidies. For Qatar, Saudi Arabia and the United Arab Emirates, the estimates of pre-tax subsidies are used.
Source: IMF 2015.

Gulf states are aware of the need to sustainably manage their water resources. Abu Dhabi is the largest and economically wealthiest emirate of the seven emirates that form the UAE. The Environment Agency Abu Dhabi has a multiprong approach to water management. It works with various stakeholders in society to raise awareness of the need for greater efficiency in water use, regularly assesses and monitors the status of the emirate's groundwater supplies and regulates water abstraction. The agency is also investigating the use of renewable energy for solar desalination plants to supply future water needs (EAD 2014). It has also developed specialized programs and publications that promote efficient water use among different sectors and consumers. In one, the agency states that "securing a safe and sustainable water supply, both now and in the future, presents a profound challenge, which, if left unaddressed, threatens Abu Dhabi's economic, social and environmental well-being." Abu Dhabi created several governmental organizations to monitor, plan and develop water resources, including the Permanent Committee for Setting and Implementing Water and Agricultural Strategies in Abu Dhabi and a Water Council (EAD 2014).

The Emirate has a five-year (2014–2018) plan that aims to (1) reduce water consumption from desalination, (2) increase the use of treated wastewater and (3) slow the depletion of groundwater reserves. Earlier initiatives that it had undertaken to bolster sustainable water management included a new billing system, where customers are sent a statement showing their consumption and the subsidy provided by the government (tariffs for water and electricity were once combined). The purpose of this information is to raise awareness and incentivize voluntary water conservation. The government also automated the reading of water meters and developed steps to reduce the water intensity of current and new buildings. By altering the agriculture subsidy structure, Abu Dhabi also managed in 2010 to contract the production of water-intensive crops.

Since around the early 2000s, GCC governments started viewing freshwater as a strategic resource. They started building storage tanks, above- and underground, and recharging depleted aquifers with the goal of using them in times of emergencies. For example, the UAE undertook a seven-year project (2010–2017) to recharge the large Liwa Aquifer with desalinated water. When the aquifer is recharged, it will be able to provide Abu Dhabi with 90 days of freshwater (EAD 2014).

Subsidies and Political Stability

Water-conservation tools include technological, economic and social measures. Regular infrastructure maintenance, the raising of public awareness of scarcity and water-pricing increases can go a long way toward reducing water consumption in the GCC (Aljamal, Bagnied, and Speece 2015). A report by a consultancy firm reported that "increases in municipal tariffs can reduce demand by 20–35 percent" (Fayad, Batri and Ayoub 2011). Water leaks, or "unaccounted for" volumes, are related to the quality and frequency of maintenance, and they vary from 23 to 45 percent in the GCC states. It is estimated that repairing leaky distribution networks could save Saudi Arabia, Oman, Qatar and Bahrain a combined total of 1.8 million cubic meters per day, which is equivalent to the output of two enormous desalination plants.[3] Kuwait has reduced its water-loss rates to between 12 and 20 percent, while Dubai has brought it down to an impressive 5 percent (Fayad, Batri and Ayoub 2011; AlA'laas 2015).

A World Bank report advocates a "principled pragmatist" approach to water pricing, instead of drastic changes such as having customers pay the full cost of water immediately. Economic principles, when applied to water management, "need to be tailored to specific, widely varying natural, cultural, economic and political circumstances, in which the art of reform is the art of the possible" (World Bank 2004, 22). This customized approach is sensitive to the complexity and subtlety of water-pricing policies that decision makers need to consider if reforms are to succeed without creating unintended socioeconomic or political consequences. As mentioned in the previous section, people–government relations in Gulf monarchies have long been anchored in a social contract where the ruling families share oil revenues with the people through tax-free incomes and comprehensive social welfare systems, including subsidies in return for deference in the political sphere (Davidson 2012; Barrett 2011). For example, after announcing the expansion of subsidies on water and electrical power to low-income Emiratis in particular, the emir of Dubai explained in his decision that "the UAE leadership" wants to provide nationals "with a prosperous life and services at every house without having to bear additional burdens." In the same statement, he also said "water and electricity are national assets which have to be protected from wasting and therefore preserved for future generations" (WAM 2011). It is unlikely that one-time broad moral prodding to conserve water will yield any significant results.

The Gulf states' provision of freshwater for free or at heavily subsidized prices has gradually created cultural norms of excessive water use and

---

3   The Ras Al Khair desalination plant is Saudi Arabia's newest (2014), and it produces over one million cubic meters daily, which makes it the world's largest. Its construction cost was about $7.2bn.

water practices that are wasteful (e.g., flood irrigation). This arid region is unique in that it has one of the highest per capita water-consumption levels and one of the lowest water tariffs in the world. The chief economist of NCB Capital (Riyadh, Saudi Arabia), Jarmo Kotilaine, said that raising water prices is the best way of cutting consumption but that, in some Gulf countries, "even the suggestion" of doing that would "provoke demonstrations" (Lidstone 2010). In this post–Arab Spring period, the political calculus of lifting subsidies is even more delicate than it once was, with governments viewing the likely economic and hydrological benefits of higher water prices as minuscule in the face of the potential social upheaval that may threaten hereditary leaders' hold on power. In other words, charging full market price for freshwater supply may well trigger objections by locals (natives) that could have political ramifications that Gulf leaders would rather avoid. Since moving to cut energy and water subsidies in early 2015, the Kuwait government has postponed any changes after a political backlash from members of parliament who argued that the currently low international price for oil should mean lower prices for consumers, despite the fact that Kuwait is projected to have a budget deficit of $27.2 billion for fiscal year 2016 (Faucon and Said 2015).[4] Subsequently, the country's oil minister, Ali Al Omair, announced that "the government had decided to postpone any removal of subsidies from petrol, electricity and water" (Reuters 2015). Discussion of major water-subsidy reforms that would impact the local population is off the table in Kuwait and in other Gulf states, which will preserve the status quo.

This ironically points to a governing system that is politically cautious, perhaps extremely so, but it is not stagnant. This is illustrated in Kuwait's determination to collect water tariffs and in Saudi Arabia's wheat self-sufficiency program. In the fall of 2014, Kuwait's minister of electricity and water Abdulaziz Al-Ibrahim warned that his ministry is serious about collecting electricity and water dues and that it will disconnect services to consumers who do not pay. He also said that data shows that Kuwait's water and electricity charges are the cheapest in the Arab world, yet he would not advocate reducing or lifting subsidies, not even for expatriates, as had been discussed in local media outlets (Garcia 2014). When the ministry started to enforce water-tariff collection, it disconnected water supply to an average of 100 homes per day because residents had not paid their water bill. This despite

---

4   Initially, Kuwait increased domestic diesel prices by threefold, but was later forced by public pressure to roll them back. Today, they are twice as high as they were in 2014 (Faucon and Said 2015).

the fact that consumers pay less than 10 percent of the actual cost of water production and delivery (AlA'laas 2015).[5] In 2015, a senior ministry official reported that as the people realized that the government is serious in its collection efforts, it spurred more delinquent consumers to come forward to pay their overdue water bills, which reduced the number of disconnections. Given that each disconnection and reconnection costs around $40, and that the enforcement was started "suddenly," the ministry ran a deficit because it had only budgeted for three or four disconnections per day (AlA'laas 2015). Kuwait's "sudden" decision may have been spurred by alarming news when, on one day toward the end of September 2013, water consumption in Kuwait reached 425 million imperial gallons, which exceeded the volume produced for that day, 411 million imperial gallons (*Kuwait Times* 2013). A frequent recurrence of deficient water supply could draw down the country's limited strategic reserve of seven days (Amery 2015). In short, even though Gulf states like Kuwait find the lifting of water subsidies to be too politically controversial to tackle head-on, they have been pursuing alternative methods to remind consumers of the value of freshwater supplies in the hopes of curbing consumption.

A dramatic yet illustrative case from Saudi Arabia pertains to farming and food security. During the Arab oil embargo of 1973, some of the targeted Western countries and their media outlets pushed back, reminding oil exporters that they are heavily dependent on food imports, which could be withheld. A few years later, Saudi Arabia initiated a wheat self-sufficiency program that by 1984 had exceeded its goal and allowed the country to start exporting wheat to 30 countries (Embassy of Saudi Arabia, n.d.). Official Saudi narrative labels the program as an "agricultural achievement" (Embassy of Saudi Arabia, n.d.), despite its immense ecological and hydrological impacts and economic costs.

Over 25 years (1980–2005), the government of Saudi Arabia spent about $85 billion on subsidies for wheat farmers (Jones 2010; See also Lippman 2011). Furthermore, the rate of utilization of groundwater supplies, the main source of irrigation in Saudi Arabia, was ten times faster than the replenishment rate (Fayad, Batri and Ayoub 2011). The general hydrological impacts of water-intensive farming have long been known to be decision makers in the kingdom. While the country's Sixth Development Plan (1995–2000) called for

---

5   This is comparable to the economics of desalinated water in Bahrain, where the costs of production, conveyance and distribution of water is US$0.78, yet the average price to municipal consumers is US$0.15 (Al-Zubari, 2014). In Saudi Arabia, however, it is reported that local citizens "only pay about one percent of what it costs the government to provide water" (CSIS, 2011).

reducing subsidies on wheat and animal-feed crops and other water-intensive crops, it also set a goal of a 3.1 percent increase in agricultural output. After considering these issues for over a decade, the government decided in 2008 to phase out the wheat program by reducing its area under cultivation by 12.5 percent per year until 2016. The area that was cultivated with wheat dropped from 450,330 ha in 2007–2008 to about 83,000 ha in 2014–2015 (Ahmed 2014). In 2003, the government stopped subsidizing barley production. While the bureaucracy was slow in responding to the fantastic wheat farming program, once the decision was made, it was carried out methodically, resulting in the gradual decline in wheat farming. Most of Saudi Arabia's wheat is now being imported from Australia, Brazil, Germany, United States, Poland, Canada, Lithuania and other countries.

Large-scale wheat farmers switched their crop of choice but not their careers; they started cultivating alfalfa and Sudan grass to be used as feed for livestock. Although such forage crops are highly water intensive, such farmers are likely to be well connected politically and tribally, and can therefore prevent the government from discontinuing their lucrative business enterprises. The area with forage crops increased from 151,000 hectares in 2007 and 187,000 ha in 2011 to almost 200,000 ha in 2014 (Clarke 2015; Ahmed 2014). The problem is that growing animal feed is water intensive, and even more so in arid environments. Forage crops "consume three times the amount of water needed for wheat production" (Ahmed 2014), which undermines the government's declared objective of slowing the depletion of groundwater supplies. However, the largest dairy farm in the world, Almarai, which is located in Saudi Arabia, did not wait for the government to introduce measures that discourage or ban the domestic production of green forage. The company voluntarily decided to start importing all of its animal feed from abroad, including from company-owned farms located in Argentina (Naffee 2014; See also Lippman 2011). While a policy reversal on the wheat cultivation program was an inevitable step, the glacial pace of the Saudi political system and its cautious nature makes this a notable achievement for the country. For the new policy to achieve its hydrological goals, it would need to be made more comprehensive so as to include all water-intensive and low-value crops.

Another, politically safer, approach to water-demand management is to increase the productivity of water by investing in research and development in the fields of plant biology and arid ecology. Rhodes grass, which consumed more than 59 percent of the 1.5 billion cubic meters of water that the UAE used for irrigation per year, was banned in 2010. In an effort to find a plant that used less water, researchers in the UAE and Syria collected and classified regional plants and tapped into the "Bedouin's (sic) knowledge to find out which were good for animals", according to Ahmed Moustafa of the International Centre for Agricultural Research in the Dry Areas (qtd. in Malek, 2012). Results from eight years of research showed that the *Cenchrus ciliaris*, an extremely drought-tolerant grass that is native to the Mediterranean and other arid regions of the world, needs less than a third of the water of Rhodes grass. However, because soil salinity levels vary, grass types need to be tailored to different parts of a country. The *Distichlis spicata* and *Sporobolus virgin*icus varieties that are native to Oman, Saudi Arabia and Mexico were found to grow well in saline soils and provide suitable feed for sheep, goats and camels (Malek 2012).

Conclusions

With the help of abundant oil and gas reserves, Gulf ruling families have "made their subjects wealthy and complacent" (Krane 2014) because their implicit social contract trades paternal provisioning for allegiance and acquiescence. Subsidizing water consumption has come to be seen as the government "sharing" hydrocarbon wealth with the local population, who have developed a certain sense of entitlement to the lucrative natural resources in their countries. Despite the significant political constraints on extensive water-subsidy reforms, Gulf governments realize that they need to contain and reduce water consumption. Public awareness programs abound in the Gulf and have undoubtedly influenced people's understanding of water issues in their respective countries. In an attempt to balance current and future demands on available freshwater resources, many Gulf States have started

1. treating water like a strategic resource and taking measures to protect subsurface water that could be used if there is a catastrophic disruption of water supply from the existing mega desalination plants;
2. treating surface and renewable subsurface water as a single, interconnected resource;
3. protecting critical environments such as wadis and aquifer recharge zones;
4. applying different quality water to distinct yet appropriate uses;
5. reducing further point and nonpoint sources of pollution;
6. taking steps to increase water-use efficiency throughout the economy and society beyond the focus that has been limited to public spaces and buildings; and
7. drafting master plans for the country that help governments manage the growing and diverse pressures on their water supplies, which would include a research center and national research priorities.

These policy measures are intended to slow aquifer depletion and to ensure that ecosystems receive the quantity, quality and timing of flows needed to support their ecological functions and services to society. Political considerations have led decision makers to rely primarily on water-demand management strategies based not on price but rather on technological changes and public education. However, despite many years of soft demand-management efforts like raising awareness, there is no evidence to indicate that per capita water consumption in the region is leveling off or declining. This is primarily because of the voluntary nature of water conservation, the absence of conservation pricing mechanisms, and farming using the vast majority of freshwater supplies, a sector that is usually spared comprehensive reforms.

Water-saving measures usually focus on campaigns to raise the public's awareness of the hydrological picture in their country, which include the need to conserve the resource. Furthermore, they sometimes include the retrofitting of wasteful water outlets in mosques, government buildings, national and city parks and manufacturing facilities. Residential quarters of the local population may be retrofitted with water-efficient faucets, showerheads and toilets. But Gulf governments steer clear of steps that may require their populations to alter their lifestyles by curbing their water use at home or by remodeling their lush green backyards (or family farms) by using Xeriscape gardening. This type of gardening cultivates low-water-use plants to reduce or eliminate the need for supplemental irrigation, thus creating landscapes that are sustainable in the arid or semiarid climate that is prevalent in the Gulf states. It is worth noting that, in recent years, the idea of farming in the GCC countries has been culturally redefined. Most locals now hire foreigners to tend to the physical labor on their land, and the farm itself is generally not a source of income but rather serves the function of a weekend family retreat from the hectic modern urban lifestyles where locals reconnect with their land and ancestral heritage.

However, even success stories in the Gulf have their limitations. Saudi Arabia's U-turn on wheat self-sufficiency was a policy reversal too focused on a single crop to yield the desired results in a timely manner. The other so-called success story, Kuwait's rigorous implementation of existing laws of water tariffs, was possible likely because the amounts that were due were relatively small on a household level. Yet it earned the government millions of dollars and let the people know that freshwater supplies come at a cost. Even there, however, the price of water remains so heavily subsidized that it is unlikely that paying water bills alone would result in much water savings. Greater levels of awareness hold a lot more promise (Aljamal, Bagnied, and Speece 2015). This effort in Kuwait was made possible because of the country's vibrant, partly free political climate. The remaining five GCC counties lag behind in the different areas of freedom (FreedomHouse, n.d.).

References

Abazza, H. 2012. *Economic Considerations for Supplying Water through Desalination in South Mediterranean Countries Sustainable Water Integrated Management-Support Mechanism (SWIM-SM)*. European Union.

Ahmed, Hassan F. 2014. *Grain Report Number SA1402*. Riyadh: Grain and Feed Annual. USDA Foreign Agricultural Service, http://gain.fas.usda.gov/Recent%20GAIN%20 Publications/Grain%20and%20Feed%20Annual_Riyadh_Saudi%20Arabia_2-19– 2014.pdf.

AlA'laas, Ali. 2015. "Water in Kuwait: 500 Liters Is the Per Capita Consumption." May 3. *AlRai* (Kuwait). In Arabic.

Aljamal, Ali, Mohsen Bagnied, and Mark Speece. 2015. "Willingness to Pay for Water in Kuwait." 15th EBES Conference, Lisbon, Portugal, January 8–10.

Al-Zubari, Waleed. 2014. "The Costs of Municipal Water Supply in Bahrain." Research paper, The Royal Institute of International Affairs, Chatham House, London. December.

Amery, Hussein A. 2001. "Islamic Water Management." *Water International* 26 (4): 1–9.

———. 2006. "Environment: Water and Pollution." *Encyclopedia of Women & Islamic Cultures*. Leiden: Brill.

———. 2012. "Water Security for Kuwait: Assessing the Feasibility of Water Imports from Iran." *International Journal for Hydrology Science and Technology (IJHST)* 2 (3): 292–305.

———. 2013. "The Geopolitics of Water Scarcity." In *Water and Food Security in the Arabian Gulf*, 61–80. Abu Dhabi: The Emirates Center for Strategic Studies and Research.

———. 2015. *Arab Water Security: Threats and Opportunities in the Gulf States*. Cambridge: Cambridge University Press.

Barrett, R. 2011. "How a Broken Social Contract Sparked Bahrain Protests." *Christian Science Monitor*, February 21.

Center For Strategic and International Studies (CSIS). 2011. "Water and National Strength in Saudi Arabia." CSIS Middle East Program. Center For Strategic and International Studies (CSIS). Analysis Paper. Washington, DC, http://csis.org/files/publication/ 110405_Water%20and%20national%20strength%20in%20Saudi%20Arabia.pdf.

Clarke, William 2015. "Policy Shifts to Send Saudi Corn, Wheat Imports to Record Highs." *Agrimoney*, March 11, http://www.agrimoney.com/news/policy-shifts-to-send-saudi-corn-wheat-imports-to-record-highs–8062.html.

Davidson, C. 2012, "The Importance of the Unwritten Social Contract among the Arab Monarchies." *New York Times*, August 29.

Dawoud, Mohamed A, Osama M. Sallam and Mahmoud A. Abdelfattah. 2012. "Treated Wastewater Management and Reuse in Arid Regions: Abu Dhabi Case Study." Paper presented at the 10th Gulf Water Conference, Doha, Qatar, April 22–24, http://www. researchgate.net/profile/Mahmoud_Abdelfattah/publication/259182543_Treated_ Wastewater_Management_and_Reuse_in_Arid_Regions_Abu_Dhabi_Case_Study/ links/00b7d52a332412fbe5000000.pdf.

Drechsel, Pay, Christopher A. Scott, Liqa Raschid-Sally, Mark Redwood and Akiça Bahri, eds. 2010. *Wastewater Irrigation and Health Assessing and Mitigating Risk in Low-Income Countries*. London Earthscan.

Embassy of Saudi Arabia. n.d. "Agricultural Achievements." Washington, DC., http:// www.saudiembassy.net/about/country-information/agriculture_water/Agricultural_ Achievements.aspx.

Environment Agency (EAD). 2013. "A Strategy for the Efficient Management and Conservation of Water Resources in Abu Dhabi Emirate Launched Alongside IWS 2014." January 21, Abu Dhabi, United Arab Emirates: EAD, http://www.ead.ae/press-centre/a-strategy-for-the-efficient-management-and-conservation-of-water-resources-in-abu-dhabi-emirate-launched-alongside-iws-2014-2/.

Environment Agency (EAD). 2014. "Protecting Our Shared Resource: Sustainable Water Use for Organisations." Abu Dhabi, United Arab Emirates: EAD, http://www.google.com/url?sa=t&rct=j&q=&esrc=s&source=web&cd=1&ved=0CB8QFjAA&url=http%3A%2F%2Fwww.ead.ae%2Fwp-content%2Fuploads%2F2014%2F04%2FWater_Guide_English.pdf&ei=GQVdVfrKMInYtQWX4IDwCA&usg=AFQjCNHB85WpS7DFKsLDARLIfptfN7OorA&bvm=bv.93756505,d.b2w.

Falkenmark, Malin. 1989. "The Massive Water Scarcity Threatening Africa: Why Isn't It Being Addressed." *Ambio* 18 (2): 112–118.

Fattouh, Bassam, and Lavan Mahadeva. 2014. "Price Reform in Kuwait's Electricity and Water Sector: Assessing the Net Benefits in the Presence of Congestion." Oxford Institute for Energy Studies, April. OIES Paper: MEP 9.

Faucon, Benoît and Summer Said. 2015. "Oil Nations See Chance to Reduce Domestic Fuel Subsidies." *Wall Street Journal*, May 5, http://www.wsj.com/articles/oil-nations-see-chance-to-reduce-domestic-fuel-subsidies-1430881494.

Fayad, Walid, Nadim Batri and Johnny Ayoub. 2011. "Gulf Must Act to Stem Heavy Water Use." *Financial Times*, October 5, http://www.ft.com/intl/cms/s/0/6bec65b8-ee6d-11e0-a2ed-00144feab49a.h.

Ferraro, Paul J., and Michael K. Price. 2013. "Using Nonpecuniary Strategies to Influence Behavior: Evidence from a Large-Scale Field Experiment." *Review of Economics and Statistics* 95 (1): 64–73.

Frederick, K. D. 1993. "Balancing Water Demands with Supplies: The Role of Management in a World of Increasing Scarcity." Technical Paper 189, World Bank, Washington, DC.

FreedomHouse. n.d. "Freedom in the World," https://freedomhouse.org/report-types/freedom-world#.VYsvnSFViko.

Garcia, Ben. 2014. "Al-Ibrahim: Pay Water and Electricity Bills or Else." *Kuwait Times*, October 15. http://news.kuwaittimes.net/al-ibrahim-pay-water-electricity-bills-else/.

Gulf Research Center (n.d.). "Population by Nationality at Dates of Census," http://gulfmigration.eu.

Hamoda, Mohamed F. 2001. "Desalination and Water Resource Management in Kuwait." *Desalination* 138: 385–393.

International Fund for Agricultural Development (IFAD). 2009. "Fighting Water Scarcity in the Arab Countries." International Fund for Agricultural Development, Rome, Italy. March, http://www.ifad.org/operations/projects/regions/pn/factsheets/WWF_factsheet.pdf.

International Monetary Fund (IMF). 2015. "Qatar." IMF Country Report No. 15/87. March. Washington, DC, http://www.imf.org/external/pubs/ft/scr/2015/cr1587.pdf.

Jones, T. C. 2010. *Desert Kingdom: How Oil and Water Forged Modern Saudi Arabia*. Cambridge, MA: Harvard University Press.

Johnston, Chris. 2015. "Desalination: The Quest to Quench the World's Thirst for Water." *The Guardian*, May 27, http://www.theguardian.com/technology/2015/may/27/desalination-quest-quench-worlds-thirst-water.

Krane, Jim. 2014. "Guzzling in the Gulf: The Inessentials Face a Threat from Within." *Foreign Affairs*, December 19, http://www.foreignaffairs.com/articles/142692/jim-krane/guzzling-in-the-gulf.

Kuwait Times. 2013. "Water Consumption Surpasses Production." October 6, http://news.kuwaittimes.net/water-consumption-surpasses-production/.

Lidstone, Digby. 2010. "Gulf Buries Its Head in the Sand over Water." *Financial Times*, January 18, http://www.ft.com/intl/cms/s/0/74174862-0458-11df-8603-00144feabdc0.html#axzz1Zbltfbmq.

Lippman, Thomas W. 2011. *Saudi Arabia on the Edge: The Perilous Future of an American Ally.* Dulles, VA: Potomac Books.

Malek, Caline. 2012. "Grass That's Always Green But Never Thirsty." *The National* (UAE), February 5.

Millock K., and C. Nauges. 2010. "Household Adoption of Water-Efficient Equipment: The Role of Socio-Economic Factors, Environmental Attitudes and Policy." *Environmental and Resource Economics* 46: 539–565.

Naffee, Ibrahim. 2014. "Saudi Firm Moves toward 100% Use of Imported Animal Feeds." *Arab News*, April 15, http://www.arabnews.com/news/555836.

Organization of American States (OAS). n.d. "Organization of American States." Washington, DC, https://www.oas.org/dsd/publications/Unit/oea59e/ch26.htm.

Pitsuwan, Fuadi 2014. "Saudi Arabia's Fossil Fuel Subsidies: Understanding the Problem." *Harvard Journal of Middle Eastern Politics and Policy*, January 24, http://hksjmepp.com/saudi-arabias-fossil-fuel-subsidies-understanding-the-problem/.

Public Broadcasting Service (PBS). n.d. "Global Connections to the Middle East." Public Broadcasting Corporation, http://www.pbs.org/wgbh/globalconnections/mideast/timeline/text/tscience.html.

Randolph, B., and Troy P. 2008. "Attitudes to Conservation and Water Consumption." *Environmental Science and Policy* 11: 441–55.

Relox, Alvin Patrick. 2013. "Desalination Method Should Be Improved to Meet Water Shortage." *Arab News*, October 22, http://www.arabnews.com/news/468436.

Reuters. 2015. "Kuwait Postpones Plan to Remove Petrol, Power Subsidies." *Arabian Business*, January 4, http://www.arabianbusiness.com/kuwait-postpones-plan-remove-petrol-power-subsidies-577281.html.

Saif, Omar 2012. "The Future Outlook of Desalination in the Gulf: Challenges and Opportunities Faced by Qatar and the UAE." United Nations University Institute for Water, Environment and Health (UNU-INWEH) Hamilton, Ontario, Canada, December 18, http://inweh.unu.edu/wp-content/uploads/2013/11/The-Future-Outlook-of-Desalination-in-the-Gulf.pdf.

Sdralevich, Carlo, Randa Sab, Younes Zouhar and Giorgia Albertin. 2014. *Subsidy Reform in the Middle East and North Africa: Recent Progress and Challenges Ahead.* Washington, DC: International Monetary Fund, http://www.imf.org/external/pubs/ft/dp/2014/1403mcd.pdf.

Shehab, F. 1964. "Kuwait: a Super-Affluent Society." *Foreign Affairs*, April 3: 461–474.

Todorova, Vesela. 2015. "Special Report: Saving Water in the UAE." *The National*, February 28.

United Nations (UN). 2013. *World Population Prospects: The 2012 Revision, Volume 1: Comprehensive Tables.* United Nations Department of Economic and Social Affairs/Population Division, http://esa.un.org/wpp/Documentation/pdf/WPP2012_Volume-I_Comprehensive-Tables.pdf.

WAM. 2011. Mohammed Doubles Free Water Quota for Nationals, *Emirates247*, October 6.

World Bank. 2004. Water Resources Sector Strategy: Strategic Directions for World Bank Engagement, Washington, DC World Bank.

World Economic Forum (WEF) 2007. *The United Arab Emirates and the World: Scenarios to 2025.* Geneva: World Economic Forum.

Chapter 4

A WATERSHED-BASED APPROACH TO MITIGATING TRANSBOUNDARY WASTEWATER CONFLICTS BETWEEN ISRAEL AND THE PALESTINIAN AUTHORITY: THE BESOR-HEBRON-BE'ER SHEVA WATERSHED

Clive Lipchin and Tamee Albrecht

Introduction

Approximately 16 streams in Israel are transboundary in nature, or shared between Israel and the Palestinian Authority (PA), and roughly two-thirds of these streams originate in Palestinian territory, flow through Israel and discharge into the Mediterranean Sea. Lack of cooperation on water management between Israel and the PA has contributed to high levels of pollution in these waterways, preventing beneficial agricultural, recreational and ecological uses. Past experience shows that effective restoration of Israel's streams requires a coordinated effort between Israelis and Palestinians. If one side invests in infrastructure to improve water quality, but the other continues to pollute, the investments will not result in meaningful improvements to the quality of the regional environment. However, to date such coordination has been minimal and cooperation is difficult.

In principle, most water experts in Israel and the PA recognize the need to adopt watershed-based approaches to water management, acknowledging that rivers, wetlands and groundwater provide important ecological services including waste assimilation, floodwater storage and erosion control. These services provide additional social and economic benefits, such as improved water resources for domestic, agricultural and recreational use. However, because water does not recognize political borders, the ongoing Israeli-Palestinian conflict makes the adoption of watershed-based approaches more challenging because most watersheds in this region, as indicated above, are transboundary in nature. While Israeli and Palestinian water experts have cooperated on transboundary water issues for decades, this cooperation has been mainly technical or research based. We believe that a comprehensive watershed management plan should incorporate ecological, historical, physical, economic and geographical terms agreed upon by both sides. This would serve the best interests of the watershed, regardless of present or future political issues. This chapter argues that since the majority of Israel's water resources (surface and groundwater) are transboundary, Israeli and Palestinian water policy should center on a transboundary approach to watershed management.[1]

General conditions

Drought, population growth and rapid agricultural, industrial and commercial expansion have widened the gap between water supply and demand in Israel and the PA. Israel has bridged this imbalance by developing sophisticated technologies to increase water supply through desalination and wastewater treatment and reuse, while Palestinian infrastructure, technology and investment lag behind. West Bank Palestinians experience frequent water shortages, and the treatment and reuse of wastewater are very limited. The PA's centralized wastewater collection networks do not service the majority of residents: 73 percent of the population relies on cesspits (Fischendler, Dinar, and Katz 2011), in contrast to Israel, where less than 10 percent of the population is not connected to the sewage network.

The poorly maintained septic tanks and cesspits used by most Palestinian households act only as holding tanks. Cesspits merely collect and store wastewater until the pit is emptied and the waste is disposed of. Most cesspits are emptied with vacuum tankers that dump untreated sewage in open areas or in wadis, polluting the environment and posing a major risk to human health.

---

1   The term "transboundary waters" refers to sources of freshwater that are shared among multiple user groups with diverse values and different needs associated with water use. In this way, water crosses boundaries—be they those of economic sectors, legal jurisdictions, or political interests. From sets of individual irrigators and environmental advocates, to urban versus rural uses, to nations that straddle international waterways, essentially all freshwater is transboundary water, and is important to society at local, national, regional and international scales. Transboundary waters share certain characteristics that make their management especially complicated, most notably that these basins require a more complete understanding of the political, cultural and social aspects of water, and that integrated management is dependent on extremely intricate awareness of the decision-making process.

Sewage stored in cesspits is either untreated or only partially treated and contains waterborne pathogens that can cause serious illness such as cholera, typhoid and dysentery. Untreated sewage can also destroy aquatic ecosystems and thus threaten human livelihoods when the associated BOD and nutrient loading deplete oxygen in the water to levels too low to sustain life. Generally the cesspits in the West Bank are unlined, allowing the inadequately treated sewage to percolate into and pollute the groundwater, which is an important source of drinking and irrigation water for both Israelis and Palestinians. Roughly 60 MCM of raw sewage is discharged into wadis in the West Bank every year (Fischendler, Dinar, and Katz 2011). Much of this sewage flows from the upstream areas in the West Bank, across the Green Line and into the downstream areas in Israel.[2]

When the cesspits are not emptied in time, the sewage not only poses serious environmental and public health risks but also contributes to the cross-border conflict. Conflict occurs primarily around the Green Line at the point where the sewage from the West Bank crosses into Israel. As raw sewage flows downstream, it harms Israeli attempts to rehabilitate surface and groundwater sources. According to Israeli law, the country is obliged to treat the sewage but has no right to use it, as the water belongs to the Palestinians according to international law. Israelis demand that the Palestinians treat their sewage, but the Palestinians counter that they are unable to do so as Israel hampers their ability to build the appropriate treatment facilities. Palestinian inability to treat the sewage limits the development of the Palestinian agricultural sector, as recycled wastewater could form an additional source of irrigation water in the West Bank. Another aspect of the conflict occurs in Area C, where Israel proposes to build wastewater treatment plants that will serve both Israeli settlements in Area C and Palestinian communities.[3] Palestinians refuse to consider such a proposition, as this would entail their recognition of the settlements, which are deemed illegal according to international law and the international community. Nonetheless, there are a few places in the West Bank where Israeli settlements and Palestinian communities share a treatment facility.

Sources of conflict

There are three specific sources of conflict over wastewater issues between Israel and the PA: (1) location and construction of treatment facilities, (2) cost

---

2 The de facto border between Israel and the West Bank.
3 Area C is that region of the West Bank where, according to the Oslo Accords signed between Israel and the Palestinian Liberation Organization (PLO), Israel retains both civil and military control.

and benefit sharing and (3) a lack of bilateral water-quality standards for reuse in irrigation.

First, the location and construction of wastewater treatment facilities is a source of conflict between the parties due to the division of the West Bank into Areas A, B and C (according to the Oslo II Accords) and unilateral actions by both parties.[4] As wastewater treatment facilities should be located outside population centers, the most suitable location for the PA to build the plants is usually the mostly rural Area C. However, all construction in Area C requires recognition, special arrangements and licensing from the Israeli Civil Administration as well as a permit from the Joint Water Committee, normally an arduous bureaucratic process.[5]

Disagreements often occur when the permit process is delayed, permission is denied or Israeli military orders halt project implementation. The Palestinian response is to focus on options that can be carried out in Area A, where Israeli approval is not needed. However, the dense urban nature of Area A makes it difficult to find an appropriate site for the construction of a wastewater treatment facility. Additionally, rather than implement joint ventures as originally envisaged by the Oslo process, Israel has unilaterally built several treatment plants on the Israeli side of the Green Line that capture the sewage flowing from the upstream regions of the West Bank. These facilities treat 33 percent (Al-Saed 2010) of Palestinian urban wastewater, but are inefficient, nonintegrated and inferior to upstream treatment solutions at the source of pollution. This Israeli move has sparked ardent protests from the Palestinians, who cannot use the treated wastewater, which is instead discharged and used downstream in Israel.

Second, wastewater crossing political boundaries leads to disputes over cost and benefit sharing. Treatment plants in Israel operate according to a "polluter pays" principle. Israel deducts the cost of treating Palestinian wastewater at Israeli facilities from jointly collected Palestinian custom and trade taxes

---

4   Administrative divisions of the Occupied Palestinian Territories as outlined in the 1995 Oslo II Accords between Israel and the PLO. Area A, according to the Accords, consists of land under full civilian and security control by the PA. Area B is Israeli controlled but PA administered, while Area C is controlled entirely by the Israeli government, with authority over both civil administration and police. Areas B and C constitute the majority of the territory, comprised mostly of rural areas, while urban areas—where the majority of the Palestinian population resides—are mostly in Area A.

5   The Israeli–Palestinian Joint Water Committee is a joint Israeli–Palestinian committee created in 1995 under the Oslo II Accords. Its purpose is to manage water- and sewage-related infrastructure in the West Bank, particularly to make decisions on maintenance of existing infrastructure and approval of new projects. Although it was originally intended to be a temporary agreement for a five-year interim period, it still existed as of 2014.

before transferring the remaining funds to the Palestinian Ministry of Finance. Over the past 15 years, Israel has charged the PA more than \$34 million in reimbursements for wastewater treatment (Al-Saed 2010). The PA objects to the offset and claims that these deductions, which are not supported by bilateral agreements, are illegal. Furthermore, the PA does not receive any of the economic and environmental benefits of the treated effluent, most importantly the return flow for irrigation. In some cases, Israel uses reclaimed Palestinian water for irrigation purposes and river rehabilitation. This is the case, for example, with the Alexander River in northern Israel. The PA demands that Israel deduct the value of these benefits from the offset treatment costs. However, in general, as mentioned above, Israel cannot use reclaimed Palestinian water under international water law. Therefore, Israel treats the wastewater—mostly at a minimum primary level of treatment—and then discharges it unused into rivers. Collaborative efforts could thus yield significant benefits for both parties in terms of additional water for irrigation, stream rehabilitation and the protection of groundwater resources from pollution.

In the case of the all-important Mountain Aquifer, the two parties would have to sign a treaty before treated effluent could be exchanged for additional extraction, and water allocations and use would have to be clearly spelled out.[6] Israel and Jordan have signed such a treaty regarding allocation of the Jordan and Yarmouk Rivers, but no such treaty exists between Israel and the PA. As the PA is not a sovereign state, it cannot enter into a formal treaty with Israel. The only agreement between the parties, the Oslo Accords, was designed as an interim accord, not a treaty. It does discuss water allocation of the Mountain Aquifer between the parties but does not cover the allocation of treated wastewater or options for an exchange scheme.

Finally, the "polluter pays" principle has triggered further disputes, with Israel insisting that the Palestinians adopt Israeli wastewater treatment and reuse standards. These standards, known as the Inbar standards, require all wastewater treatment plants to treat wastewater to a tertiary level for unrestricted use in irrigation.[7] Many facilities in Israel currently treat

---

6   The Mountain Aquifer is one of the most significant sources of water for both Israelis and Palestinians. Nearly the entire Palestinian population in the West Bank is dependent on springs, wells or water extracted from the Mountain Aquifer for drinking and other uses. In Israel, the Mountain Aquifer supplies water to major population centers.

7   As part of Israel's continued commitment to improving wastewater recovery and reuse, in 2005 a draft set of wastewater reuse standards was published containing 38 updated water-quality parameters. These are known locally as the Inbar standards after the interministerial committee chairman, Dr. Yossi Inbar, who oversaw the standard review. The Israel Ministry of Environmental Protection and the Ministry of Health adopted

wastewater to a secondary level and are required to upgrade their facilities to tertiary level. The PA insists that paying for treatment of their wastewater according to Israeli standards is unfair, especially when they do not get to use the treated wastewater for irrigation. This unilateral approach to water-quality standards further exacerbates the conflict because, as the PA has a very limited wastewater treatment capacity, it is unreasonable for Israel to require treatment to tertiary level in compliance with the Inbar standards.

The Besor–Hebron–Be'er Sheva watershed

The Besor–Hebron–Be'er Sheva watershed is an example of a transboundary watershed that is highly polluted. Streamflow in the Israeli city of Be'er Sheva is present year-round because untreated wastewater continuously pours into upstream drainages in the West Bank near Hebron. This sewage flows through several Palestinian communities with limited domestic wastewater infrastructure as well as active stone-cutting and olive oil industries that contribute additional wastewater streams. The polluted streamflow crosses into Israel at the Green Line north of Meitar, where it is partially treated. The treatment, however, is minimal because Israel legally cannot use this treated wastewater, which belongs to the PA; therefore, all Israel can do is return the wastewater to the stream. By the time the water enters the city of Be'er Sheva, Israeli's seventh-largest city, it has picked up additional untreated wastewater from the surrounding Bedouin villages and towns and is essentially a constant sewage flow that fails to match the beauty of the Be'er Sheva river park that is being created around it (Figure 4.1).

Treating this wastewater effectively and efficiently is the impetus for adopting a transboundary watershed management approaching the Besor–Hebron–Be'er Sheva basin. This approach aims to address local water-quality degradation and water-supply issues by taking into account interlinked hydrological, economic and social systems at the watershed level. Our research

these standards in 2007. This new policy requires all future wastewater treatment plants to be able to produce wastewater at a level that allows for "unlimited irrigation or discharge to streams," while existing wastewater treatment plants must be upgraded to meet the new standards. The purpose of the Inbar regulations is to protect public health, prevent pollution of water resources from sewage effluents and enable the use of wastewater recovery for safe discharge back into streams while protecting the environment, including ecosystems and biodiversity, soil and crops.

Figure 4.1 Untreated sewage flowing in the stream at Umm Batin, a Bedouin village northeast of Be'er Sheva
Source: Arava Institute for Environmental Studies.

considers the entire Besor–Hebron–Be'er Sheva watershed, meaning the region where any flowing water or runoff is interlinked and would eventually converge to exit the watershed into the Mediterranean Sea via Gaza at the same place. This region is roughly triangular, defined by Hebron in the northeast, Sde Boqer in the south and Gaza in the west.

While water flows freely across political borders, the management of this transboundary watershed remains fractured. The diverse group of settlements and industries situated along the stream all contribute to its degraded quality, yet they blame each other and rarely coordinate, simply making the situation worse for all. Current water management in the area often looks at water quality from only one side of the Green Line or considers only physical factors, while overlooking the underlying political tensions that have led to the current situation. We seek to understand potential sources of pollution throughout the entire watershed from both a hydrologic and socioeconomic perspective. This research provides a platform for identifying transboundary water-management strategies that will be sustainable and provide benefits throughout the watershed.

Figure 4.2 Besor–Hebron–Be'er Sheva watershed in Israel and the PA
Source: Arava Institute for Environmental Studies.

The work of the Arava Institute for Environmental Studies

Work at the Arava Institute's Center for Transboundary Water Management (CTWM) has recruited a diverse group of students and interns to work on this watershed-based approach.

The Arava Institute is also working together with the Department of Geography at Ben-Gurion University; the Zuckerburg Water Resources Institute at the Jacob Blaustein Institute for Desert Research; the Israel Water and Sewerage Authority; and the Besor–Shiqma River Authority (Figure 4.2).

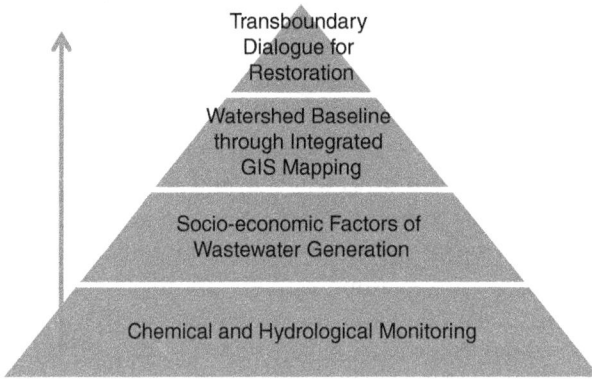

Figure 4.3 Model of analysis framework for transboundary stream restoration
Source: Arava Institute for Environmental Studies.

In collaboration with the Department of Geography at Ben-Gurion University and the Besor–Shiqma River Authority, we at the Arava Institute have begun to establish a joint effort to determine the water quantity and quality in the stream around Be'er Sheva. When completed, three advanced hydrological monitoring stations will collect data along the Hebron–Be'er Sheva stream. These stations will operate continuously, providing water quantity and quality data in real time. The first station will be installed on the Hebron stream, the major drainage of the Besor–Hebron–Be'er Sheva watershed. It will be located at the outlet of the sewage-treatment facility situated at the Metarim checkpoint, close to the Green Line (Figure 4.3).

In addition to our efforts to expand stream monitoring in the watershed, we are conducting a watershed characterization. This combines physical and socioeconomic information to establish a baseline status of the watershed, which in turn enables us to better understand the extent of pollution. We are using geographic information systems (GIS) to conduct scientific watershed analyses and to improve communication of management issues to stakeholders throughout the watershed. Data collected represent both Israeli and Palestinian communities from throughout the watershed.

Gathering Data for a Watershed Approach to Integrated Management

Understanding the nature and extent of pollution is crucial to stream restoration. Pollution can be caused by point and nonpoint sources. Point sources have a distinct location of origin, such as a sewer pipe or a mine tailings pile discharging directly into a water body. Nonpoint sources are diffuse or distributed over a large area, and collectively become a source of pollution when aggregated. For example, runoff that flows over agricultural fields picks up nutrients from fertilizers and carries these contaminants into streams. Nonpoint sources of pollution are more difficult to identify and regulate than point sources. Nevertheless, over the last 15 years nonpoint pollution loads to streams have decreased by 50–80 percent in Israel. Similarly, point source pollution sites have decreased from 130 sources to 80 sources. This is largely due to daily on-site supervision, inspection and enforcement. The issue of pollution prevention in streams has gained great momentum over the last few years following the establishment of the Inbar effluent (wastewater) quality regulations.

As indicated earlier, Israel has adopted (2007) a new set of wastewater reuse standards (Inbar standards), containing 38 updated water-quality indicators. This policy requires that all future wastewater treatment plants be designed to produce wastewater at a quality that allows for "unlimited irrigation or discharge to rivers," while existing wastewater treatment plants must be upgraded to abide by the new regulations. The purpose of the Inbar regulations is to protect public health, prevent pollution of water resources from sewage effluents and enable the utilization of wastewater recovery for safe discharge back into streams while protecting broader environmental factors such as ecosystems, biodiversity, soils and crops. These stringent standards place Israel as a leader among developed nations in terms of wastewater management for environmental protection and reuse.[8]

Again, however, the implementation of these progressive policies is complicated by the fact that most of the major streams that flow westward to the Mediterranean Sea originate in the West Bank, and are thus transboundary systems. Lack of sufficient wastewater treatment and water-quality regulations in the PA results in significant pollution entering streams in the West Bank that flow across the Green Line into Israel, a case in point being the Besor–Hebron–Be'er Sheva stream. Stream water flowing across the Green Line in the Besor–Hebron–Be'er Sheva stream is composed almost entirely of untreated wastewater (Tal et al. 2007), and elevated concentrations of contaminants are observed downstream, even below Be'er Sheva.

Our model of integrated watershed management focuses on a long-term methodology to serve the needs of all of the watershed's stakeholders over time. Stakeholders are not only recipients of the impacts of a

8   Israel's achievments in wastewater management were recognized by the UN World Water Development Report in 2009. (World Water Assessment Programme. 2009. "The United Nations World Water Development Report 3: Water in a Changing World," UN, available online at: http://unesdoc.unesco.org/images/0018/001819/181993e.pdf).

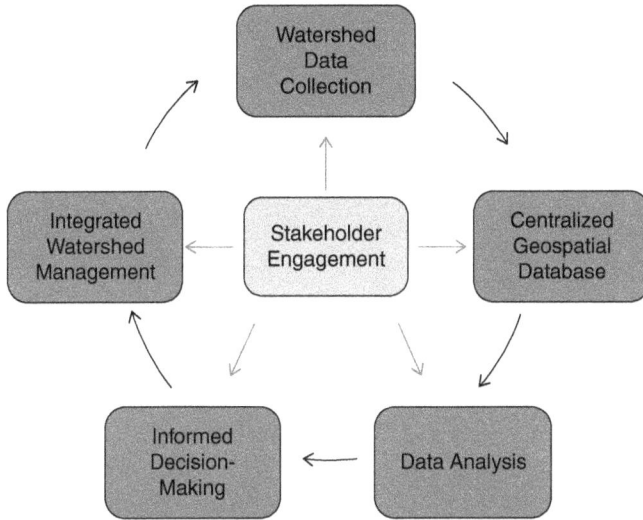

Figure 4.4 Schematic of integrated watershed management process
Source: Arava Institute for Environmental Studies.

management plan but they are also key sources of the information needed to develop a workable plan. Often, stakeholders can provide data or help with watershed monitoring (FAO 2006). In addition, in order for a management plan to have a long-term impact, the recommendations of science and policy experts must be merged with stakeholders' preferences and interests (FAO 2006).

Figure 4.4 represents the watershed approach as an iterative process of data collection, centralized data management and data analysis, leading to informed decision-making and, ultimately, integrated watershed management practices. The first step in this approach is comprehensive data collection to help develop a baseline characterization of the condition of the watershed. A baseline characterization provides a starting point for evaluating how water quality and pollution in the watershed change over time. Initially, data collection supports baseline characterization. In the iterative process, long-term monitoring programs are required to evaluate the effectiveness of management strategies. For the initial baseline characterization, we collected information about streamflow, climate, soils, lithology, surface water quality, groundwater, population, demographics, land use, wastewater treatment and other potential sources of pollution. These data are described in more detail in the next section. Since watershed processes operate at multiple spatial and temporal scales, it is important to obtain both current and historic data whenever available from locations throughout the watershed, as was done here.

Compiling data into a centralized database is the next step. A centralized database is necessary to organize and manage data, integrate data from different sources, provide access to multiple users and adapt dynamically to expanding datasets. To these ends, our model utilizes a GIS. A GIS is not only a useful tool to manage data, for example, in a geographically referenced database called a geodatabase, but it also provides the ability to analyze and visualize the data in their spatial context.

Further, a GIS can be a powerful tool for data analysis that informs decision-making. A GIS can integrate scientific and socioeconomic data to help evaluate interactions between land-use activities and the environment. Visualizing watershed information on maps and in other graphical representations, as quantitative results and as explicit representations of potential future scenarios, can help stakeholders better understand the implications of impending decisions and the interdependencies between watershed management and other sectors. Not only can datasets be overlaid on a map to explore their spatial interaction but GIS can also assist in modeling potential future scenarios, such as changes in the watershed condition over time and the impact of different management interventions. GIS analysis also helps target priority areas. Scenario modeling using computer-based tools such as GIS has been extremely useful in supporting watershed decision-making (Carmona, Varela-Ortega and Bromley 2013). Our hope is that by engaging stakeholders throughout the watershed approach, we will enable and implement better-informed decisions over the long term.

Problems in Data Collection

Since the Besor–Hebron–Be'er Sheva watershed is a transboundary system, the most significant challenge was the availability of and access to reliable data. Data were obtained from various Israeli sources, mainly universities, government ministries, nongovernmental organizations (NGOs) and international aid organizations. Data were also obtained from other researchers. Because of this, information regarding the origin of the data, date of collection and method for compiling the GIS layers was often unknown. Data were sometimes not up to date or not freely shared. Although CTWM has strong connections with Palestinian partners, data are even more difficult to acquire from Palestinian organizations, either due to a lack of monitoring or hesitancy to share information with a cross-border organization. Our efforts to date have focused on obtaining data from Israel and the West Bank, since our partners are in these locations. We have not yet tried to collect data for locations in Gaza.

Fragmented data sources and the lack of a centralized system to access information were observed in both Israel and the West Bank. These problems have been described by many researchers in the region (Comair et al. 2014). Therefore, developing a database structure to organize, manage and improve access to information is particularly important.

It was also challenging to assess the quality and accuracy of the data obtained. Data tables and GIS files were reviewed for internal consistency, and spatial data were correlated to known locations where possible. Nonetheless, data quality remains a problem inherent in relying on external sources of information.

Data collected and sources

Table 4.1 GIS database datasets and sources

Dataset	Source
Physical environment	
Soils for Israel and West Bank	Ben-Gurion University
Lithology	Ben-Gurion University
Land cover for West Bank	Friends of the Earth Middle East (FOEME)
Land use for Israel	Ben-Gurion University
Watersheds	Ben-Gurion University
Aquifers and aquifer recharge areas	Digitized from Israel Hydrological Service
Rivers	Ben-Gurion University
Rain	Ben-Gurion University
WWT plants and collection sites (Israel only)	Israel Water Authority and Mekorot (2006/07)
Digital Elevation Model (DEM)	Ben-Gurion University
Water quality	
Surface water quality	Israel Nature and Parks Authority, Nagouker Cohen, N. 2007, Ben-Gurion University
Wastewater	
Type of treatment used by municipality	Israel Water Authority, Arafeh 2012; House of Water & Environment (HWE); Hareuveni, E. 2009
Wastewater treatment facilities in Israel	Mekorot
Collection sites and reclamation projects (Israel)	Mekorot
Stonecutting facility locations	Al-Joulani, N. 2008

(Continued)

Table 4.1 (*cont.*)

Dataset	Source
Socioeconomics	
Population areas	Israel Institute of Technology
Populations by town/city	Israel Water Authority, Israel Central Bureau of Statistics, Palestinian Central Bureau of Statistics
Community ethnicity	Israel Central Bureau of Statistics, Palestinian Central Bureau of Statistics, Israel Institute of Technology
Bedouin community status	Negev Coexistence Forum for Civil Equality and Rudnitzky, A. 2012
Israel districts, sub-districts and natural regions	Israel Central Bureau of Statistics
West Bank governorates	Ben-Gurion University
West Bank administrative area	USAID
Jurisdiction and national boundaries	Israel Central Bureau of Statistics
Data Created	
Hill slope layer	Calculated in ArcGIS from DEM

Source: Arava Institute for Environmental Studies.

Data processing and integration (Geodatabase Functionality Upgrades)

A preliminary geodatabase was constructed in ArcGIS during the previous stages of this project. The current phase of work has built upon the existing geodatabase structure by adding many new GIS layers, data tables and lookup tables, and expanding the functionality of the geodatabase. This section describes the additions and modifications that were made.

The data collected were obtained as GIS files, Excel spreadsheets (or reports with data that could be transcribed into a spreadsheet) and image files. Each file and data type required a different extent of preprocessing before it could be integrated into the geodatabase.

Beyond the preliminary phases, we sought to increase the functionality of the geodatabase to facilitate investigation of spatial relationships between various data types. For example, in order to integrate socioeconomic data, these data had to be linked to other data that are spatially referenced. To accomplish this, a master GIS layer showing all communities within the watershed was compiled from multiple data sources. An initial file of community locations had been obtained from the Israel Institute of Technology, but more than 45 percent of these locations were unnamed. Through research and investigation, names were added wherever possible, and in the final file only 25 percent of locations remain unnamed. The remaining unnamed locations were typically

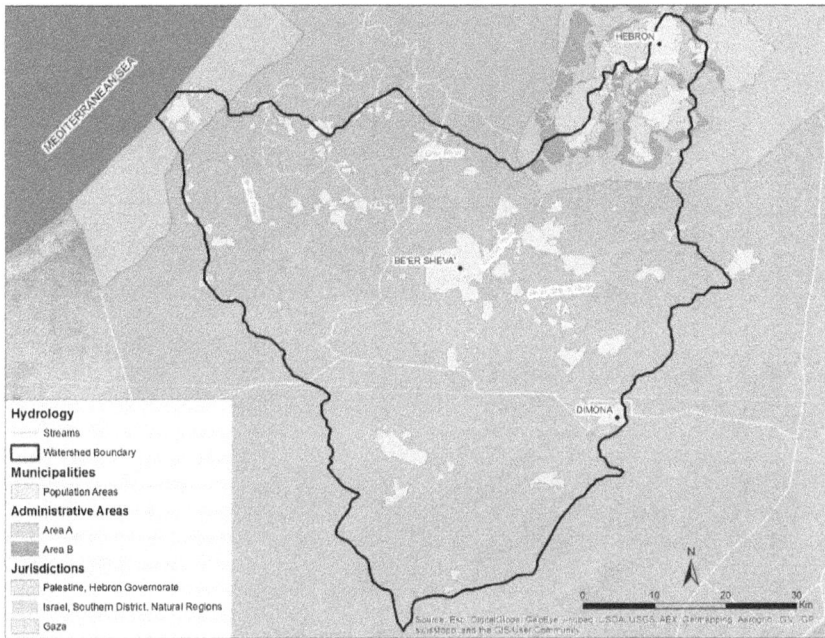

Figure 4.5 The complexity of governance within the watershed
Source: Arava Institute for Environmental Studies.

small and have low populations. The spelling of the English transliteration of each community name was standardized throughout the geodatabase so that these names could be used as a unique identifier to link the nonspatially referenced socioeconomic data with the communities. This link enabled us to visualize and evaluate spatial relationships between socioeconomic indicators and hydrologic characteristics to better understand pollution sources, the upstream–downstream connection, and the location of high-risk areas.

Results

This project is currently ongoing. Preliminary results and observations based on our ongoing research are discussed herein. Results thus far are primarily based on historic and recent water-quality measurements and spatial investigation of hydrologic, geographic and socioeconomic datasets. This section presents the prepared maps, interpretations and water-quality results.

Boundaries and demographics

Figure 4.5 shows the complexity of governance within the watershed. The Besor–Hebron–Be'er Sheva watershed overlies areas of Israel, the West Bank and Gaza. These areas of governance are further subdivided by different

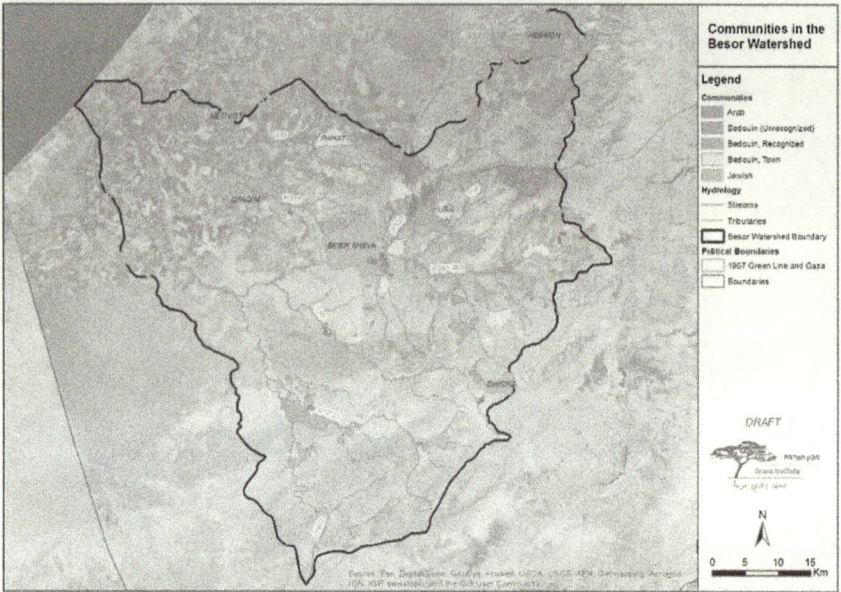

Figure 4.6 Municipalities color coded by demographic
Source: Arava Institute for Environmental Studies.

administrative areas. In Israel, the natural regions subdivide the Southern District. In the West Bank, Areas A and B denote important differences in civil and security administration. Additionally, over two hundred different municipalities lie within the watershed.

Communities in this area tend to have a dominant demographic. Figure 4.6 shows municipalities color-coded by demographic: Palestinian, Bedouin or Jewish Israeli. Bedouin communities are further subdivided based on the status of the community. Established Bedouin towns are recognized by the Israeli government and have access to infrastructure such as water and sewer networks and electricity. Unrecognized Bedouin villages are regarded as illegal by the Israeli government and do not have access to infrastructure or services.[9] In 2003, Israel decided to recognize 13 Bedouin villages in the Negev. Since then, improvements in infrastructure and access to services in these villages have been occurring, however slowly.

Seven Jewish communities are located in the West Bank within the Besor–Hebron–Be'er Sheva watershed. These include Kiryat Arba, Otniel, Haggai, Tene, Shim'a, Mezodot Yehuda and Suseya (separate from Palestinian Suseya).

---

9   Negev Coexistence Forum for Civil Equality. Website accessed June 1, 2014. http://www.dukium.org/eng/

Population data were compiled from the Israel Central Bureau of Statistics (2011), the Palestinian Central Bureau of Statistics (2013) and the Israel Water Authority (2006–2007). We have not yet been able to obtain reliable population data for some Bedouin communities, including Um Batin, Bir Hadaj, Al Sayyid, Abu Qureina and others. Estimates for population areas in Gaza are even more difficult to obtain, but the United Nations Relief and Works Agency estimates that approximately 124,000 people live in the area of Gaza within the Besor–Hebron–Be'er Sheva watershed. Our approximation suggests that, in total, about nine hundred thousand people live within the watershed boundaries, of whom 75 percent live in the northeastern quadrant. Estimations of demographic information compiled from surveys conducted between 2006 and 2013 suggest that about two-thirds of the watershed population is Palestinian (including Gaza), one-third is Jewish Israeli and a small percentage (approximately 1 percent) is Bedouin living in Israel. Hebron and Be'er Sheva are the largest population centers in the southern West Bank and Southern District of Israel, respectively. Each has a population of approximately two hundred thousand.[10]

Hydrologic Characterization

Drainages within the Besor–Hebron–Be'er Sheva watershed are naturally ephemeral. They do not support base flow year-round, but instead flow in response to significant precipitation events that tend to occur six or seven times per year (Tal et al. 2007). However, the natural system has been altered by overallocation and overuse of surface water and releases of wastewater directly into the wadis. Releases of untreated domestic and industrial wastewater from leather tanneries, stonecutting operations and olive presses in the urban area of Hebron have created a perennial base flow in the Hebron drainage (also known as Wadi As Samen). The average annual streamflow varies from less than 5 million to nearly 10 million cubic meters/year. The Hebron and Besor drainages are the basin's primary drainages.

The climate in the Besor–Hebron–Be'er Sheva watershed varies from semi-arid to arid. Average annual rainfall in the south is less than 50 mm/year; however, in the north, it can be as much as 550 mm/year. The watershed is characterized by high topographic variability, rising from the Mediterranean Sea to over one thousand meters above sea level in the northeast extent near Hebron. Higher elevations in the northeast and southeast constitute the

---

10 According to data from the Palestinian Central Bureau of Statistics for 2013. Website accessed 1 June, 2014. According to data from the Israel Central Bureau of Statistics from 2011.

headwaters of the watershed. Drainages flow through the basin and eventually converge at the outlet to the Mediterranean Sea.

The headwaters near Hebron are mountainous, with steep slopes, minimal soil cover, permeable soils and shallow bedrock. The headwaters overlie the southern extent of the structural anticline that forms the Judean hills. Bedrock in this area is generally Late Cretaceous limestone and dolomite of the Judea Group, which hosts the Mountain Aquifer, an important source of drinking water for the region. Groundwater is stored in a lower zone and in a karstic upper zone separated by low-permeability chalk and marl (GSI 1998). Groundwater flow is toward the south/southwest in the upper zone and toward the south in the lower zone (Livshitz 1999). The Western Mountain Aquifer is bounded to the east partly by the crest of the anticline and partly by hydraulic controls. The Eastern Mountain Aquifer, the expression of the Mountain Aquifer on the eastern side of the anticline crest, underlies the northeast corner of the watershed and has a groundwater flow direction to the northeast. Outcroppings and shallow Judea Group limestone in the southeast and northeast of the basin, where soils are thin and permeable, provide recharge areas for the groundwater aquifer (Livshitz 1999). In these areas, there may be some seepage from the upper zone into the lower zone of the Mountain Aquifer (GSI 2014). The center of the basin is primarily chalk, chert of the Eocene Avedat Group, overlaid by conglomerate, sand and alluvium (GSI 1998).

Soil type also affects infiltration to groundwater. Water infiltrates more easily through rendzinas than through loessial soils (Livshitz 1999). Soils in the northeast headwaters vary from terra rossas to brown and pale rendzinas. South of the Green Line, an east-west band of brown lithosols, loessial soils and brown soils stretches across the basin. The southern quadrant of the basin can be characterized by loessial serozems and brown lithosols. Areas of sand dunes, bare rocks and desert lithosols extend into the basin from the southwest.

Based on the geologic and hydrologic characteristics of the watershed, areas where surface water, groundwater or both are vulnerable to pollution can be identified. Low flow in naturally ephemeral streams throughout the basin makes these drainages susceptible to impact. Natural processes, such as self-purification, dilution and sedimentation, can help degrade pollutants, but without a substantial natural baseflow of clean water, these processes are reduced. Baseflow in the Hebron stream is almost entirely untreated wastewater. Although flood events typically increase pollutant loading by flushing pollutants from paved surfaces in runoff, in the Hebron stream, even runoff is a source of dilution to improve the extremely degraded streamflow (Nagouker Cohen 2007). Groundwater is most vulnerable in the headwaters in the northeast corner of the basin. Here, shallow groundwater, thin soil coverage and outcropping bedrock provide for recharge to the groundwater aquifer. Previous

studies have estimated that between 40 and 90 percent of surface water infiltrates the subsurface within the first 8.5 km of measurable flow in the Hebron
drainage (Tal et al. 2007). Recharge areas in the southeast may also be vulnerable to pollution, though cover of loessial soils reduces infiltration rates.

Pollution Sources

The most problematic source of pollution in the Besor–Hebron–Be'er
Sheva watershed is untreated domestic and industrial wastewater released
in the upper catchment in and around the city of Hebron. This region is
known for three main industries that all produce problematic wastewater: stonecutting, leather tanning and olive oil production. Due to the serious lack of sufficient wastewater treatment infrastructure, these industrial
wastewater streams drain into the Hebron drainage, contributing significantly to its degradation. Currently 22,730–25,150 m^3/day of wastewater
is generated in the city of Hebron. Most of this is not treated and eventually ends up in the Besor–Hebron–Be'er Sheva watershed (Al-Zeer and
Al-Khatib 2008).

Other industrial areas are found in the central part of the basin, particularly
near Be'er Sheva and at the industrial complex of Ramat Hovav. Industrial
areas in the center of the basin tend to be located along streams and may be
potential sources of pollution to the surface water. Groundwater is less vulnerable in the center of the basin because the depth to groundwater is greater
than in recharge areas, and a thick alluvial unit covers the bedrock and is an
unconfined aquifer in some areas. Soils are also less permeable. Groundwater
recharge areas in the southeast do not spatially overlap identified pollution
sources.

Wastewater treatment methods for Jewish Israeli communities in Israel and
in the West Bank were tabulated by the Israel Water Authority in 2006 and
2007. The main population center of Be'er Sheva and some nearby communities are serviced by the Mekorot water company's Be'er Sheva Wastewater
Treatment facility, which treats 14.4 million cubic meters of wastewater per
year (Mekorot 2014). Other regional wastewater treatment facilities serve
additional communities. Less populous Jewish Israeli communities use cesspits, settlement ponds or oxidation ponds. Settlement ponds and oxidation
ponds are considered primary or secondary levels of treatment and can be
slow and inefficient. In settlement ponds solids are allowed to settle out of
the wastewater, and in oxidation ponds algae growth produces oxygen to fuel
the breakdown of organic material by microorganisms. Cesspits are used to
collect and store wastewater underground. In a porous cesspit, liquid waste
percolates into the subsurface. The remaining solid waste needs to be cleaned

out periodically. In a tight cesspit, a watertight liner is utilized to prevent infiltration, but emptying is required more often.

More than 80 percent of Hebron is connected to sewer pipes, but the raw domestic wastewater collected in these pipes is discharged directly into the Hebron drainage south of the urban area (Hareuveni 2009). The Jewish Israeli community of Kiryat Arba, which is adjacent to Hebron, also discharges wastewater without treatment. Less populous Palestinian communities in the West Bank primarily use cesspits for wastewater treatment (House of Water and Environment (HWE) 2014, unpublished report), most of which are porous (according to the Palestinian Central Bureau of Statistics (PCBS) 2014), which means that leakage of untreated wastewater into the groundwater is common. Arafeh (2012) reports the use of household septic tanks in Yatta, Bani Na'im, Dura, As Samu and Ar Rihiya. In a septic tank, solids within the underground tank undergo some degradation and liquids are released into a drain field, where they are dispersed. This allows septic tanks to be cleaned out less often than cesspits. In both septic tanks and cesspits, compromises to the construction integrity and lack of maintenance increase the risk to groundwater. Cesspit use in communities within Israel is dispersed in the north-central part of the basin.

Wastewater treatment methods for many recognized and for all unrecognized Bedouin villages are unknown; however, they are assumed to be rudimentary. Only two established Bedouin towns are connected to centralized wastewater treatment facilities: Rahat and Segev Shalom. Laqye and Hura, which are also established towns, are documented as using cesspits for wastewater as of 2006/2007 (Nagouker Cohen 2007). Other established towns and recognized villages use cesspits or settlement ponds.

In addition, widespread agricultural land cultivation is a dispersed source of nitrogen, phosphorus and other nutrient pollution from pesticide and fertilizer use. Based on the available data, the majority of the 3.5 million dunums of land within the Besor–Hebron–Be'er Sheva watershed is open land, forests or grasslands (approximately 64%).[11] However, approximately 37 percent (1.3 million dunums) is used for agriculture or agriculture-related activities. An additional 1.4 percent (47,000 dunums) is covered by olive groves. Irrigated lands can be a source of increased nitrogen and phosphorus in surface water. Approximately 44,000 dunums of land (1.3 percent of the watershed) are zoned for industry or commercial use, which can be a highly concentrated source of contaminants. Mining areas are small (1,600 dunums) and restricted to the mountainous areas in the West Bank.

---

11 One dunum is approximately 1,000 square meters.

Our research shows that multiple pollution sources tightly clustered in the headwaters in the northeastern corner of the watershed overlay the natural recharge areas of the Western Mountain aquifer. Additionally, previous studies have estimated that infiltration from surface water to groundwater in the upper reaches of the Hebron stream is significant. Estimates suggest that 40–90 percent of water from the stream drainage infiltrates into the subsurface in the first 8.5 km of flow, and that infiltration rates are high throughout the upper 40 km (Nagouker Cohen 2007).

Water-Quality Monitoring Results

Water-quality monitoring can help characterize the current stream health and provide a baseline from which to monitor future impacts. Measuring water quality at both upstream and downstream locations can shed light on the patterns and mechanisms of pollutant transport in the stream and the location of potential sources. This section reviews the water-quality data that have been collected and analyzed thus far. First, a historical record from the Israel Nature and Parks Authority is presented. Next, samples that CTWM coordinated in 2013 are presented.

Historical Trends in Water Quality

A historical record of surface water quality was available for only four locations within the watershed, two of which are on the Besor–Hebron–Be'er Sheva stream. These locations, the Shama Roadblock and the Southern Delivery Station, are useful in evaluating changes from upstream to downstream along this drainage. The Shama Roadblock station is located at the Green Line near Meitar, and the Southern Delivery Station is located downstream of Be'er Sheva. Surface water-quality samples have been taken by the Israel Nature and Parks Authority biannually since 2002 in the spring (April, May or June) and fall (September, October or November). Data from 2002 through 2012 have been acquired to date.

The water-quality data show that concentrations of total suspended solids (TSS), BOD, fecal coliforms and total nitrogen are generally higher upstream than downstream. Industrial wastewater from the stonecutting industry in the Hebron area of the West Bank is a major source of elevated TSS, a measure of the amount of suspended particles in the water. Suspended particles diffuse sunlight and absorb heat, which can increase water temperature and reduce light available for algal photosynthesis. Suspended sediment can foul gravel beds, smother fish eggs and benthic insects and transport pathogens, pollutants and nutrients. The data show a seasonal variation in TSS concentrations, with peaks at the Shama Roadblock occurring in spring before 2008, and in fall after 2008. This seasonal shift may reflect the installation of the Shoquet treatment facility at the Green Line near the Metarim checkpoint, just upstream of this sampling location. Wastewater treatment at the Shoquet plant is minimal, but some reduction in sediment and suspended solids could be expected from this process. At the Southern Delivery Station, elevated TSS typically occurs in the spring. Spring peaks suggest that flushing due to precipitation runoff increases the transport of TSS to the stream. Seasonal peaks both upstream and downstream exceed the Inbar standard of 10 mg/L by two or three orders of magnitude.

BOD and fecal coliform are indicators of domestic wastewater pollution. BOD concentrations are generally higher at the Shama Roadblock than the Southern Delivery Station. Concentrations upstream peaked at nearly 800 mg/L in 2006, whereas downstream concentrations have been below 300 mg/L between 2002 and 2012. Seasonal fluctuations are observed, both upstream and downstream, where peaks occur in the spring season. Fecal coliforms are plotted on a logarithmic scale, since their concentrations are extremely elevated compared to the Inbar standard of 200 units per 100 mL. Upstream concentrations were close to or above 1,000,000 units per 100 mL since 2007. Downstream, fecal coliforms vary more dramatically. This and the reduction in BOD downstream may suggest that some self-purification occurs within the Hebron stream. Elevated BOD and fecal coliforms confirm that domestic wastewater is a significant source of pollution to the Hebron stream, that this is not a new problem and that it most likely relates to the minimal wastewater treatment infrastructure in the West Bank. Elevated concentrations were observed even in 2002. Additionally, since greatly elevated amounts of fecal coliforms persist downstream, there are likely additional inputs of pollution south of the Green Line.

Agricultural uses can increase concentrations of nutrients (such as nitrogen and phosphorus) and salt in runoff that reaches surface water and groundwater (Causapé, Quílez and Aragués 2004). Total nitrogen concentrations are elevated far above the Inbar standard of 10 mg/L at both the Shama Roadblock and Southern Delivery Station since 2005. Upstream concentrations vary between 60 and 160 mg/L, whereas downstream concentrations are slightly lower and vary from less than 20 mg/L to almost 120 mg/L. Total nitrogen shows seasonal peaks in the fall since 2009. However, seasonality is not observed downstream. This is likely due to self-purification and the complex cycling of nitrogen in the environment. The meaning of seasonal fluctuations is difficult to diagnose in arid and semiarid climates, since the first flood of the season can be responsible for washing 60–70 percent of the contaminants built up on the ground surface into the stream (Skipworth et al. 2000). It is unknown whether sampling events in the spring season were coordinated with the first flood. Chloride, a salt indicating irrigation of arid soils, is near the Inbar standard of 400 mg/L at the Shama Roadblock. At the downstream location, concentrations above 2,500 mg/L observed in 2002 and 2003 decreased dramatically in the fall of 2003, and in recent years concentrations have been at or near 400 mg/L. Seasonal variability downstream shows peaks in the fall during 2005, 2006, 2007 and 2009, and a peak in the spring in 2004.

These data show that historical records of water quality are helpful to gain a better understanding of the spatial and temporal variations, that is, long-term changes and seasonal fluctuations that elucidate the sources of pollution and the magnitude of their impact. Adding more monitoring stations on the Hebron stream where a long-term record of water quality is available would help characterize the baseline condition of the watershed, clarify the upstream/downstream connection and monitor the positive impacts due to changes in water management in the watershed. Our recommendations for further long-term monitoring are included in the concluding section, "Going Further."

Stream Sampling and Results

In order to address data gaps in water-quality information, water samples were collected from locations on the Hebron stream. Locations were selected to help clarify upstream conditions in the West Bank, where data are sparse and potential pollution sources are nearby. Grab samples were collected in the West Bank near Hebron, at the Green Line and at two locations downstream. Two sampling events have been conducted: one in June 2013 and one in December 2013. During the second sampling event, an additional location on the Be'er Sheva stream, a tributary to the Hebron stream that enters the Hebron near the Bedouin town of Tel Sheva (upstream of Be'er Sheva), was sampled (Table 4.2).

In Table 4.2, concentrations that exceed the Inbar standard for discharge to rivers (also included in the table) are shown in bold. In general, many values exceed the Inbar standards in both June and December. TSS concentrations exceeded the Inbar standard in June and December for all stations; however, concentrations were lower at all stations in December than in June. More specifically, a decrease of two orders of magnitude was observed in TSS from June to December at the upper catchment stations near Hebron and the Meitar checkpoint in the West Bank. Total phosphorus and sodium concentrations exceeded the Inbar standards of 1 mg/L and 200 mg/L respectively in almost all samples. Chemical oxygen demand (COD) decreased from June

Table 4.2 Results of water quality from grab samples collected in June and December 2013

Parameter	Unit	Inbar standards discharge to streams	Upper catchment – West Bank, outskirts of Hebron		Meitar checkpoint – southern West Bank		Tel Sheva, east of Be'er Sheva		Near Kibbutz Hatzerim, west of Be'er Sheva		Be'er Sheva stream, near Tel Sheva, upstream of Hebron stream	
			June	Dec	June	Dec	June	Dec	June	Dec	June	Dec
Total suspended solids	mg/L	10	**1,260**	**96.7**	**2,721**	**18.0**	**62.0**	**14.0**	**63.0**	**28.0**	N/A	**100**
Chemical oxygen demand	mg/L	70	**1,210**	**320**	**1,230**	2.00	**186**	65.6	**170**	**72.0**	N/A	**420**
Total nitrogen	mg/L	10	**85.4**	6.18	**85.9**	1.86	**52.2**	**27.0**	**48.8**	3.15	N/A	6.00
Total phosphorus	mg/L	1	**9.35**	**13.3**	**11.7**	0.04	**12.2**	**8.48**	**10.3**	**4.23**	N/A	**15.9**
Chloride	mg/L	400	247	196	252	14.0	348	182	**411**	323	N/A	172
Sodium	mg/L	200	N/A	**246**	**208**	24.5	**287**	**218**	**285**	**272**	N/A	**244**
pH	mg/L	7.0–8.5	7.91	7.96	8.19	8.34	8.31	8.30	**8.67**	7.79	N/A	7.62

N/A = not applicable because not measured

Bold values exceed the Inbar standard for discharge to streams.

Source: Arava Institute for Environmental Studies.

to December in all locations that were sampled in both months. Decreases of between one and three orders of magnitude were observed, with the greatest magnitude of decrease occuring at the station at the Meitar checkpoint. Sodium concentrations follow a different trend. Decreased sodium is observed in December only at the Meitar checkpoint station. At the Tel Sheva and Hatzerim stations, upstream and downstream of Be'er Sheva respectively, sodium concentrations are consistently elevated in both June and December with no significant seasonal change.

COD is an indicator of the amount of organic compounds present in water. Wastewater effluent would cause COD levels to increase. COD concentrations vary by two orders of magnitude from upstream to downstream—concentrations are over 1,000 mg/L in the West Bank and less than 200 mg/L in Israel during the June sampling event. These show the effect of untreated wastewater discharge in the upper reaches of the Hebron stream.

Approximately 100 stonecutting companies are located in Hebron and lie primarily within the industrial zone in the southern corner of the city (Kahrmann 2013). Stonecutting activities are a primary source of TSS in the Hebron stream. Water is used to cool rock saws, and the used water mixes with calcium carbonate dust. It is estimated that the stone-cutting industry produces 3,300 metric tons/year of calcium carbonate solids (El-Hamouz 2010). TSS data are by orders of magnitude much higher in the West Bank, further indicating that significant quantities of industrial wastewater are being discharged into the Hebron stream.

These results show that significant pollution is observed, specifically with regard to sodium, COD and TSS. Elevated sodium is an indication of agricultural runoff from farms due to high rates of fertilizer and pesticide use. Since the topography in Israel is more conducive to agricultural use than the mountainous areas of the West Bank, it makes sense that more impact from agricultural runoff would be observed in downstream areas near Tel Sheva and Hatzerim. Additionally, nonpoint source pollution shows a different trend than point source pollution, such as wastewater treatment discharges. In general, water quality is worse in the summer, when flows are reduced and chemicals become more concentrated. For point source discharges, additional input from precipitation in the winter would be expected to cause a reduction in concentrations due to dilution. For nonpoint sources, however, increased precipitation causes an increase in runoff, which mobilizes agricultural chemicals from fields.

In summary, the water-quality results indicate a complex situation of pollution with sources in both Israel and the West Bank and illustrate the different transport mechanisms of point and nonpoint source pollution throughout the watershed. Very few parameters meet the Inbar standards, reflecting a high level of pollution throughout the Besor–Hebron–Be'er Sheva stream. In some cases, the data are orders of magnitude above the Inbar standard. The locations included in this sampling effort begin to address an important gap in water-quality data from locations in the upper reaches of the Hebron stream in the West Bank.

A comprehensive dataset that covers both the upstream and downstream areas of a polluted watershed is necessary in order to develop a clear baseline understanding of the water quality. Upstream and downstream sampling locations help clarify the nature and extent of pollution, and elucidate potential sources of pollution. Collecting samples in both dry and wet seasons can be useful to understand the mechanisms of pollutant transport as well as the seasonal variations caused in part by natural fluctuations, chemical transport mechanisms and variations in loading from the sources of pollution.

In addition to a baseline characterization, long-term monitoring is required to evaluate the effectiveness of any stream restoration. Seasonal variability and other natural fluctuations will only be apparent in an extended record of sampling. Long-term monitoring can also elucidate the fate and transport of pollution in the watershed. For example, what is the self-purification capacity of the stream? And is the groundwater vulnerable to impact from polluted surface water? In addition, long-term trends can help evaluate and quantify improvements in water quality caused by changes in water management or point source control.

Cooperation among Stakeholders

The Arava Institute's experience working with cross-border organizations and extensive network of research place the Institute in a unique position to address transboundary water management challenges. CTWM regularly connects with researchers from across the region during workshops, conferences and trainings held in the region. On June 26, 2014, CTWM had the opportunity to present current research to a group of watershed stakeholders during a workshop cosponsored by international aid agencies and NGOs from Israel and the PA.[12] The workshop participants are listed in Table 4.3. Out of over thirty participants, approximately 37 percent were Palestinian, 37 percent were Israeli (including Israeli-Arabs) and 25 percent were internationals. The benefit of this workshop is twofold: by sharing research results we can begin to increase the stakeholders' understanding of the watershed, and we can develop new relationships with researchers and stakeholders.

By presenting the results of preliminary research in the Besor–Hebron–Be'er Sheva watershed, stakeholders can learn about the scientific aspects of

---

12 The workshop was cosponsored by USAID, the Arava Institute for Environmental Studies, Ben-Gurion University, the Water and Environmental Development Organization (WEDO) and the House of Water & Environment.

Table 4.3 Participant affiliations from the June 26, 2014, stakeholder meeting in Beit Jala

Participant affiliations
Al Quds University
Arava Institute for Environmental Studies
Ben-Gurion University
Bethlehem Western Southern Joint Council
Black and Veatch Consulting
Colorado State University
Friends of the Earth Middle East
GIZ Ramallah
Hebrew University
Independent
Israel/Palestine Center for Research and Information (IPCRI)
United Nations Development Programme, Ramallah
US Agency for International Development (USAID)
Water and Environmental Development Organization (WEDO)
Yarkon River Authority

Source: Arava Institute for Environmental Studies.

watershed management and increase their knowledge of the specific challenges faced in this watershed (Carmona, Varela-Ortega and Bromley 2013). Further, stakeholders can participate in the data collection process, as engaging in discussion about active research may make them more likely to share their existing knowledge. More specifically, data visualizations, such as maps and graphs (described in the first part of this chapter), are especially effective in promoting a holistic understanding of watershed processes (Carmona, Varela-Ortega and Bromley 2013). For example, seeing a map of water-quality samples can clearly show how upstream activities can impact the water quality downstream.

Since the watershed is interconnected, so too should be the research and data collection throughout the watershed. This requires collaboration between scientists and researchers from Israel and the West Bank. At the workshop in June 2014, CTWM was able to make connections with other researchers, both Israeli and Palestinian, who are working in the watershed. Our hope is that these relationships become productive avenues for sharing data and knowledge and for increasing the possibility of collaborative solutions that address water-quality challenges. Unilateral solutions have been attempted by Israel to reduce the impact of polluted streamwater. A wastewater treatment facility was constructed on the Hebron stream at the Green Line to treat sewage from the West Bank as it flows into Israel (Hareuveni 2009). Although political conflict and economic asymmetries between the governing bodies of Israel and the PA can make unilateral solutions seem more viable, treating wastewater so far from its source is problematic (Fischendler, Dinar and Katz 2011; Tal et al. 2010). Research has shown that over the 40 km where sewage flows in wadis before entering Israel, between 40 and 90 percent may seep into the groundwater aquifer, causing additional pollution to this important resource (Nagouker Cohen 2007). Since unilateral solutions—though they have the least political and bureaucratic obstacles/resistance—are often severely deficient in addressing the source of pollution, we believe that collaboration at the watershed level can produce more sustainable solutions for minimizing environmental degradation on both sides of the political border.

Going Further

The focus of our continued work is twofold: to further our scientific understanding and to promote cooperation among stakeholders, both on a watershed level. Specifically, our next tasks will include deepening our understanding of baseline environmental conditions, establishing a long-term monitoring program and promoting stakeholder engagement to develop feasible recommendations for restoration of the watershed. Ultimately our goal is to improve the

Figure 4.7 The Be'er Sheva River Parkway as it is today with untreated sewage flowing in the stream

health of the Besor–Hebron–Be'er Sheva stream through implementation of a transboundary, watershed-based approach.

In this chapter we have demonstrated the importance of building and maintaining a comprehensive database in GIS. We have been able to conduct some analyses with the information that has been collected up to this point, but gaps in the database must continue to be addressed. Our preliminary analysis has identified areas where additional water-quality information (both surface water and groundwater) is needed, specifically in the West Bank and in Gaza. It is also apparent that an understanding of the connection between surface water and groundwater would be critical for evaluating the potential risk to water resources.

However, in addition to analyzing existing data, a long-term monitoring plan is needed. Grab samples in wet and dry seasons should be conducted annually in order to understand how rainfall and flooding impact the quality of wastewater in the stream. This schedule would be coordinated and supported in part by the Israeli Water and Sewerage Authority. In addition, automatic sampling stations, now in the process of being implemented, would add important real-time information about water quantity and quality and would constitute a significant contribution to our understanding of flow and chemical transport in the stream.

Arriving at viable solutions to improve the water quality in the watershed depends not only on science but also on the establishing of cooperative relationships with stakeholders. We believe that engaging stakeholders in the process of data collection and analysis will set the stage for cooperative relationships to develop in other areas as well. Through sharing information and learning about the watershed, stakeholders are more likely to consider watershed-wide solutions that positively benefit multiple parties (Carmona, Varela-Ortega and Bromley 2013). Following the stakeholder workshop in June 2014, we continued to build upon relationships started there by engaging with researchers working in the Besor–Hebron–Be'er Sheva watershed and sharing information about water quality and pollution. This workshop also demonstrated how GIS can be used as a visual tool for communicating complex information to stakeholders from different professional backgrounds (e.g., scientists and decision-makers). Our next steps are to continue to develop the capacity of GIS as a tool for engaging and educating stakeholders and for conducting analysis for decision support. The GIS database that we have developed is the first step toward conducting quantitative modeling of scenarios that reflect different management options for watershed restoration. For example, we could model the effect that removing the point source discharge of untreated wastewater in Hebron would have on the flow and water quality downstream, such as near Be'er Sheva. Visual representations of quantitative results derived from observed data would be an extremely effective tool in helping decision-makers understand the effects of different decisions, and therefore enable them to choose the most beneficial decision for the entire watershed.

References

Al-Sa'ed, Rashed. 2010. "A Policy Framework for Trans-Boundary Wastewater Issues along the Green Line, the Israeli-Palestinian Border." *International Journal of Environmental Studies* 67 (6): 937–954.

Al-Joulani, N. 2008. "Soil Contamination in Hebron District Due to Stone Cutting Industry." *Journal of Applied Science* 10 (1): 37–50.

Al-Zeer, I., and I. Al-Khatib. 2008. "Potential Reuse of Treated Wastewater for Irrigation in Hebron District, Imad Al-Zeer and Issam Al-Khatib." In *Proceedings of First Symposium on Wastewater Reclamation and Reuse for Water Demand Management in Palestine*. April 2–3, 2008, Birzeit University, Palestine (p. 87).

Arafeh, Ghadeer 2012. "Process Monitoring and Performance Evaluation of Existing Wastewater Treatment Plans in Palestinian Rural Areas / West Bank." Master's thesis, Birzeit University.

Carmona, G., Consuelo Varela-Ortega and John Bromley. 2013. "Participatory Modelling to Support Decision Making in Water Management under Uncertainty: Two Comparative Case Studies in the Guadiana River Basin, Spain." *Journal of Environmental Management*, 128: 400–412.

Causapé J., D. Quílez and R. Aragués. 2004. "Salt and Nitrate Concentration in the Surface Waters of the CR-V Irrigation District (Bardenas I, Spain): Diagnosis and Prescriptions for Reducing Off- Site Contamination." *Journal of Hydrology* 295: 87–100.

Comair, Georges, Daene McKinney, David Maidment, Gonzalo Espinoza, Harish Sangiredy, Abbas Fayad and Fernando Salas. 2014. "Hydrology of the Jordan River Basin: A GIS-Based System to Better Guide Water Resources– Management and Decision Making. *Water Resources Management* 28 (4): 933–946.

El-Hamouz, Amer. 2010. "The Development of a National Master Plan for Hazardous Waste Management for the Palestinian National Authority (PNA)." An-Najah National University.

Fischhendler, Itay, Shlomi Dinar and David Katz. 2011. "Spatial and Temporal Politics of Unilateral Environmentalism: Cooperation and Conflict over Water Management along the Israeli- Palestinian Border." *Global Environmental Politics* 11 (1): 36–61.

Food and Agricultural Organization of the United Nations (FAO), Paper 150. 2006. "The New Generation of Watershed Management Programmes and Projects." Accessed July 7, 2014, http://www.fao.org/docrep/009/a0644e/a0644e00.htm.

Geological Survey of Israel Jerusalem (GSI). 1998. "Geological Map of Israel 1:200,000 (4 Sheets)." State of Israel, Ministry of National Infrastructures. Accessed June 15, 2014, http://www.gsi.gov.il/Eng/Index.asp?ArticleID=159&CategoryID=112.

Hareuveni, Eyal. 2009. *Foul Play: Neglect of Wastewater Treatment in the West Bank*. B'Tselem. Accessed at: https://www.btselem.org/download/200906_foul_play_eng.pdf

Kahrmann, David. 2013. "USAID Keeps West Bank Trade—Not Slurry—Flowing." *USAID*. IIP Digital. Accessed June 4, 2013, http://iipdigital.usembassy.gov/st/english/article/2013/06/20130604275415.html#axzz2ZQg75Prr.

Livshitz, Y. 1999. "The Influence of Natural and Artificial Factors on the Chemical Composition of the Groundwater in the Northwestern Negev and the Southern Portion of the Shfela." PhD diss. Ben-Gurion University of the Negev, Beer Sheva.

Nagouker Cohen, N. 2007. "Hydrological and Chemical Characterization of Baseflow and Small Flow Events along the Trans-Boundary Besor Basin." Master's thesis. Ben-Gurion University of the Negev. Jacob Blaustein Institutes for Desert Research and Albert Katz International School for Desert Studies.

"Palestinian Central Bureau of Statistics (PCBS)." 2014. Accessed June 1, 2014, http://www.pcbs. gov.ps.

Rudnitzky, A., and T. Abu Ras. 2012. "The Bedouin Population in the Negev." The Abraham Fund Initiatives. Accessed at: http://www.abrahamfund.org/webfiles/fck/Research%20-%20Beduin%20English%20Final.pdf

Skipworth P. J., S. J. Tait and A. J. Saul. 2000. "The First Foul Flush in Combined Sewers: An Investigation of the Causes." *Urban Water* 2 (4): 317–325.

Tal, A., N. Al Khateeb, L. Asaf, A. Assi, A. Nassar, M. Abu Sadah, A. Gasith, J. Laronne, Z. Ronen, Y. Hirshkowitz, D. Halawani, N. Nagouker, R. Angel, H. Akerman, M. Diabat and A. Abramson. 2007. "Watershed Modeling: BioMonitoring and Economic Analysis to Determine Optimal Restoration Strategies for Transboundary Streams. Covering the period from September 2004 to December 2007." Final MERC Report project M23-019. Unpublished. The Arava Institute for Environmental Studies (AIES; Israel), Water and Environmental Development Organization (WEDO; PA), House of Water and Environment (PA), The Institute for Nature Conservation Research (Tel Aviv University, Israel). Submitted to the US Agency for International Development: Bureau for Economic Growth, Agriculture and Trade (Middle Eastern Regional Cooperation).

Tal, A., N. Al Khateeb, N. Nagouker, H. Akerman, M. Diabat, A. Nassar, R. Angel, M. Abu Sadah, Y. Hershkovitz, A. Gasith, A. Aliewi, D. Halawani, A. Abramson, A. Assi, J. Laronne and L. Asaf 2010. "Israeli/Palestinian Transboundary Stream Restoration and Management: Lessons for the Future." *International Journal of River Basin Management* 8 (2): 207–213.

Weinberger, Gavriel, Yakov Livshitz, Amir Givati, Michael Zilberbrand, Adi Tal, Menachem Weiss and Arik Zurieli. 2012. "The Natural Water Resources Between the Mediterranean Sea and the Jordan River." Israel Hydrological Service. Accessed June 9, 2015.

‎2007–2006 – ‏.א, כהן, פיימן,. ד., מ. ארצי סקר ,חקלאית להשקיה קולחים וניצול בשפכים וטיפול איסוף .2008 לדל. רשות המים (Collection and treatment of sewage and the reuse of effluent for agricultural irrigation A national survey. M. Feiman and D. Cohen. The Israel Water Authority: 2006–2007).

Chapter 5

THE EVOLUTION OF ISRAELI WATER MANAGEMENT: THE ELUSIVE SEARCH FOR ENVIRONMENTAL SECURITY

Alon Tal

"Then Abraham complained to Abimelek about a well of water that Abimelek's servants had seized."

—Genesis 21:25

Introduction: Water, Conflict and the Land of Israel

The first book of the Bible is full of quarreling between the Israelite patriarchs and the surrounding communities (Audu 2013). Water was undoubtedly a critical resource for survival in an agrarian society, and apparently there was not always enough to go around. Indeed, it was lack of rains and famine that forced the children of Israel into an Egyptian exile which lasted 430 years, much of it enslaved. While a source of tension and intermittent conflicts, control of water resources appears in retrospect to have been largely amenable to reconciliation, giving rise to occasional covenants for water sharing and cooperation. In a region where recent climate change and reduced precipitation along with rapid population growth makes water scarcity more acute than ever (Mariotti 2015), is the underlying optimism of the Biblical narrative still valid?

While pervasive water scarcity does seem to have changed in the Middle East during the Holocene era, technologically, there is little that remains the same. In this context, this chapter evaluates Israel's experience in water management and its ongoing quest for water security. Although control over water resources has rarely, if ever, been the sole casus belli in modern war between nations, it has certainly exacerbated tensions (Wolf 1998). Israel along with its neighbors is often given as an example of such dynamics. Water management for most of Israel's history was driven by an underlying sense that water resources were limited and critical for survival and that ensuring their availability was a paramount policy objective. This contributed to making the country's hydrological history a particularly unique story where local water managers took a path less traveled. In many cases, solutions were pursued that at the time were altogether unexplored in other countries. Israel's ensuing water management strategy has certainly generated interest internationally. But is it sustainable?

Most retrospective chronologies of water management in Israel present the narrative essentially in a favorable light (Teschner 2013; Tal 2006a). At a time when demographic proliferation in countries surrounding Israel has compromised the regularity of water supplies and crisis-like hydrological dynamics are pervasive, Israel has largely managed to increase the reliability and quality of its water supply. It can be argued that Israel developed its water resources much as it did its security forces. On the one hand, there was great confusion, with different agencies alternatively vying for domination and then evading accountability for water-quality problems. Yet, from the competing interests of a pluralistic governmental bureaucracy, a distinct idiosyncratic policy orientation emerged. A combination of technological innovation and nimble policy shifts ostensibly came to provide a secure water supply for the growing urban population at the tap and phenomenal yield increases among its farmers. But as we shall see, there are still great uncertainties and vulnerabilities that the Israeli system faces.

This chapter examines the different challenges associated with the establishment of Israel's water-management program. It is well to ask whether the Israeli experience still constitutes a relevant model for other dryland nations given the emergence of desalination as a technological solution to water scarcity. Despite dramatic accomplishments, which can and should be recognized, Israel has made many mistakes that have created fundamentally ethical dilemmas: Given present exigencies and economic demands, does mining an aquifer, diverting water sources to the Dead Sea or irreversibly contaminating groundwater compromise notions of transgenerational justice? Are the institutional frameworks that have emerged to manage these resources adequate to address the growing population and demands for regional water sharing? In particular, can Israel's water-management successes be translated into cooperative transboundary efforts that produce collective sustainability and true water security for the Israeli, Palestinian and Jordanian peoples?

Overcoming Scarcity: Israel's Water History, the First 55 Years

From its inception, Israel's Zionist nationalism and socialist economics were soon manifested in local water-management strategies. The challenges were not trivial. Among the most salient and challenging characteristics of Israel's

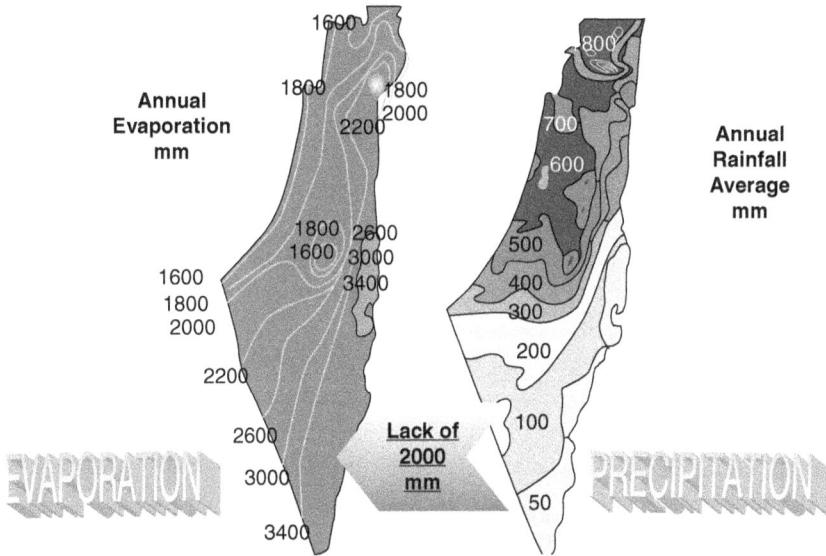

Figure 5.1 Geographic asymmetry: Israel's evaporation and precipitation levels
Source: Alon Tal.

hydrological reality are the country's temporal and geographic asymmetry. As seen in figure 5.1, Israel is located along a very steep rain gradient, where the southern hyperregions frequently receive only 10–20 mm of rain annually, but small sections of the north receive tropical levels of precipitation.

With the doubling of the local population within a few years due to immigration after the Holocaust, the expansion of agriculture was deemed a top national priority. This was both to guarantee food self-sufficiency and to provide employment to the many unemployed refugees. In order to provide water to the new rural settlements, two major water carriers were constructed to deliver water from the Yarkon River and the Kinneret Lake (Sea of Galilee) to the more desiccated southlands. As a result, 16 years after declaring political independence, Israel had more than doubled its available water resources. The country was able to merge natural resource and social policy by subsidizing water for a quickly growing agricultural sector. This so-called hydrological socialism allowed Israel's water commissioner to offer consumers a uniform price for water in their sector, regardless of their geographic location (Tal 2002). Most importantly, the country's water policies had made it food independent.

The interface between Israel's military security and its hydrological security was prominent during Israel's first decades. The objection of Syria and Jordan in the 1950s to the transfer of water from the Jordan River to southern Israel was sufficiently virulent to lead to formal appeals and a heated debate in the

UN Security Council (Blass 1973). Israel capitulated to international pressure and moved its national water carrier away from the upper Jordan River downstream to the Kinneret Lake. It took almost eight years to build the entire network of pumps, tunnels and pipes. The initial capital cost came to 175 million dollars at a time when the country was extremely poor (Shoham 1995). And that was just the start.

The national water carrier that brought the water south relied on gravitation. The Kinneret Lake is the lowest freshwater lake in the world. The pumping required to physically lift the water uphill from the Kinneret Lake to the newly created Eshkol Reservoir for treatment required copious quantities of energy, at the time a substantial percentage of that generated in the country. But, over budget and a little bit late, the carrier did work. Soon, the country had literally doubled the amount of water it could deliver to farmers and, to a lesser extent, urban residents. But while the project increased the absolute of amount of water, it did not guarantee water security. Israel's water managers remained very nervous that Arab armies would manage to sabotage the water carriers or bomb the supporting electrical facilities, bringing pumping to a halt. These negative scenarios were never realized, largely because the country's new and vaunted water infrastructure enjoyed the protection of a high-security asset.

When the National Water Carrier began operations in 1964, the country could rely on a national grid of water delivery. At the time, much of the uncertainty associated with the water supply that had been part of the reality for farmers in the land of Israel since Biblical patriarchs prayed for rain ceased to be a salient factor in day-to-day life (Tal 2002). Overnight, the country's irrigation and drinking water supply became dependent on robust flows in the upper Jordan River basin. This was deemed a sufficiently critical strategic interest that in 1966, when the Syrian army began to divert certain tributaries to the Jordan within its jurisdiction, Israel perceived the act as an attack on a vital interest. Without thinking twice, its air force bombers simply took out the Syrian bulldozers, halting its northern neighbors' attempt to impair its water supply (Sachar 1976).

For engineers at the time, the National Water Carrier was an unqualified water-security success. Water delivery expanded dramatically. Even during drought years, copious quantities of water were delivered at subsidized rates. Close to nine hundred thousand acres of land could now be designated for farming with the promise that water would be delivered to the newly cultivated fields and orchards for irrigation (Hann 2013). For much of the country's history, the water carriers constituted a substantial contribution to local food security.

But an environmental price was paid for the new policy of water transfer. Highly saline, the Kinneret water delivered salt onto agricultural soils all over the country. The Kinneret frequently was pumped to levels below the "red lines" recommended by the hydrological community. Because of underlying saline springs, the water-quality implications were treacherous, with a real threat of long-term salinization (Tal 2006). During most years, the entire amount of rainfall and runoff reaching the Kinneret was diverted to the carrier and its consumers. Practically no water was released from the lake via the Degania Dam to the southern Jordan River. Eventually the Dead Sea began to disappear. Water levels dropped roughly a meter each year, with unhappy aesthetic, economic and geological implications (Filin et al. 2014).

The delivery of water to Israel's southland represented a profound national commitment to water-supply and agricultural development. To ensure that this would continue, new institutions were created: a water commission was established and run by a water commissioner who, for most of the country's history, was a professional with an understanding of hydrological dynamics. A water law was enacted that created the statutory basis for the water policies; it revolutionized the landscape and the way farming was done throughout the country. It left responsibility for drinking water and effluent treatment standards in the hands of the Ministry of Health. Further, just as the British had perceived sewage to be a local issue, Israel left these critical environmental services in the hands of individual municipalities. Many had neither the resources nor the political will to address what soon become a significant health and ecological hazard.

But the new surfeit of sewage also created a water-management opportunity. As immigration continued apace, water demand grew relentlessly. The additional water provided by the water carriers was simply not enough. Sanitation engineers at the Ministry of Health came to realize that wastewater recycling could be a significant boost to local supplies (Shuval 1980).

It would be natural to expect the Ministry of Agriculture or the water commission itself to have taken the lead in advocating for sewage reuse. But neither of these institutions had a keen sense of the country's hydrological constraints, and they did not yet see the potential hazards associated with drawing down the groundwater. The Ministry of Health's alacrity in encouraging recycling of effluents was based on an entirely different consideration: the rapidly growing population created exponentially greater quantities of sewage that could no longer be contained by cesspools and septic tanks. The overflow soon emerged as a full-blown health hazard. Indeed, Israel suffered from cholera outbreaks (Schwartz 1971), and beaches were deemed unsafe for bathing due to the high bacterial levels created by the discharge of raw sewage directly or via westerly flowing streams. But the Ministry of Health saw that the farming community in Israel was already taking matters into its own hands and recycling its sewage without any regulation. It opted not to fight the trend but to try to control it by recommending guidelines for wastewater reuse and integrating effluents into the national water strategy (Tal 2006).

A national master plan for wastewater reuse envisioned Israeli farmers benefiting from the recycling of 150 million cubic meters of effluent for local irrigation (Wachs 1971). By then, already, a psychological transition had occurred among the farming community: wastewater was considered a valuable resource. Despite initial concerns of exposure to pathogens, epidemiological studies failed to find long-term impacts on human health. Environmental impacts, however, increasingly emerged as an "inconvenient truth" that water managers often chose not to address. Some of the problems, such as the concentrations of boron in the effluents, could be controlled by regulating the contents of laundry detergents (Tal 2013). But other problems were less given to magic bullet solutions. For instance, the salts added to agricultural soils were assessed by Technion professor (and former water commissioner) Dan Zaslavsky as an agronomic disaster in the making (Zaslavsky, Guhteh and Sahar 2004).

These problems were particularly acute, as wastewater treatment often was conducted at a minimal *primary* level. The water that was released still contained a host of biological and chemical contaminants. Due to poor pretreatment in Israeli factories, industrial solvents found their way into the municipal sewage stream and from there to farmers' fields and underlying aquifers (Muszkot 1990). For most of its history, institutionally, agricultural interests dominated the Israel Water Commission. Commissioners were first and foremost committed to providing farmers with plentiful and inexpensive irrigation water. They were loath to regulate polluters or intervene in a way that would reduce water supply for agricultural operations. This led to decades of extremely contaminated streams across Israel and percolation of sewage or partially treated effluents into aquifers, especially along Israel's coastline. High levels of nitrates were recorded in many wells, leading to their discontinuation. Recently, a range of pharmaceuticals, including antibiotics, was identified in wells underlying fields with a history of wastewater reuse (Avisar, Lester and Ronen 2009).

It would take many years before Israel's wastewater infrastructure would be sufficiently robust to handle the daunting task of eliminating the potential hazards associated with massive effluent recycling. It is ironic that waster infrastructure for delivery of freshwater was considered a sufficiently significant priority for Israel's security and economy to warrant an unprecedented investment, while ensuring its long-term sustainability had been neglected for decades. The first plant to introduce activated sludge to allow for safe wastewater reuse, the Shafdan plant, remains Israel's largest facility, treating the sewage of greater Tel Aviv. Slowly but surely, however, secondary treatment was introduced in wastewater treatment plants across Israel. By 2009, over 90 percent of the country's sewage treatment facilities had reasonable effluents that could be delivered to agriculture (Israel Water Authority 2015a).

The trouble was that over time it became clear that when wastewater is discharged into dry stream beds or is utilized for irrigating vegetables or fruits, even *secondary* treatment is not a sufficiently stringent standard for a sustainable water supply. During the late 1990s, government bureaucrats at the Ministry of Agriculture and the Ministry of Environment (and their stable of so-called independent scientists) argued over what the new standard for wastewater recycling should be. Eventually, a compromise was reached. The new standards are locally still known as the Inbar standards, after the government official who chaired the interministerial committee. They were much more extensive than the earlier regulations that only addressed suspended solids and chemical oxygen demand, covering dozens of hitherto unregulated chemicals. They also were tougher. In practice the committee, and eventually the Knesset, approved bifurcated standards that pose different expectations on wastewater that is to be recycled by agriculture than wastewater that is directed to streams (Lawhon 2006).

Present trends appear to be encouraging: Israeli farmers recycle 86 percent (400 million m³) of the sewage that arrives at the country's treatment plants. This level of wastewater reuse is unprecedented internationally. (By way of contrast levels, Spain reports some 17 percent recycling of its sewage with Italy and Australia at 10 percent or less.) About half of the wastewater undergoes tertiary treatment, with the remainder utilizing secondary treatment, generally based on some form of activated sludge technology. In the not-so-distant future, all of the wastewater utilized by Israeli farmers will be treated at tertiary levels (Israel Water Authority 2015b). Even at secondary levels, a well-run plant can eliminate many of the endocrine-disrupting compounds that can affect human reproductive and hormonal functioning. A recent study found that Israeli wastewater treatment plants perform better on average than comparable facilities in Europe in this regard. Even at those plants that have not yet introduced tertiary treatment, activated sludge almost completely eliminates a range of the chemicals present in the raw sewage such as octylphenol (OP), nonylphenol (NP), bisphenol A (BPA), estrone, estriol, 17β-estradiol, testosterone (TES), triclosan (TCS) and carbamazepine (CBZ) (Godinger et al. 2015).

In short, the introduction of recycled wastewater revolutionized Israel's water sector and brought with it a higher level of security for agriculture. Whether or not it is a rainy year, people produce sewage, and it has to go somewhere. So effluents are considered to be a most reliable source of water. Israeli farmers receive more treated wastewater for irrigation than freshwater. From a water-security as well as a food-security perspective, the country's investment in wastewater infrastructure and regulation in the short run appears to be largely positive. With a predictable sewage supply, Israeli farmers are increasingly free of the uncertainties associated with the stochastic fluctuations of rainfall in the region. Yet given concerns about the long-term impact of soil salinization, the long-term prospects for water security are by no means clear. The primary threat to future land fertility is salinization from wastewater, the cumulative impact of which is still unknown. Many experts warn that the impacts could eventually be disastrous for agriculture as more and more salts slowly compromise the physical properties of the soil.

Part of the reason why Israel could expand wastewater irrigation so dramatically during the past two decades involves a network of reservoirs that provides storage infrastructure throughout the country. During the rainy winter months, farmers typically do not need to irrigate their fields. That means that the sewage treated during this period ordinarily is not directed to agriculture. In order to store these effluents during the rainy season, 240 reservoirs were established at a price exceeding one billion dollars. The projects generally were funded by international private donors through the Jewish National Fund, a public corporation and philanthropy with offices around the world. Today, over half of the effluents used by Israeli agriculture spend a period of time in storage in an effluent reservoir. The storage capacity allows water managers to "finesse" the climatic asymmetry and accommodate the differential irrigation needs of Israel's farmers (KKL 2015).

The utilization of reservoirs, and the aeration that takes place during storage, may offer a modest water-quality dividend. But at present, reservoirs are not designed to make a significant contribution to water quality. A 2012 national survey of 60 wastewater-reuse reservoirs looked at the quality of effluents being sent for irrigation. Most of the water leaving reservoirs for irrigation is clean enough to meet Israel's old standards (65 percent), but the majority fails to meet the stringent new Inbar standards (Kfir et al. 2012).

The lesson from the experience is clear: Israel's success in recycling wastewater provides a sizable and reliable alternative source of water. But it is not clear whether this is a "Faustian" deal that will be paid for by future generations. At the very least, other countries that consider emulating the strategy should be prepared to invest heavily in tertiary treatment plants that can remove much of the minerals and contaminants as well as in storage capacity to optimize effluent utilization. Otherwise, short-term improvement in water security may bring about unacceptable environmental consequences and make a suboptimal economic contribution.

The environmental history literature speaks of a "frontier" approach to natural resource development (Patterson and Glavovic 2013). Unaware of any physical limitations, young societies frequently pursue constant growth, expanding their extraction of raw materials until they become exhausted. Only later do they begin to understand that there must be limits on demand. Israel's hydrological history conforms to this general model. The initial phases of the country's water-management strategy were large informed by an obsessive effort to expand water supply with no compelling sense that they were dealing with finite resources. Eventually, physical limits were reached and the overpumping of aquifers led to seawater intrusion and the decommissioning of wells due to salinity. Israeli water managers came to understand that in order to offer water security, they had to start placing limits on demand.

Given Zionists' historic glorification of agriculture and the powerful political patronage protecting farmers, this was easier said than done (Tal 2007). Fairly substantial water subsidies created cheap water for irrigation, and the results were highly predictable. Farmers often wasted precious freshwater because it was so inexpensive. Israel's utilization of sprinklers and even flood irrigation exacerbated the excessive exploitation of groundwater and during dry years, drawing down the water level of the Kinneret Lake below the "red lines" that had been established as hydrologically sustainable markers.

This insouciant and often profligate attitude toward irrigation changed rather suddenly, as Israeli farmers came to be the most efficient water users in the word. Dramatic reductions in agriculture utilization of irrigation water did not come about due to hard political choices between competing sectors but rather because of technological innovation. The introduction of drip irrigation during the 1960s took some time to take off, but eventually the new efficient irrigation systems became positively ubiquitous throughout Israel (Ben-Gal, Tel-Tsur and Tal 2006). It would not take long before local farmers could sit back and allow computers to assess the water needs of fields and orchards, turn irrigation systems on while they slept comfortably at night and control the amount of fertilizers delivered to the root zones of the plants and trees being cultivated (Hillel 2008). As the technologies improved, eventually involving minimal evaporation and subsurface drippers, so did the yields. While not the only factor, the 1,600 percent increase in the value of produce grown by Israeli farmers during the past 60 years has a great deal to do with innovations in irrigation and a savvy cohort of farmers who seamlessly integrated the new drip technologies for optimal results. (Kislev and Tsaban 2013).

Conservation was not only a matter for farmers, and soon became part of the lifestyle and personal ethos among Israelis in the country's predominantly urban population. Public bathrooms increasingly relied on waterless urinals; dual-flush toilets became the norm; cities distributed low flow fixtures and faucet aerators, free of charge to taxpayers; water-intensive garbage disposals were replaced with compost bins. Most of all, the country got serious about plugging the leaks in the pipes delivering water in its towns and metropolises. Through a combination of positive incentives and penalties, infrastructure was monitored and maintained. Today, Israel's cities lose only about 10 percent of the water delivered to them (Gvirtzman 2012), a very low rate by international standards and an unthinkably low percentage for the Middle East.

No longer a reflection of Israeli farmers' most-favored status, water pricing became an important policy instrument for ensuring sustainability. Subsidies for freshwater were removed altogether and were priced higher than the recycled effluents that are available at reduced rates. To encourage water among urban consumers, a "two-block tariff system" was introduced: a cubic meter of water costs only $2.30 for households if they use less than 3.5 m^3/month. The price goes up 50 percent if they use more. During drought years, supermodels and pop singers were drafted to go on television and remind the public that the Kinneret Lake was drying up. This appeal to citizens' higher sense of duty is not unlike the kinds of campaigns that are rolled out during Israel's intermittent military conflicts. The results were no less impressive. When asked, the public consistently and voluntarily reduces its water consumption. But it was harder to make the case for self-discipline and collective denial once Israel embraced desalination as the cornerstone of its new water strategy.

Israel Enters the Era of Desalination

Desalination has been around for some time, and even in days of old was recognized as having military benefits. The Romans knew how to distill seawater and saw desalination as a critical component of their strategy for helping soldiers avoid dehydration. As secretary of state in 1791, Thomas Jefferson required all ships in the US Navy to have desalination units as a contingency for when freshwater stocks ran out (Rensselaer Polytechnic Institute 2011). But it would take a couple of centuries before significant improvements in salt removal efficiency—through the introduction of reverse osmosis (RO) membranes—brought the price down to levels that justified widespread adoption. By the end of the 1990s in Israel, the drop in the costs of producing freshwater from the sea (or from brackish aquifers) was sufficient for Israeli water managers to convince the country's all-powerful Finance Ministry that this was an investment that made sense.

The April 4, 2002, cabinet decision approving the establishment of four plants on the Mediterranean coastline stands as a watershed date in Israel's hydrological history. But the new phase was run quite differently than the earlier initiatives. Gone were the days when the Israeli government would fund such massive infrastructure projects. Rather, private capital was enlisted. In response to tenders issued by Israel's Water Authority, international

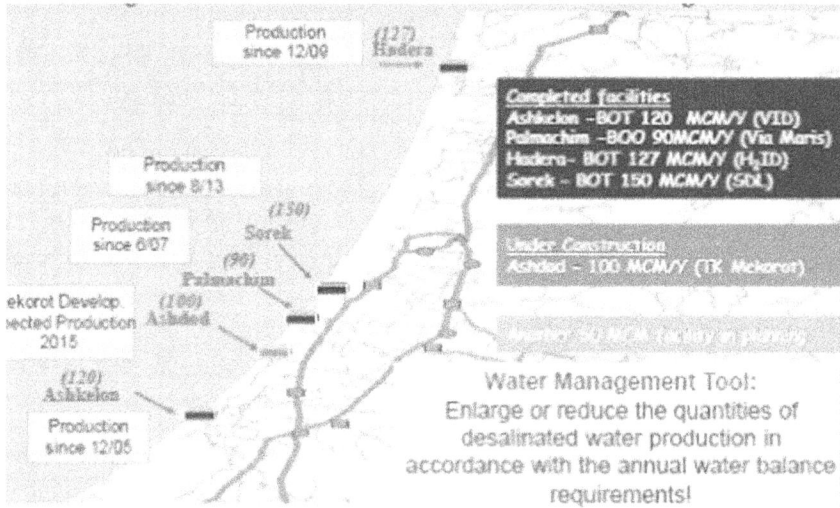

Figure 5.2 Israel's desalination production centers
Source: Israel Water Authority, 2015.

consortiums (typically with an Israeli partner) filed bids. Within no time at all, four new desalination plants emerged along Israel's Mediterranean coasts (Mandell 2012). Although initial plans called for an annual capacity of 250 million cubic meters (250 billion liters) within a decade, Israel's new hydrological juggernaut had roughly double that amount. Another 50 million cubic meters of freshwater was now produced in the Negev southlands from brackish aquifers in the Negev. By the end of 2016, an additional facility in Ashdod went on line, increasing local capacity by an additional 100 MCM (Israel Water Authority 2015c). This "sea change" has just begun: the Water Authority publicly pronounces the likelihood that this amount may double or even triple in the foreseeable future.

Based on most evaluation criteria, Israel's grand experiment with desalination appears to be succeeding. Costs have stayed well within the contractual limits, notwithstanding intermittent increases in energy prices worldwide. Depending on the terms of specific contracts, typically a thousand liters of water range between 50 and 60 cents—not much more than the price of transporting natural freshwater from the Galilee down to the south of Israel. The quality of the desalinated water is excellent. Because Israel recycles its wastewater, desalination facilities include a stage of boron removal. This was deemed necessary because most of the desalinated water produced will eventually be recycled and sent to farmers, and boron in excessive quantities can be toxic to plants. Indeed, the initial "pure H2O" produced was found to be "too pure" for optimal irrigation of plants. After removing all minerals in the seawater, desalination facilities have begun to dissolve limestone into the freshwater prior to its release. This ensures that critical minerals are available when the water is reused by agriculture.

The strategic decision to address water scarcity through desalination encountered no significant opposition from Israeli environmentalists, not that there were not fears and misgivings about a range of adverse outcomes as well as unexpected consequences. There have been always three fundamental environmental concerns about desalination:

- the space that the facilities take up and the recreational open spaces supplanted
- the impact of the brine and the chemicals it contains when released via outflow in the sea
- the energy demands and the additional greenhouse gas emissions created

But many of the anticipated environmental hazards associated with extensive seawater desalination that were envisioned at the project's outset (Einav and Lokiec 2003) never surfaced.

Regarding the issue of loss of coastal lands, Israel's desalination plants thus far (especially electric plants) have largely been integrated into existing coastal infrastructures so that beachfront property is not compromised. The brine released from the pipes lay 20 meters below the sea surface, which stretch out for 1.8 kilometers into the sea (Water-technology 2015) was another source of apprehension. Yet, monitoring shows nothing even remotely catastrophic. There appear to be very modest effects on plankton around the outfall, but thus far any damage is very limited and immediate in its dimensions (Drami et al. 2011). There may even be benefits to certain fish populations that take advantage of the additional iron and other nutrients in the otherwise nutrient-poor Mediterranean Sea.

The one disquieting area of desalination's environmental performance that remains germane involves the prodigious amounts of energy required to create the enormous pressure that pushes saltwater through the RO membranes. Energy efficiency in the desalination plants themselves has improved significantly through energy-recovery systems that capture residual energy and recycle it back into the water-purification process. Even so, desalination plants consume enormous amounts of electricity, making greenhouse gas emissions the most troublesome environmental impact associated with Israel's new desalination infrastructure.

There are any number of ways to characterize the energy demands of a 100 MCM desalination plant: the associated 60 mw/hour electricity demands can generate greenhouse gases commensurate with those in a city of 45,000 people (Tal 2011). These emissions come to roughly five hundred thousand tons of carbon dioxide equivalent, comparable to the emissions of 120,000 cars on the highway (Israel Water Authority 2015a). Typically, one liter of petrol is required for every 1,000 liters of water desalinized (Dickie 2007). Regardless of the comparison, desalination plants require a significant amount of energy, and their expansion flies in the face of Israel's international commitment to reduce its carbon footprint.

Israel's Future Water Security: The New Challenges of Desalination

Three key challenges affecting Israel's water security emerge from the recent desalination revolution. One is ethical/ideological, one economic and one geopolitical. They are

- the effect on Israel's environmental conservation ethic;
- the ensuring of equal access to inexpensive water for the entire public; and
- Israel's relationship with its neighbors and water's role in conflict mitigation.

Some environmentalists are uncomfortable with the expansion of desalination because it creates an impression of unlimited resources. It took some time for Israel to develop a national ethos that is thrifty about its water usage. Conservation campaigns rely on the same kind of rhetoric that induces Israelis to volunteer for combat units in the military or to donate blood subsequent to terrorist attacks: sacrifice is needed to address compelling, collective national dangers. Yet the ability to produce water from the sea in unlimited qualities can create complacency: why forego a swimming pool or allow a lawn to dry up when water is as easily purchased as gravel?

There is concern that desalination may begin to undermine the Israeli public's positive environmental ethics and shared sense of humility as travelers on the proverbial spaceship earth. In an era of both individualism and global affiliations, Israel's military survival remains dependent on a strong sense of patriotism and voluntarism. In the environmental context, the educational challenge involves maintaining selflessness and national pride as inherent parts of the public's relationship to natural resources. Notwithstanding its newfound unlimited availability, can water retain its key role in reinforcing solidarity and a collective sense of national commitment?

With all of the country's internal diversity and divisions, a strong common sense of purpose is critical to Israel's security. Nothing does more to undermine this than the country's growing social gaps, which make notions of equal opportunity appear to be empty rhetoric. One out of every seven Israelis took to the streets in the summer of 2011 to demand social justice. Historically, Israel has tried to make equity a central part of its water policies. Water was always offered at a price that did not distinguish between citizens living in the north who are hydrologically wealthy and their poorer countrymen living in the arid southlands. If experiences in other countries are at all relevant, privatization of water can undermine such an egalitarian approach (Perreaulta 2014).

By transferring water production to profit-maximizing, private corporations, Israel risks retreating from its fundamentally egalitarian heritage in water-management and policy. The past decade has seen a dramatic geographical transformation in water delivery, where most of the country's water utilized in Israel no longer originates in the Galilee. Rather, recycled effluent and desalinated water, both of which originate in the center of the country, provide much of the water to agriculture and to municipal consumers respectively (Feitelson and Rosenthal 2012).

This is just as well, as the north of Israel has seen a reduction in precipitation in recent years that appears to be a new, climate-change-driven rainfall pattern. There is no reason a priori to believe that the geographical shift will affect the equal-pricing structure that has always been offered to Israelis, regardless of where they reside or purchase their water. But the increasing role of private corporations in the production and delivery of water in Israel introduces the profit motive into water-management considerations, something that was never a factor before and that needs to be monitored closely.

Along with these threats, desalination also offers a remarkable opportunity. Low-cost, desalinated water offers a country that has constantly battled uncertainty and unreliable water supply a modicum of predictability and stability. In the not-so-distant future, the Mediterranean Sea should be able to provide for all of Israel's water needs. Already, the hydrohysteria that once made Israelis so nervous when winter rains were late in coming is subsiding. The Israeli public was only vaguely aware of the droughts that struck the country during many of the past several years, largely because seawater supply was fundamentally unaffected. Indeed, the surfeit of water was sufficient to lead Israel's water managers to decide to not even utilize their full desalination production capacity during a recent summer (Udasin 2014). It would seem that Israeli water supply is, at long last, secure.

But like all matters of security, there is never room for complacency. Despite the reliable flow from the Mediterranean Sea, Israel's water supply actually remains vulnerable. The first area of vulnerability is economic. Given desalination's high embedded-energy profile, any rise in electricity prices will immediately affect local water prices. Oscillations in the price of fuels on international markets will immediately affect the real costs of water locally (Garb 2010). Here the solution is fairly self-evident, even as it involves Israel's energy sector. Reduced reliance on fossil fuels and the adoption of solar and other renewable energy sources will immediately make Israel's water supply more secure. It will also make Israel's water policy less susceptible to criticism in international forums that seek to reduce global carbon footprints. It is fortuitous that, institutionally, the same government minister responsible for water is also responsible for energy. Tedious interministerial coordination will not be necessary because the minister of energy and infrastructure can oversee a full integration of Israel's energy and water policies.

Another source of vulnerability is the inherently unstable and violent dynamics of the festering Israel–Arab conflict. Desalination plants are not located far below the surface and outside the range of neighboring forces' bombs and missiles (although perhaps they should be). They can clearly be identified in Google Images and undoubtedly are seen by Israel's enemies as an inviting strategic target. A few well-directed missile strikes could set back a decade of progress in water security and totally disrupt local water supply. Even if Hamas's and Hezbollah's rockets do not end up reaching the major desalination facilities, the sewage discharged from Gaza inevitably will. It is impossible for Israel to ignore its fundamentally transboundary hydrological reality.

Israel must engage its neighbors in a constructive way to reduce these vulnerabilities. The good news is that the new ability to inexpensively produce water through desalination means that water politics no longer needs to be perceived as a zero-sum game. Expanding the pie is a compelling option now, and Israel should work to ensure that its Mediterranean desalination bonanza benefits residents of Amman and Ramallah as well as the residents of Tel Aviv and Jerusalem. The ancillary bonus from any proactive and munificent hydrological gestures is that Palestinians and Jordanians will increasingly have a real stake in Israel's water security (Tal and Abed-Rabbo 2010). To the extent that these countries' water supply is linked to Israel's desalination capacity, incentives to damage water infrastructure are reduced during the region's intermittent conflict.

The recent 2015 agreement between Israel, Jordan and Palestine, brokered through the World Bank, is an excellent example of the mutually beneficial possibilities that water sharing in the Middle East brings. Under the accord, Jordan is to establish an 80 MCM desalination facility in the Gulf of Aqaba. It will utilize 30 MCM of water for domestic use in and around Aqaba, while Israel will purchase the remaining 50 MCM. In exchange, Israel will transfer 50 MCM of water to Jordan in the center and north of the country, where a growing Jordanian population is desperately in need of expanded water supply (Coren 2015). The Aqaba desalination brine is to be piped north along the Arava Valley and discharged in the Dead Sea as a pilot venture to start the process of refilling the depleted saltwater lake via a Red-Dead conduit. Although in the past Jordan was unwilling to purchase water from Israel, scarcity today has become so acute that its position appears to have changed. Publicly, it has expressed interest in buying Israel's surplus desalinated water. The Palestinians have not yet signed onto the most recent round of agreements, but the pact left that possibility open.

Integration between the three countries' water-delivery systems makes sense for Israeli, Jordanian and Palestinian water managers. It also makes sense for peace advocates. Not only are suspicions and animosity attenuated by working together to meet all parties' water needs, but quality of life is improved. Ultimately, Israel's water security is linked to the country's overall security and its relationship with its neighbors. Economic development is a key component in any sustainable peacemaking strategy. Undoubtedly, the best way for Israel to ensure that the sewage pouring from Gaza into the Mediterranean does not compromise its southern desalination facilities, is to make sure that Gaza has the resources to build and to operate a high performing, tertiary-level wastewater treatment plant.

Israel's history of water management offers a basis for optimism. Unlike its other environmental challenges, such as biodiversity loss or greenhouse gas emissions, real progress has been made during the past decades. A reliable and potable supply of water for humans, along with reasonably priced irrigation water for farmers, is a vision that can be realized. Ready or not, desalination has arrived and it appears to be a game changer. While this new technology solves a traditional source of insecurity—the region's unpredictable rainfall— it introduces several others. Only through cooperation and reconciliation can these be eliminated and sustainability achieved.

References

Audu, Sunday Didam, and Afolarin Olutunde Ojewole. 2013. "Conflict over Water in Genesis 26:12–33: Implications for the Church in Sub-Sahara Africa in Relation to Support for the Millennium Development Goals." *Research on Humanities and Social Sciences* 3 (19): 15–21.

Avisar, Dror, Lester Yael and Daniel Ronen. 2009. "Sulfamethoxazole Contamination of a Deep Phreatic Aquifer." *Science of the Total Environment* 407: 4278–4282.

Ben-Gal, Alon, Noemi Tel-Tsur and Alon Tal. 2006. "The Sustainability of Arid Agriculture: Trends and Challenges." *Annals of the Arid Zone* 45 (2): 1–31.

Ben-Gurion, David. 1969. "Southbound." In *Studies in the Bible*, 132–144. Tel Aviv: Am Oved.

Coren, Ora. 2015. "Israel, Jordan Sign Red-Dead Canal Agreement." *Haaretz*, February 27. http://www.haaretz.com/israel-news/business/.premium-1.644601

Crawford, Stanley Holling. 1978. *Adaptive Environmental Assessment and Management.* New York: John Wiley and Sons.

Dickie, Phil. 2007. *Making Water: Desalination: option or distraction for a thirsty world?* Report for the WWF's Freshwater Programme, June 2007.

Drami, Dror, Yosef Yacobi, Noga Stambler and Kress, Nurit. 2011. "Seawater Quality and Microbial Communities at a Desalination Plant Marine Outfall: A Field Study at the Israeli Mediterranean Coast." *Water Research* 45 (17): 5440–5462.

Einav, Rachel, and Fredi Lokiec. 2003. "Environmental Aspects of a Desalination Plant in Ashkelon." *Desalination* 156 (1–3): 79–85.

Elizur. Yuval. 2014. "Over and Drought: Why the End of Israel's Water Shortage Is a Secret." *Haaretz*, January 24, http://www.haaretz.com/news/national/1.570374.

Engle, Nathan. 2011. "Adaptive Capacity and Its Assessment." *Global Environmental Change* 21(2): 647–656.

Fattal, Badri, and Hillel Shuval. 1981. "Historical Prospective Epidemiological Study of Wastewater Utilization in Kibbutzim in Israel, 1974–77." In *Developments in Arid Zone Ecology and Environmental Quality*, edited by Hillel Shuval, 333–343. Philadelphia: Balaban ISS.

Feitelson, Eran, and Gadi Rosenthal. 2012. "Desalination, Space and Power: The Ramifications of Israel's Changing Water Geography." *Geoforum* 43 (2): 272–284.

Filin, Sagi, Yoav Avni, Amit Baruch, Smadar Morik, Reuama Arav and Shmuel Marco. 2014. "Characterization of Land Degradation along the Receding Dead Sea Coastal Zone Using Airborne Laser Scanning." *Geomorphology* 206 (1): 403–420.

Galnoor, Itzhak. 1980. "Water Policy Making in Israel." In *Water Quality Management under Conditions of Scarcity, Israel as a Case Study*, edited by Hillel Shuval, 287–314. New York: Academic Press.

Garb, Yaakov. 2010. "Desalination in Israel, Status, Prospects and Context." In *Water Wisdom, A New Menu for Palestinian and Israeli Cooperation in Water Management*, edited by A. Tal and A. Abed-Rabbo, 238–245. New Brunswick, NJ: Rutgers University Press.

Godinger, Tal, Pniela Dotan, Ludmila Groisman, Alon Tal and Shai Arnon. 2015. "Occurrence and Fate of Endocrine Disrupting Compounds in Wastewater Treatment Plants in Israel." Master's thesis, Sede Boqer, Ben-Gurion University, Israel.

Gvirtzman, Haim. 2012. *The Israeli-Palestinian Water Conflict: An Israeli Perspective*. Ramat Gan: Begin-Sadat Center for Strategic Studies, Bar Ilan University.

Hann, Iris. 2013. "Open Space in an Urban Society." In *Between Ruin and Restoration, An Environmental History of Israel*, edited by Daniel Orenstein, Alon Tal and Char Miller, 146–167. Pittsburgh: University of Pittsburgh Press.

Hillel, Daniel. 2008. "40 Years of Drip Irrigation: Reviewing the Past, Prospects for the Future." *CSA News* 53: 3–7.

Hughes, T. P., L. H. Gunderson, C. Folke, A. H. Baird, D. Bellwood and F. Berkes. 2007. "Adaptive Management of the Great Barrier Reef and the Grand Canyon World Heritage Areas." *Ambio* 36: 586–592.

Israel Water Authority. 2015a. "The Wastewater and Treated Effluents Infrastructure Development in Israel." Presentation at the World Water Forum, 2015, http://www.water.gov.il/Hebrew/ProfessionalInfoAndData/2012/05-Water%20Sector%20in%20Israel%20-%20Zoom%20on%20Desalination.pdf.

———. 2015b. "Water Sector in Israel, IWRM Model." Presentation at the World Water Forum, 2015, http://www.water.gov.il/Hebrew/ProfessionalInfoAndData/2012/02-Israel%20Water%20Sector%20-%20IWRM%20Model.pdf.

———. 2015c. "Water Sector in Israel, Zoom on Desalination." Presentation at the World Water Forum, 2015, http://www.water.gov.il/Hebrew/ProfessionalInfoAndData/2012/05-Water%20Sector%20in%20Israel%20-%20Zoom%20on%20Desalination.pdf.

Keren Kayemeth L'Yisrael (KKL). 2015. "KKL Assistance to the Water System," http://www.kkl.org.il/water-activity/water-for-israel/water-resources/.

Kfir, Ofir, Alon Tal, Amit Gross and Eilon Adar. 2012. "Assessing the Effectiveness of Waste Water Reuse Reservoirs in Israel: Results of a National Survey." *Resources, Conservation and Recycling* 68: 76–87.

Kislev, Yoav, and Shaul Tsaban. 2013. *Statistical Atlas of Israeli Agriculture, 2013*. Beit Dagan: Israel Ministry of Agriculture, http://www.moag.gov.il/agri/Files/atlas_haklaut.pdf.

Lawhon, Phoenix, and Moshe Schwartz. 2006. "Linking Environmental and Economic Sustainability in Establishing Standards for Wastewater Re-use in Israel." *Water Science and Technology* 53 (9): 203–212.

Mandell, Meredith. 2012. "Water from the Sea: The Risks and Rewards of Israel's Huge Bet on Desalination." *International Business Times*, June 17, http://www.ibtimes.com/water-sea-risks-and-rewards-israels-huge-bet-desalination-723429.

Mariotti, Annarita, Pan, Yutong, Zeng, Ning and Alessandri, Andrea. 2015, "Long-term Climate Change in the Mediterranean Region in the Midst of Decadal Variability." *Climate Dynamics* 44 (5–6): 1437–1456.

Muszkot, Leah. 1990. "Large Scale Contamination of Deep Groundwaters by Organic Pollutants." *Advances in Mass Spectrometry*, 11B: 1628.

National Research Council. 2004. *Adaptive Management for Water Resources Project Planning*. Washington, DC: National Academies Press.

Pahl-Wostl, Claudia. 2007. "Transitions towards Adaptive Management of Water Facing Climate and Global Change." *Water Resource Management*, 21: 49–62.

Patterson, Murray, and Bruce Glavovic. 2013. "From Frontier Economics to an Ecological Economics of the Oceans and Coasts." *Sustainability Science* 8 (1): 11–24.

Perreaulta, Tom. 2014. "What Kind of Governance for What Kind of Equity? Towards a Theorization of Justice in Water Governance," *Water International* 39 (2): 233–245.

Rensselaer Polytechnic Institute. 2011. "The History of Desalination," http://www.rpi.edu/dept/chem-eng/Biotech-Environ/Environmental/desal/history.html.

Sachar, Howard. 1976. *A History of Israel*. New York: Knopf.

Schwartz, T. A. 1971. "The Jerusalem Cholera Outbreak: The Course of the Epidemiological Investigation." *Public Health* 13 n.p.

Shoham, Yael, and Ofra Sarig. 1995. *The National Water Carrier*. Sapir: Mekorot.

Shuval, Hillel. 1980. "Quality Management Aspects of Wastewater Reuse in Israel." In *Water Quality Management under Conditions of Scarcity, Israel as a Case Study*, edited by Hillel Shuval. New York: Academic Press, 211–242.

Tal, Alon. 2002. *Pollution in a Promised Land: An Environmental History of Israel*, Berkeley: University of California Press.

———. 2006a. "Seeking Sustainability: Israel's Evolving Water Management Strategy." *Science* 313: 1081–1084.

———. 2006b. *The Environment in Israel: Natural Resources, Crises, Campaigns and Policy from the Advent of Zionism until Twenty-first Century*. B'nei Brak: HaKibbutz HaMeuhad Press.

———. 2007. "To Make a Desert Bloom: The Israeli Agriculture Adventure and the Quest for Sustainability." *Agricultural History* 81 (2): 228–258.

Tal, Abed Rabbo, ed. 2010. *Water Wisdom, A New Menu for Palestinian and Israeli Cooperation in Water Management*, New Brunswick, NJ: Rutgers University Press.

———. 2011. "The Desalination Debate: Lessons Learned Thus Far," *Environment* 53 (5): 35–49.

———. 2013. "Management of Transboundary Wastewater Discharges." In *Shared Borders, Shared Waters*, edited by S. B. Megdal, R. G. Varady and S. Eden, 221–232. Leiden: CRC Press/Balkema Taylor & Francis Group in cooperation with UNESCO.

Tal, Alon, and David Katz. 2012 "Rehabilitating Israel's Streams and Rivers." *Journal of River Basin Management* 10 (4): 317–330.

Tenne, Abraham. 2010. *Sea Water Desalination in Israel: Planning, Coping with Difficulties, and Economic Aspects of Long-Term Risks*. Tel Aviv: Israel Water Authority, http://www.water. gov.il/Hebrew/ProfessionalInfoAndData/2012/12-Desalination-in-Israel.pdf.

Teschner, Na'ama, and Maya Negev. 2013a. "The Development of Water Infrastructures in Israel: Past, Present and Future." In *Shared Borders, Shared Waters*, edited by S. B. Megdal, R. G. Varady and S. Eden. Leiden: CRC Press/Balkema Taylor & Francis Group in cooperation with UNESCO, 7–20.

Teschner, Na'ama, Yaakov Garb and Jouin Paavola. 2013b. "The Role of Technology in Policy Dynamics: The Case of Desalination in Israel." *Environmental Policy and Governance* 23: 91–103.

Udasin, Sharon. 2014 **"Desalination Facilities to Run at 70% Capacity for 2014."** *Jerusalem Post*, February 1, http://www.jpost.com/Enviro-Tech/Desalination-facilities-to-run-at-70-percent-capacity-for-2014–336935.

United Nations University. 2011. "Former National Leaders: Water a Global Security Issue," March 20, http://unu.edu/media-relations/releases/water-called-a-global-security-issue.html.

Wachs, Alberto. 1971. "The Outlook for Wastewater Utilization in Israel." In *Developments in Water Quality Research*, edited by Hillel Shuval, 109–111. Ann Arbor, MI: Ann Arbor Science Publishers.

Walters, C. 1986. *Adaptive Management of Renewable Resources*. New York: MacMillan.

Water-technology. 2015. "Sorek Desalination Plant, Israel," http://www.water-technology. net/projects/sorek-desalination-plant/.

Wolf, Aaron. 1998. "Conflict and Cooperation along International Waterways." *Water Policy* 1: 251–265.

Yermiyahu, Uri, Alon Tal, Alon Ben-Gal, Asher Bar-Tal, Jorge Tarchisky and Ori Lahav. 2007. "Rethinking Desalinated Water Quality and Agriculture." *Science* 318: 920–921.

Zaslavsky, Dan, Rami Guhteh and Ayal Sahar. 2004. *Policies for Utilizing Sewage in Israel: Sewage Treatment for Effluent Irrigation or Desalinating Effluents to Drinking Water Quality*. Haifa: Technion.

Chapter 6

ADAPTING TO CLIMATIC VARIABILITY ALONG INTERNATIONAL RIVER BASINS IN THE MIDDLE EAST

Neda A. Zawahri

"Climate Change will require a more severe adjustment of water resources management in MENA [Middle East and North Africa] than any other region."
—World Bank (2007a, 4)

Various climate-change models are predicting an increase in temperature, a decrease in precipitation and an increase in the evaporation rate for the riparian states sharing international rivers in the Middle East, such as the Jordan, Euphrates and Tigris Rivers. Experts also anticipate an increase in weather extremes, such as floods and droughts, and a decrease in the overall freshwater supplies throughout the Middle East (Evans 2009; Alpert et al. 2008; World Bank 2007b; Verner 2012; IPCC 2014). In this region of the world that is already plagued by severe freshwater shortages, any decrease or variability in supplies is likely to intensify an already stressful crisis and contribute to significant direct and indirect losses (Verner 2012). It can also exacerbate interstate and intrastate conflicts and compromise states' ability to comply with existing treaties or protocols governing the region's international rivers.

To minimize the social, economic and political losses from the anticipated changes produced by climate variability, experts have searched for means by which society, states and the international community can build adaptive capacity to minimize their vulnerability (Adger, Arnell and Tompkins 2005; Koch, Vogel and Patel 2007). One area that will require improved adaptive capacity but that has been largely neglected by the existing literature is

The Faculty Scholarship Initiative Award from Cleveland State University funded field research in Jordan, Palestine and Israel during April and May 2012.

interstate institutions, in particular river basin commissions established to manage international rivers.[1] Drawing on neoliberal institutionalism, an international relations theory about the role of institutions in facilitating cooperation, this chapter explores the role and resilience of Middle Eastern river basin commissions in managing the transition to the anticipated decrease in freshwater availability and the likelihood of increased tension between riparian states. Through an analysis of the design and capabilities vested in the region's existing commissions, the chapter proposes that they in fact lack adaptive capacity to manage uncertainties and address interstate disputes. To minimize the potential threat of increased regional tensions or conflict, the chapter argues that existing commissions need to be redesigned and empowered with additional capabilities.

Data for this chapter come from field research in Jordan, Israel, Turkey, Syria and Palestine in 2000, 2001 and 2012. During field research, regional newspapers were searched along with interviews with government officials, representatives of the international donor community, nongovernmental organizations and university scholars.

Before demonstrating this argument concerning the lack of adaptive capacity with respect to institutions, in the following section I characterize the nature and degree of change that can be expected as a result of climate variability in the Middle East. Drawing on neoliberal institutionalism, I examine the role, function and design of river basin commissions as facilitators of adaptation to climate variability. The capacity of the various bilateral and trilateral river basin commissions established to govern the Jordan, Yarmouk, Euphrates and Tigris Rivers to respond to climate variability is then analyzed. After a summary of the findings, the chapter closes with a consideration of some policy prescriptions for redesigning Middle Eastern river basin commissions.

Climate Change and Middle East Freshwater

The Middle East is known for its aridity and variability of rainfall (Verner 2012). With the exception of Lebanon and Turkey, most Middle Eastern states have been experiencing the highest scarcity of freshwater in the world. Water availability in this region is well below 1,000 m^3 per person per year, which is less than the quantity needed for individual water security (World Bank 2007b). To meet their ever-increasing demand for this essential natural

---

1 Institutions are "persistent and connected sets of rules (formal and informal) that prescribe behavioral rules, constrain activity, and shape expectations" (Keohane 1989, 3).

resource, states like Jordan, Israel and Syria have overexploited their renewable and nonrenewable sources of freshwater.

Several forces are interacting to aggravate the region's freshwater crisis. Some of these factors include high population growth rates, industrialization and climate change (World Bank 2007b, 2012). Middle Eastern states confront some of the highest population growth rates in the world. Yemen's average annual population growth rate is 3 percent, while the West Bank and Gaza Strip confront a 4 percent growth rate (World Bank 2007b). Jordan's population growth rate is 2.2 percent per year (Department of Statistics 2013), but since 1948 Jordan has also experienced several waves of refugees from war-torn or conflict-torn neighboring states. The war in Iraq is estimated to have brought to Jordan about eight hundred thousand refugees (Hummel 2008). The recent turmoil in Syria has increased the number of refugees in Jordan. As of December 2014, the United Nations High Commission on Refugees listed 620,441 registered Syrian refugees in Jordan (UNHCR 2015). These various waves of refugees have placed additional stress on Jordan's limited supply of freshwater (Fagen 2009). As Middle Eastern nations developed and industrialized, residents experienced improvements in their living standards, which further increased demand for scarce freshwater. Finally, most of the climate-change scenarios are warning that the Middle East's freshwater crisis will worsen in the near future (IPCC 2007 and 2014; Alpert et al. 2008).

Impact of climate change on the Middle East

Due to a combination of natural occurrences and human activities that resulted in the emission and concentration of greenhouse gases (GHGs) in the atmosphere, the global climate is in transition (IPCC 2014). Predicting the exact quantity of climate change and the adverse consequences it is expected to have on the ecosystem and society is complicated by several factors (Sowers, Vengosh and Weinthal 2011). Experts remain uncertain about the consequences of past and present emissions of GHGs for the climate, and they are unable to anticipate future emission rates. Moreover, there are substantial uncertainties about future population growth rates, energy consumption, technological innovations and economic growth, all of which are expected to influence the extent and rate of climate change. Despite the uncertainties associated with the magnitude and rate of change, the majority of existing climate-change scenarios indicate several trends, many of which are already occurring in the Middle East (IPCC 2014).

Most of the existing climate-change models predict that the temperature in the Middle East will rise, but they disagree on the exact magnitude. Some models expect an increase in temperature between 0.8 and 2.1 degrees

Centigrade (°C) by 2020 (Bou-Zeid and El Fadel 2002), while others anticipate an increase between 3°C and 6°C for 2070 to 2100, depending on the GHG emission rate (Alpert et al. 2008; Suppan et al. 2008). In fact, experts discovered that the climate in the Middle East has already transitioned. An analysis of the region's weather from 1950 to 2003 revealed an increase in the temperature, a decrease in the number of cold days and an increase in the amount of warm days (Zhang et al. 2005). In Israel, an analysis of past temperature trends revealed an increase in the summer temperature between 0.25°C and 0.21°C per decade (Issar 2008).

The precipitation and evaporation rates are also expected to be affected by climate change (Verner 2012). Some models suggest a decrease in the precipitation rate between 10 and 40 percent for 2070 to 2100, depending on GHG emissions, while the overall evaporation rate is set to increase from 47 percent to 54 percent (Issar 2008; Suppan et al. 2008). Data analysis of the past 45 years revealed a decrease in annual precipitation between 5 and 20 percent in the majority of the country of Jordan, a decrease in the number of rainy days and an overall warming trend (Assi and Ajjour 2009). In fact, precipitation in the region has already shifted in frequency, intensity and distribution. Jordanian and Israeli government officials have noticed not only a decrease in precipitation rates but also both a distributional shift and intraseasonal variability. This shift was noted by an Israeli government official who complained about a decrease in the precipitation rate in the north of the country, where the population and hydrological infrastructure are concentrated, and an increase in the middle and somewhat in the south (Nolga Blitz, pers. comm. February 22, 2001; Pinhas Alpert, pers. comm. May 24, 2012). Empirical analyses of past precipitation patterns have documented and quantified this shift in the precipitation pattern (Alpert et al. 2008). Decreased precipitation and increased evaporation will decrease the soil moisture, which is likely to have a negative impact on agricultural productivity. Variability in the timing and intensity of precipitation in Jordan has already had a negative impact on farmers as late and heavy rains are contributing to crop failures (Al Sharif, pers. comm. May 14, 2012).

Climate-change scenarios also anticipate an increase in the occurrence of extreme weather events, such as flash floods and droughts, in the Middle East (IPCC 2007). Throughout the region, droughts have already plagued states during recent decades. Water-rich Turkey has been experiencing recurrent droughts that have strained its domestic water supplies (Sonmez et al. 2005). An analysis of past precipitation rates in Israel revealed an increase in the number of dry years (Issar 2008). Droughts are not only occurring more often but they also tend to last longer than in the past. The increasing occurrence of droughts and flash floods is contributing to a decrease in soil moisture and ultimately a decrease in agricultural productivity in Jordan (Sharif, pers. comm. May 14, 2012).

Sea levels in the Mediterranean Sea and the Persian Gulf are expected to rise 0.1 to 0.9 by 2100 because of climate change. The rise in sea levels could result in the flooding of major cities in Egypt and the Persian Gulf and contribute to saltwater intrusion into coastal aquifers, which can contaminate freshwaters and diminish their utility. Thus, the Intergovernmental Panel on Climate Change (IPCC) (2014) has concluded that the Middle East and North Africa are the regions that will be most severely influenced by climate change, which will involve shorter, warmer winters; summers that are hotter and dryer; and a weather pattern that is more variable with extreme events.

Climate change and transboundary freshwater

Across the Middle East, states receive 60 percent of their water supplies from international rivers, which represents the highest percentage of dependence on shared freshwater resources in the world (World Bank 2007b). When considering the dependence on international waters of specific countries, the degree ranges from 100 percent for Kuwait to 72.36 percent for Syria and to 27.21 percent for Jordan (Economic and Social Commission for Western Asia 2013).

The rise in the region's temperatures and the decrease in precipitation rates will have a negative impact on the runoff of international rivers in the Middle East (Verner 2012). The Jordan River system, which already fails to carry sufficient water to meet the domestic demands of its five riparians, is likely to be severely affected by climate change. According to experts, an increase in the region's temperature by 1°C can reduce the Jordan River's average annual water yield between 9 and 17 percent (Oroud 2008). The Global Change and the Hydrological Cycle (GLOWA) Jordan River Project expects precipitation in the headwaters of the Jordan River to decrease 25 percent and the temperature to increase 4.5°C, which combine to decrease the river's runoff by 23 percent for the period from 2070 to 2100 (Suppan et al. 2008). The combination of climate change and increased upstream consumption has depleted the discharge of the Yarmouk River, a tributary of the Jordan River. The substantial decrease in the Yarmouk's runoff has prevented Jordan from filling the Unity Dam despite its completion in 2006. In fact, as of the summer of 2012, the dam had only reached 18 of its 100 mcm storage capacity (Hazim El Nasser, pers. comm. May 1, 2012).

The discharge of the Euphrates and Tigris Rivers is also expected to decline because of decreased precipitation and increased evaporation brought about by climate change (Bozkurt and Sen 2013; Özdoğan 2011). Since the Euphrates and Tigris Rivers are heavily dammed, their capacity to absorb disturbances brought about by climate change is weaker than less dam-impacted basins (Bozkurt and Sen 2013). Increased sedimentation from flooding is expected to decrease the reservoir's life span, which can ultimately increase the risk for dam failures or breaches that threaten downstream livelihoods. Large reservoirs along the basin can increase the evaporation rate and decrease discharge threatening downstream ecosystems, biodiversity and water quality (ibid.). With declining river runoff, the quality of the remaining water is expected to deteriorate substantially because of the reduction in the river's ability to dilute pollution. The increase in the evaporation rate can also raise the salinity level in reservoirs and lakes and increase the sedimentation of reservoirs.

Given the Middle East's dependence on and overuse of transboundary aquifers, such as the Disi Aquifer, West Bank Mountain Aquifer and the Basalt Aquifer shared by Jordan and Syria, any further depletion may contribute to the permanent contamination of renewable aquifers. The increasing occurrence of droughts and floods will minimize the recharge capacity of the region's aquifers, while exploitation of nonrenewable waters could lead to their destruction. Experts estimate that climate change will decrease groundwater recharge between 20 and 30 percent for Middle Eastern aquifers for the 2070 to 2100 period (Margane, Borgstedt and Subah 2008; Issar 2008). Waterborne diseases such as cholera and dysentery, which already plague Syria, Jordan and the Palestinian Authority, are likely to increase as the quality of existing supplies in shared aquifers and rivers decrease (El-Fadel and Maroun 2008).

The consequences of climate change on Middle Eastern states' domestic water supplies are expected to be significant especially for Jordan, the West Bank, the Gaza Strip and Yemen (Verner 2012). In the case of Jordan, a 20 percent decrease in precipitation and a 4°C increase in the temperature can increase its annual water deficit from the current 200 mcm/yr to 803 mcm/yr by 2020 (Abu-Taleb 2000). States, such as Lebanon and Turkey, which have historically had an abundant supply of freshwater, are expected to confront shortages. By 2020, Lebanon's water supply is expected to decrease between 5 and 15 percent, depending on GHG emissions (Bou-Zeid and El Fadel 2002). The MENA region as a whole is likely to confront an increase in unmet demand for freshwater from the current rate of 16 percent to 37 percent in 2020–2030 and 51 percent in 2040–2050 (Verner 2012, 112).

Potential interstate consequences

Existing shortages of freshwater supplies and the increasing stresses produced by climate change, as well as the region's macropolitical conflicts, have led some to argue that certain regions (such as the Middle East, North Africa, sub-Sahara Africa and South Asia) in the world are likely to experience an increasing potential for intrastate and interstate disputes or tensions (Gleditsch 2012; Salehyan 2008; Trondalen 2009, Verner 2012). Others have suggested that regional peace, which is linked to meeting domestic demand for fresh-water, may be threatened by climate change (Suppan et al. 2008). Tension or possible conflict may arise because of the increasing dependence on shared waters. As states struggle to meet increasing demands for domestic freshwater supplies, they are likely to augment their use of international rivers, which can result in interstate tensions over increasing dependence on shared waters (United Nations 2007; Verner 2012). Water officials in several states in the Middle East, such as Jordan, Israel and Palestine, perceive the building of adaptive capacity to enable them to respond to climatic variability predomi-nantly in terms of augmenting domestic water supplies through the construc-tion of a large hydrological infrastructure, such as desalinization plants and the Red Sea-Dead Sea Canal (Sowers, Vengosh and Weinthal 2011). But this form of adaptation may contribute to regional tensions because riparian states may not only be more interested in developing international water resources but they may also be less likely to forgo control over or share existing resources. While government officials have argued that trilateral projects such as the Red Sea-Dead Sea conveyance system between Israel, Jordan and Palestine are needed to help adapt to climate change and contribute to regional coopera-tion, in reality such projects may exacerbate tension. In terms of the afore-mentioned conveyance system, the Palestinians have felt coerced into signing on to an agreement that leaves them with little to no additional water supplies, and this has led some to argue that the project can ultimately harm regional peace building as the Palestinian population realizes the imbalance in the gains between the parties (Zawahri and Weinthal 2014).

Increasing upstream consumption and decreasing river water may also con-tribute to tension between riparians as downstream states' ability to continue operating dams to generate hydropower, manage floods or droughts, allocate irrigation water according to seasonal demand or meet ecological and recrea-tional demand continues to decrease. While dams have the potential benefit of helping states survive through periodic or relatively short-term droughts, they are less able to assist riparians through multidecade or prolonged droughts. Such prolonged droughts can challenge downstream riparians' ability to replenish their dams' live storage capacity. Droughts can also contribute to domestic and regional instability through direct impact on livelihoods. As farmers lose their capacity to generate income, they are likely to migrate to cit-ies and neighboring states in search of more stable livelihoods. However, these environmental refugees can place added pressures on cities, neighboring states and government resources and ultimately contribute to tension and conflict.

In fact, some have suggested that the Syrian government's poor response to a consecutive drought contributed to the 2012 uprising and subsequent civil war (Weinthal, Zawahri and Sowers, 2015). As Syrians fled the conflict into Jordan, they placed added pressure on scarce water resources, challenging the government's capacity to meet domestic needs and contributing to social protests in Jordan over inadequate domestic water supplies (Zawahri 2012). Environmental refugees fleeing droughts in sub-Saharan Africa contributed to tension, protests and rioting inside of host states such as Israel (Weinthal, Zawahri and Sowers, 2015).

Rapid floods can also challenge upstream or downstream dams' storage capacity and riparians' ability to meet growing demands. If the timing of floods does not coincide with demands and riparians are unable to store sufficient waters, their capacity to generate hydropower and meet demands also decreases. Increases in seasonal variation in runoff because of climate change can also challenge states' capacity to rely on dams to meet their needs. Consequently, the presence of dams along international basins, such as the Yarmouk, Euphrates and Tigris, has the potential of contributing to conflict as riparians compete to generate hydropower along with meeting agricultural and municipal needs (Özdoğan 2011). The more dependent riparian states are on an international basin for meeting energy and water needs, the more likely that tension will arise as they confront challenges in meeting these needs (Verner 2012).

Tension is also expected to surface in international basins without treaties and even those with accords. The region has few ratified treaties governing shared water resources, and many that do exist tend to govern the basin in a fragmented manner with bilateral or subbasin accords governing multi-lateral basins. Riparian states with treaties, accords or protocols regulating their use of the river can experience tension because climate change may challenge their ability to comply with allocation commitments, especially if those allocations are fixed numbers and not percentages. For those riparian states sharing international basins without accords to regulate their development of the resource, they are likely to be susceptible to increasing interstate tension as they attempt to secure access to the resource. To mitigate, manage or minimize the increasing potential for interstate political flare-ups over ever-decreasing supplies of freshwater, it is important to consider the factors that are likely to assist states in acquiring adaptive capacity.

Adapting to Climate Change

According to an IPCC (2007) report, "adaptive capacity is the ability of a system to adjust to climate change (including climate variability and extremes) to moderate potential damages, to take advantage of opportunities, or to cope with consequences" (21). The study of adaptive capacity and adaptation in general has several research objectives, one of which considers the alterations in policies that can help mitigate or minimize climate change, while another considers the shifts in polices needed to minimize the anticipated negative impacts (Smit and Wandel 2006). Adaptation to climate change can also be analyzed at several levels or scales that include the individual, local, national and international (Adger, Arnell and Tompkins 2005; Koch, Vogel and Patel 2007). In these various scales, adaptation can vary in terms of its timing, in that societies or states can embrace a new policy in anticipation of climate change or they may simply alter policy or behavior spontaneously as a direct reaction to events (Smit and Wandel 2006).

Experts have investigated extensively society's planned and anticipatory ability to adapt to the anticipated changes from climate change (Kane and Yohe 2000). However, there has been insufficient consideration of interstate adaptive capacity building that could minimize the vulnerabilities associated with the potential regional conflict resulting from global environmental changes. One particular area of planned adaptive capacity building is the establishment of effectively designed interstate institutions or improvement of the capacity of existing institutions to manage international basins. Existing empirical analysis suggests that states sharing basins with institutionalized mechanisms are more likely to select the negotiation path to address their water disputes and less likely to confront conflict (Wolf, Yoffe and Giordano 2003; Hensel, Mitchell and Sowers 2006). Recent research has also revealed that joint river commissions or institutions can assist riparian states in managing transboundary river disputes and help build adaptive capacity to climatic variability (Tir and Stinnett 2012; Dinar et al. 2015).

The role and function of river basin commissions

To appreciate the role and function of river basin commissions in managing disputes and providing states with adaptive capacity to respond to climate variability, it is necessary to consider states' interest in establishing commissions. States dependent on international rivers to meet domestic demands need to communicate in order to exchange hydrological and meteorological data, allocate the waters, dredge the river and maintain drainage systems. Otherwise, the lack of communication may result in social, economic or political losses for states, as they are unable to respond effectively to natural hazards, meet their domestic demand for water or generate hydropower (Zawahri 2008a). To facilitate this communication, states tend to establish formal or informal joint river commissions. An informal commission may rise spontaneously and may not be a byproduct of a written agreement, while a formal one is a byproduct of an official agreement between member states (Puchala and Hopkins 1982).

According to neoliberal institutionalists, states concerned with their self-interest and with behaving rationally have an interest in cooperating, but they are caught in a Prisoner's Dilemma: if all defect, the commons is destroyed; if one cooperates, while the other defects, the "sucker's payoff" involves substantial losses; if all cooperate, significant losses are avoided (Stein 1990).

Even when riparian states are adversaries with a rich history of conflict, such as Middle Eastern riparian states, they have an interest in cooperating to manage disputes and minimize the potential losses they may incur from their interdependent relationship. To collaborate, states need to reduce their uncertainty about their riparian neighbors' compliance and fear of cheating.

Concomitant with their important role as facilitators of cooperation, effectively designed river basin commissions can also help states to respond, anticipate and manage oncoming variability. That is, these interstate institutions can assist riparians to adapt to the uncertainties that are likely to be the byproducts of climate changes. Commissions can guide states through the adjustment to ever-decreasing and variable water resources. River basin commissions can also provide states with conflict-resolution mechanisms to select the negotiation path to address disputes as they arise.

Since river basin commissions tend to be operated by engineers, if properly designed they can enable this epistemic community to respond to problems and cope with increasing complexities.

They also enable commissioners to be more responsive to changing conditions that are brought about by increasing environmental variability and improve the efficient flow of timely hydrological data. By contrast, weakly designed institutions undermine states' ability to respond to climate change, to adapt and to recover.

Designing institutions

Empirical research has revealed that the simple presence of a river basin commission is not sufficient to prevent conflict (Mitchell and Zawahri 2015). Rather, an institution's capacity to mitigate conflict and perform its function is dependent on its design. In the case of adaptation to climate change, a properly designed institution can increase a country's resilience and enable it to survive through climate change (Tir and Stinnett 2012). Institutional design may be laid out in a formal agreement or it may simply be a shared understanding, but once in existence an institution's design or attribute has a direct impact on states' ability to maintain cooperation (Stein 1990; Mitchell 1994;

Yoffe, Wolf and Giordano 2003; Zawahri 2009). To overcome this collective action problem, neoliberal institutionalists argue that states need an institution to monitor members' activities, make commitments more credible, sanction defectors, lower transaction costs and gather information (Keohane, 1984; Keohane and Martin 2003). The design and capabilities vested in river basin organizations can influence riparian states' adaptive capacity to respond to climate change.

For the management of international rivers, several design features appear to be important. These include regular meetings, direct communication, monitoring and conflict-resolution mechanisms. Direct communication enables commissioners to schedule upcoming meetings, compile the agenda before meetings, exchange information outside of meetings and schedule maintenance work. Regular meetings permit commissioners to perform the necessary tasks for managing the river, such as dredging silt deposits or fixing metering stations. They also facilitate the process of implementing the treaty or agreement and enable commissioners to negotiate the design of hydrological infrastructure.

The ability of commissioners to travel throughout the river basin permits them to collect data to implement the treaty, confirm the accuracy of exchanged data and overcome fear of cheating. The capacity to inspect the basin permits commissioners to receive assurances that the necessary maintenance work is completed. Monitoring permits members to collect information on the intentions, preferences and actions of their riparian neighbor in developing the river.

Since riparian states are likely to confront continuous disagreements over the management of their shared basin, they require conflict-resolution mechanisms. Without set procedures involving steps to be taken in negotiating a settlement of disputes, states might opt to cheat. This in turn can lead to deterioration in relations and defection from cooperation. The ability to draw on conflict-resolution mechanisms can guide members through periods of high tension. Thus, an effectively designed commission is more likely to maintain cooperation. As the commission's capabilities decline, so does its capacity to fulfill its functions.

Middle Eastern River Basin Commissions

The Middle Eastern region has several river basin commissions that have been established either formally or informally to manage international rivers. The common feature of these commissions has been weak capacity. Due to the prevalence of weak river basin commissions, Middle Eastern states' existing adaptive capacity to climate change and variability is inadequate to minimize the increasing potential for interstate disputes or manage oncoming complexities. In the Middle East, river basin commissions exist to manage the Jordan, Euphrates and Tigris Rivers.

Jordan River system

"By world standards, the Jordan [River] is a small stream" (Lowi 1993, 28). Although shared between Lebanon, Syria, Israel, Jordan and the Palestinians, this stream is the only perennial river available to the latter three societies. As a result, despite its relatively small size, this river is critical for the survival of the communities that rely on it.

The Jordan River system is divided into two parts, an upper and lower portion. The upper Jordan originates from springs that receive their water from melting snow along Jebel el-Sheikh (Mount Herman). These springs feed the Dan, Banias and Hasbani Rivers, whose confluence forms the upper Jordan. The river then flows through the Huleh Basin, after which it descends in height until it reaches Lake Tiberias (also known as Lake Kinneret or the Sea of Galilee). Upon its departure from the lake, the now lower Jordan River is fed by the Yarmouk tributary, and it then flows through the Jordan valley until it reaches its terminus in the Dead Sea. To manage this multilateral basin, the riparians have reached several bilateral agreements that resulted in the basin's fragmented governance. The riparians also established several formal bilateral river basin commissions.

Joint Water Committee

The formal Israeli-Jordanian Joint Water Committee (JWC) was established by the 1994 Israel-Jordan Peace Treaty to implement the treaty and facilitate the management of the riparians' water disputes. Due to its relatively weak capabilities, the JWC struggles to manage its member states' water disputes, and it has not prevented periodic flare-ups along with periodic deterioration in bilateral relations (Zawahri 2008b). Three members from each country comprise the JWC. The commission has the ability to "specify its work procedures, the frequency of its meetings, and the details of its scope of work," but only with the prior approval of its member states (Peace Treaty, annex II, article VII, 2, 1994). The JWC consists of high-ranking government officials, whose assigned task is to manage their respective government's domestic water resources.

Members of the JWC do communicate directly with one another and hold regular meetings, but the treaty bequeathed the commissioners with weak monitoring capabilities and inadequate conflict-resolution mechanisms. Commissioners can monitor Israeli wells inside Jordan's Wadi Araba/Arava

(Peace Treaty, annex II, article IV, 4b, 1994) and they have opted to tour these wells regularly. Meetings can be held in the field, but commissioners depend on government permission for such meetings, which have taken place in the Jordan Valley, Beit Shean/Beasan, Lake Tiberias and Adasiyya. During the JWC's tenure, member states have sometimes postponed or refused to grant permission to inspect sites (Zawahri 2008b).

The treaty does not directly stipulate conflict-resolution mechanisms for the JWC, but some have suggested that commissioners may draw on the general conflict-resolution mechanisms specified in article 29 of the Peace Treaty (Shamir 1998). According to this article, disputes arising from the treaty's implementation should be settled via negotiations, conciliation or arbitration (Peace Treaty, article 29, 1 and 2, 1994). Commissioners have sought to negotiate settlements to disputes as they arise during their meetings and as they attempt to implement the treaty. When disputes occur between technicians in the field or members of the commission, they attempt to resolve them. If they fail, the disputes are sent to the JWC for further discussion. On several occasions the JWC's inability to manage disputes has contributed to a deterioration in relations to a degree that required emergency meetings between the states' national leaders. Examples include the attempt to build the Adasiyya weir and desalination plant and the attempt to manage droughts that prevented meeting the treaty's fixed allocation commitments.

As these disputes arose, commissioners attempted to resolve them. When negotiations failed, a telephone call or an emergency meeting between the Israeli prime minister and Jordan's monarchy often succeeded in resolving issues (Zawahri 2008b). These moments of tension have been punctuated by moments of cooperation. Yet, as climate change is projected to place additional pressures on the region's scarce water resources, the riparians are expected to confront more tension and disputes. However, the JWC lacks the strong capacity to peacefully address these continuous disputes. The JWC's weak monitoring power and weak conflict-resolution mechanisms diminish its ability to fully address the riparian's water disputes.

Syria-Jordan Water Committee

In contrast to the Israeli and Jordanian negotiations, Jordan and Syria have signed several bilateral agreements to develop the Yarmouk River as it flows between their borders. The riparians reached their first agreement in 1953 to construct several dams along the Yarmouk in attempt to store irrigation water and generate hydropower.[2] To implement the treaty, oversee construction of

---

2 Agreement between the Syrian Arab Republic and the Hashemite Kingdom of Jordan Concerning the Utilization of the Yarmuk Waters, 1953.

the planned infrastructure and address disputes, the Joint Syro-Jordanian Committee was established. The commission was given monitoring capabilities and conflict-resolution mechanisms. Commissioners and their assistants had the capacity to tour the study areas without prior permission from government officials. Should the commissioners be unable to resolve a dispute, they could send the issue to an arbitration committee consisting of three individuals.

Israel's control of the Golan Heights after the 1967 Arab–Israeli war increased its access to the Yarmouk tributary, which resulted in renewed mediation efforts by the United States to assist in constructing the Maqarin Dam and necessitated negotiation of a new accord. In 1987, Jordan and Syria signed their second agreement on the Yarmouk River, which focused on the construction of the Maqarin Dam (now also known as the Unity or Wahdah Dam). The accord established the Joint Syria-Jordan Commission, which consisted of three members from each state. Unlike the previous agreement, the 1987 accord decreased the commission's capabilities, especially its conflict-resolution mechanisms and monitoring capacity. If commissioners were unable to resolve disputes, their only option under the new treaty was to send the issue to their respective governments for settlement. Use of an arbitration committee consisting of three experts to resolve a dispute was purged from the 1987 accord. Furthermore, the commissioners were no longer authorized to travel freely within each state to collect information. Rather, commissioners were permitted to travel through the construction site only with prior permission.

The Joint Syria-Jordan Commission is a relatively weak commission. It has little power to assist states through the increasing challenges of climate change. In fact, the commissioners depend on directions from higher government officials to perform their tasks. Due to this weakness, it took years of negotiations until the riparians agreed to begin construction on the dam in 2004. The initiation of construction has not resolved the tensions between Syria and Jordan over the Yarmouk. Continuous upstream consumption has prevented Jordan from filling the dam. Increasing consumption of this tributary by Syrian farmers has reduced its flow to a trickle. The decrease in the Yarmouk's flow has resulted from the construction of dams (which increased from 26 to 48 since the signing of the agreement) by the Syrian government and over 3,500 wells extracting groundwater feeding the Yarmouk in upstream Syria (Namrouq 2012). As a result, Jordan has claimed that Syria is in violation of its treaty commitments. This also means that Jordan is not receiving enough water in the Yarmouk to meet its own treaty commitment to downstream Israel. Since the outbreak of the civil war in Syria, the commission has confronted additional difficulties in performing its assigned tasks. While Syria and Jordan do need to consider the redesign of their commission to improve its ability to address the anticipated tensions brought about by climate change, such efforts are not likely to be accomplished until the postconflict reconstruction period begins. At this stage the donor community can work with Syria and Jordan to help stabilize regional water disputes, and encouraging the redesign of the commission can be part of this task.

Euphrates and Tigris Rivers

The Euphrates and Tigris Rivers originate in the mountains of eastern Turkey within 40 kilometers of each other and travel from there to Syria and then Iraq. Despite the proximity of their origins, they take completely separate paths until they meet in southern Iraq to form the Shatt al-Arab and empty into the Persian Gulf. It is in Turkey that these rivers receive the majority of their waters: 90 percent of the Euphrates and 53 percent of the Tigris. Of these riparian states, Iraq is the most dependent on the two rivers, which help meet 98 percent of its domestic water supplies. For this predominantly arid country, these rivers are its only source of water. Syria is much more dependent on the Euphrates River, which represents 86 percent of its available domestic water supply. Although Turkey is the least dependent on these waters for its existence, it nevertheless relies on the rivers to meet its desperate need for hydropower.

Since 1960, these riparian states have experienced periods of conflict that were punctuated by attempts at cooperation. As with the Jordan River system, the riparians sharing the Euphrates and Tigris Rivers have elected to negotiate and reach bilateral protocols rather than multilateral treaties. But, unlike in the case of the Jordan River system, these riparians have been able to form a multilateral river basin commission.

Joint Technical Committee

The Joint Technical Committee (JTC) was created in 1964, when Turkey, Syria and Iraq attempted to coordinate the construction and the impoundment of water for dams along the Euphrates. It was revived briefly in 1974 in an attempt to coordinate further development of the Euphrates and again in 1980 when it was assigned short- and long-term objectives (Savas Uskay, pers. comm. August 13 and 17, 2001). In the short term, members were expected to exchange information on planned or completed infrastructure and schedules for the impounding of reservoirs. In the long term, the institution was intended to negotiate a final agreement on allocating the rivers. The JTC succeeded in meeting its short-term objective of exchanging information, but it failed to reach a final agreement. This failure can be attributed to its weak design.

All communication between JTC members has been carried out through diplomatic channels. As a result, JTC members have spent the first day of every meeting compiling their agenda. The inability to prepare the agenda ahead of time has left room for intense disputes over the schedule. At the 15th JTC meeting, for example, the first two days were spent arguing about the order of issues on the agenda (JTC meeting notes, March 7–12, 1990). Moreover, the fact that all communication must proceed through diplomatic channels has weakened the JTC's ability to make any progress on its long-term objective because, at times, letters were misplaced on their route through diplomatic channels. This occurred in 1989, when the Iraqi delegation sent via diplomatic channels a proposal for sharing the rivers, but, after four months, it failed to reach either the Syrian or Turkish delegation (JTC meeting notes, March 13–20, 1989).

The JTC lacks the ability to monitor the rivers' development or select sites to inspect. During their meetings, commissioners do generally visit sites, but the site selection rests completely in the hands of the state hosting the meeting. Despite the host states' unilateral decision about site selection, these visits remain a source of information gathering. Such a possibility exists because the selected site can be used by the host state to send messages regarding its future intentions. This occurred during the 12th JTC meeting when members were taken on a visit to the Ataturk Dam. Turkey used this opportunity to signal its intentions to begin impounding the reservoir.[3] For the Syrian and Iraqi delegates, this was the first opportunity to tour the mammoth structure that could store the entire flow of the Euphrates, and this proved to be an important trip.

Before one can conclude from the above that the JTC has some monitoring power, however, it is important to note that autonomy in site selection means that host states can select sites unrelated to the rivers. This occurred during the 15th JTC meeting when members toured the irrigation networks of Turkey's Black Sea region. This weak monitoring ability means that, when information is exchanged, states lack an institutionalized mechanism to confirm its accuracy. States attempting to gain additional information must rely on the generosity of their riparian neighbors to release it. Sometimes the neighbor is generous in releasing information, but at other times it is not so forthcoming.

Concomitant with its lack of authority to select sites to inspect, the JTC also lacks any mechanism or standard operating procedure to manage disputes. When a dispute arises, such as over impounding a reservoir, member states'

---

3   This statement is based on reports by JTC members in attendance.

only recourse is to declare their opinion. Other members may listen, but they are not obligated to negotiate to reach a consensus. In other words, the JTC has no set procedure for resolving disputes when they arise. Therefore, states can fulfill their domestic needs with total disregard for the impact on other members.

To appreciate the consequences of the lack of conflict-resolution mechanism, consider Turkey's filling of its Ataturk reservoir. In 1989, Turkey convened a JTC meeting to inform members of its intention to stop the river for one month to hasten the impounding process. The Syrian and Iraqi delegations pleaded with Turkey not to block the Euphrates by pointing to the negative social and economic consequences this move would impose on them. The Syrians drew attention to the fact that their major cities receive their drinking water from this river, their industrial and agricultural sectors depend on it and dams located along the river provide a significant portion of their energy needs. The Iraqi delegation raised similar concerns. Syrian and Iraqi engineers proposed new plans by which Turkey might fill its reservoir without stopping the river for one month. After a heated discussion, the Turkish delegation announced that the issue was not open for negotiation and the decision was final. According to the Turkish delegation, the meeting was convened to inform JTC members of its plans and intentions, so they could relay this information to their respective governments. The Syrian and Iraqi delegation pleaded again with Turkey by pointing to the potential damage to their citizens, but the Turkish delegation refused to continue discussions.

Once it was clear that Turkey intended to stop the river at the Ataturk Dam, the Syrians asked about the quantity of water feeding the river below the dam. The Turkish delegation refused to release this data, but suggested that the states prepare to accept less than 120 m3/sec.[4] In response, Syria and Iraq pleaded with Turkey to extend the meeting to continue discussions, but Turkey refused. The Syrian and Iraqi delegations prepared and signed the meeting's notes, but the Turkish delegation refused to sign, arguing that this was not a typical meeting but rather an emergency session to inform the states of Turkey's intentions. Had the JTC contained some conflict-resolution mechanisms, it is less likely that these states would have experienced such an acrimonious meeting and produced an outcome that benefited one state while severely harming its downstream neighbors. The failure to bequeath the JTC with direct communication between its commissioners, regular meetings and the ability to monitor the rivers' development or with conflict-resolution mechanisms has prevented it from managing disputes or meeting its long-term objective.

---

4 JTC meeting notes, March 13–20, 1989.

After 1992, the JTC stopped holding meetings (Kibaroglu and Scheumann 2011). But the riparians do continue to discuss their riparian disputes at bilateral and trilateral meetings between high-ranking government officials. These meetings produce many bilateral memorandums of understanding and communiqués between the riparians. For example, Syria and Turkey reached the 1998 Adana Security Agreement and a Joint Communique in 2001. Similarly, Turkey and Iraq also reached a minor agreement about the establishment of a joint high-level council to discuss and reach cooperative agreements or understandings over various issue areas, including energy, trade, investment, security and water. But all these bilateral protocols failed to address the underlying hydropolitical conflict between the riparians. From 2007 through 2010 another series of JTC meetings were held—first bilaterally between Turkey and Syria, and then trilaterally in 2008. During these meetings, the riparians exchanged hydrological information and data on water quality, and they continued discussions on the utilization and allocation of the shared waters (Kibaroglu and Scheumann 2011). Nevertheless, the JTC remains a weak commission dependent on higher-ranking government officials to hold its meetings and to function. Currently, the riparians do not have any means of adapting to climatic variability along the Euphrates and Tigris Rivers. The basin's JTC will need to be redesigned to empower it to mediate riparian disputes brought about by climate change. However, the 2012 civil war in Syria and the lack of a stable government in Iraq have complicated the ability to build an effective river basin commission.

Conclusion

Despite uncertainty regarding the exact quantities of the anticipated changes in precipitation and temperature brought about by the presence of GHG in the environment, the majority of experts are in consensus that freshwater scarcity will increase in the Middle East because of an overall increase in drier conditions (Sowers et al. 2011). As states search for means to meet their ever-increasing needs for freshwater supplies, they are likely to look toward their international water resources, which can increase interstate tensions. To minimize the potential for interstate disputes, effectively designed interstate institutions can assist riparians in peacefully managing their hydrological disputes (Tir and Stinnett 2012; Mitchell and Zawahri 2015). According to neoliberal institutionalism, an institution that provides member states with the ability to communicate directly, meet regularly and monitor members' activities, and which contains conflict-resolution mechanisms, can assist in facilitating and maintaining cooperation.

Through an analysis of the joint river basin commissions governing international rivers in the Middle East, this chapter has demonstrated that the region's existing institutions are too weak to provide the necessary mechanisms to see the region through climate variability. The commissions governing the Jordan, Yarmouk, Euphrates and Tigris Rivers lack the ability to guide member states in adapting to climate change. Consequently, they will need to be restructured and redesigned to minimize the adverse impacts of climate change and help build adaptive capacity between riparian states.

Given this desperate need to redesign existing commissions, what factors are likely to influence states' decisions to invest in designing effective river basin commissions? First, the international epistemic community of scientific experts needs to draw attention to the need to redesign commissions and build institutional adaptive capacity. In my view, neoliberal institutionalist theory can impart vital ideas about the role, function and design of institutions as opposed to the resolution of disputes through military conflict or other forms of violence. Second, the donor community can actively promote the construction of effectively designed interstate institutions to mitigate conflict. Donors can tie the allocation of aid to the construction of effectively designed interstate institutions. The international donor community has influence in persuading Middle Eastern riparian states to alter their policies. In fact, when it comes to building adaptive capacity to mitigate the negative impact of climate change, field research has revealed that the interest and pressure come from the international donor community and not from individual riparian states. To date, Middle Eastern states have been focused on surviving droughts and desperately attempting to meet immediate needs for domestic freshwater rather than preparing to respond to climatic changes that may arise in years. As the donor community attempts to guide states in building adaptive capacity, they can also encourage the building of better and more effective river basin commissions to govern the region's international rivers. Finally, the region's existing river basin commissioners need to learn about the operation of institutions of effectively designed river basin commissions—such as the Permanent Indus Commission established for managing the Indus River, among other river basin commissions—in order to appreciate the weakness of their own commissions and to learn how to redesign their own commissions.

References

Abu-Taleb, Maher F. 2000. "Impacts of Global Climate Change Scenarios on Water Supply and Demand in Jordan," *Water International* 25 (3): 457–463.

Adger, Neil, Nigel Arnell and Emma Tompkins. 2005. "Successful Adaptation to Climate Change across Scales." *Global Environmental Change* 15: 77–86.

Agreement between the Syrian Arab Republic and the Hashemite Kingdom of Jordan Concerning the Utilization of the Yarmuk Waters. 1953. Copy provided to the author by the Jordanian Ministry of Water.

Alpert, P., S. O. Krichak, H. Shfir, D. Haim and I. Osetinsky. 2008. "Climatic Trends to Extremes Employing Regional Modeling and Statistical interpretation over the E. Mediterranean." *Global and Planetary Change* 63: 163–170.

Assi, Rafat, and Ruba Ajjour. 2009. Jordan's Second National Communication to the United Nations Framework Convention on Climate Change. The Hashemite Kingdom of Jordan. Ministry of Environment of Jordan and the United Nations Development Programme.

Bou-Zeid, E., and M. El-Fadel. 2002. "Climate Change and Water Resources in Lebanon and the Middle East." *Journal of Water Resources Planning and Management* 128 (5): 343–355.

Bozkurt, Deniz, and Omer Lutfi Sen. 2013. "Climate Change Impacts in the Euphrates–Tigris Basin Based on Different Model and Scenario Simulations." *Journal of Hydrology* 480: 149–161.

Department of Statistics. 2013. Population and Growth Rate Estimation, 1999–2012. Accessed 10 February 2013, http://www.dos.gov.jo/dos_home_e/main/index.htm.

Dinar, Shlomi, David Katz, Lucia De Stefano and Brian Blankespoor. 2015. "Climate Change, Conflict, and Cooperation: Global Analysis of the Effectiveness of International River Treaties in Addressing Water Variability." *Political Geography* 45: 55–66.

Economic and Social Commission for Western Asia. 2013. Compendium of Environment Statistics in the Arab Region. New York United Nations.

El-Fadel, Mutasem, and Rania Maroun. 2008. "Virtual Water Trade as an Adaptation Demand Management of Climate Change Impact on Water Resources in the Middle East." In *Climatic Changes and Water Resources in the Middle East and North Africa*, edited by Fathi Zereini and Heinz Hötzl. Berlin: Springer, 93–108.

Evans, Jason P. 2009. "21st Century Climate Change in the Middle East." *Climate Change* 92: 417–432.

Fagen, Patricia Weiss. 2009. "Iraqi Refugees: Seeking Stability in Syria and Jordan." Institute for the Study of International Migration, Georgetown University, and Center for International and Regional Studies, Georgetown University School of Foreign Service in Qatar. Occasional Paper No. 1. Accessed May 5, 2015, https://repository.library.georgetown.edu/bitstream/handle/10822/558297/CIRSOccasionalPaper1PatriciaFagen2009.pdf?sequence=5&isAllowed=y.

Gleditsch, Nils Petter. 2012. "Whither the Weather? Climate Change and Conflict." *Journal of Peace Research* 49 (1): 3–9.

Hensel, Paul, Sara McLaughlin Mitchell and Thomas Sowers. 2006. "Conflict Management of Riparian Disputes." *Political Geography* 25 (4): 383–411.

Hummel, Diana. 2008. "The interaction of population dynamics and transformations in water supply systems in the Jordan River Basin." In *Climatic Changes and Water Resources in the Middle East and North Africa*, edited by Fathi Zerein and Heinz Hotzl. Berlin: Springer, 497–518.

Intergovernmental Panel on Climate Change (IPCC). 2014. Climate Change 2014: Synthesis Report. Contribution of Working Groups I, II and III to the Fifth Assessment Report of the Intergovernmental Panel on Climate Change (Core Writing Team, R. K. Pachauri and L. A. Meyer (eds.)). IPCC, Geneva, Switzerland.

————. 2007. *Climate Change 2007: Impacts, Adaptation and Vulnerability*. New York: Cambridge University Press.

Issar, Arie S. "Progressive Development in Arid Environments: Adapting the Concept of Sustainable Development to a Changing World." *Hydrogeology Journal* 16.6 (2008): 1229–1231.

Kane, Sally, and Gary Yohe. 2000. "Societal Adaptation to Climate Variability and Change: An Introduction." In *Societal Adaptation to Climate Variability and Change*, edited by Sally Kane and Gary Yohe. Berlin: Springer, 1–4.

Keohane, Robert O. 1984. *After Hegemony*. Princeton, NJ: Princeton University Press.

————. 1989. *International Institutions: Two Approaches*. VS Verlag für Sozialwissenschaften.

Keohane, Robert, and Lisa Martin. 2003. "Institutional Theory as a Research Program." In *Progress in International Relations Theory*, edited by Colin Elman and Miriam Fendius Elman. Cambridge, MA: MIT Press, 71–107.

Kibaroglu, Aysegul, and Waltina Scheumann. 2011. "Euphrates–Tigris Rivers System: Political Rapprochement and Transboundary Water Cooperation." In *Turkey's Water Policy*, edited by Aysegul Kibaroglu and Argun Baskan. Berlin and Heidelberg: Springer, 277–299.

Koch, Ingrid Christine, Coleen Vogel, and Zarina Patel. 2007. "Institutional Dynamics and Climate Change Adaptation in South Africa." *Mitigation and Adaptation Strategies for Global Change* 12 (8): 1323–1339.

Lowi, Mariam. 1993. *Water and Power: The Politics of a Scarce Resource in the Jordan River Basin*. Cambridge, UK: Cambridge University Press.

Margane, Armin, Ariane Borgstedt and Ali Subah. 2008. "Water Resources Protection Efforts in Jordan and Their Contribution to a Sustainable Water Resources Management." In *Climatic Changes and Water Resources in the Middle East and North Africa*, edited by Fathi Zerein and Heinz Hotzl. Berlin: Springer, 325–345.

Mitchell, Ronald. 1994. "Regime Design Matters: Intentional Oil Pollution and Treaty Compliance." *International Organization* 48 (3): 425–458.

Mitchell, Sara, and Zawahri, Neda. 2015. "The Effectiveness of Treaty Design in Addressing Water Disputes," *Journal of Peace Research* 52 (2): 187–200.

Namrouqa, Hana. 2012. "Yarmouk Water Sharing Violations Require Political Solution." *Jordan Times*, 28 April.

Oroud, Ibrahim. 2008. "The Impacts of Climate Change on Water Resources in Jordan." In *Climatic Changes and Water Resources in the Middle East and North Africa*, edited by Fathi Zerein and Heinz Hotzl. Berlin: Springer, 109–123.

Özdoğan, M. 2011. "Climate Change Impacts on Snow Water Availability in the Euphrates-Tigris Basin." *Hydrology and Earth System Sciences* 15 (9): 2789–2803.

Puchala, Donald, and Raymond Hopkins. 1982. "International Regimes: Lessons from Inductive Analysis." *International Organization* 36 (2): 245–275.

Salehyan, Idean. 2008. "From Climate Change to Conflict? No Consensus Yet." *Journal of Peace Research* 45 (3): 315–326.

Shamir, U. 1998. "Water Agreements between Israel and Its Neighbors." In *Transformations of Middle Eastern Natural Environments*, edited by J. Albert. New Haven, CT: Yale University Press, 274–296.

Smit, Barry, and Johanna Wandel. 2006. "Adaptation, Adaptive Capacity and Vulnerability". *Global Environmental Change* 16 (3): 282–292.

Sonmex, F. Kemal, Ali Umran Komuscu, Ayhan Erkan and Ertan Turgu. 2005. "An Analysis of Spatial and Temporal Dimension of Drought Vulnerability in Turkey Using the Standardized Precipitation Index." *Natural Hazards* 35: 243–264.

Sowers, Jeannie, Avner Vengosh and Erika Weinthal. 2011. "Climate Change, Water Resources, and the Politics of Adaptation in the Middle East and North Africa." *Climatic Change* 104 (3–4): 599–627.

Stein, Arthur A. 1990. *Why Nations Cooperate*. Ithaca, NY: Cornell University Press.

Suppan, Peter, Harald Kunstmann, Andreas Heckl and Alon Rimmer. 2008. "Impact of Climate Change on Water Availability." In *Climatic Changes and Water Resources in the Middle East and North Africa*, edited by Fathi Zerein and Heinz Hotzl. Berlin; Heidelberg: Springer, 47–58.

Tir, Jaroslav, and Stinnett, Douglas. 2012. "Weathering Climate Change." *Journal of Peace Research* 49 (1): 211–225.

Trondalen, Jan Martin. 2009. "Climate Change, Water Security, and Possible Remedies for the Middle East." United Nations World Water Assessment Programs. Accessed May 5, 2015, http://unesdoc.unesco.org/images/0018/001818/181886e.pdf.

United Nations High Commissioner for Refugees (UNHCR). 2015. "Syria Regional Refugee Response: Inter-agency Information Sharing Portal." UNHCR: The UN Refugee Agency. Last modified June 17, 2015. Accessed December 16, 2014, http://data.unhcr.org/syrianrefugees/regional.php.

Verner, Dorte. 2012. *Adaptation to a Changing Climate in the Arab Countries: A Case for Adaptation Governance and Leadership in Building Climate Resilience*. Washington, DC: World Bank.

Weinthal, Erika, Neda Zawahri and Jeannie Sowers. 2015. "Securitizing Water, Climate, and Migration in Israel, Jordan, and Syria." *International Environmental Agreements: Politics, Law and Economics* 15 (3): 293–307.

Wolf, Aaron, Shira Yoffe and Mark Giordano. 2003. "International Waters: Identifying Basins at Risk." *Water Policy* 5 (1), 31–62.

World Bank. 2007a. *Regional Business Strategies to Address Climate Change*. Washington, DC: World Bank.

———. 2007b. *Making the Most of Scarcity Accountability for Better Water Management in the Middle East and North Africa*. Washington, DC: World Bank.

Yoffe, Shira, Wolf, Aaron T. and Mark Giordano. 2003. "Conflict and Cooperation over International Freshwater Resources: Indicators of Basins at Risk." *Journal of the American Water Resources Association* 10: 1109–1126.

Zawahri, Neda. 2008a. "International Rivers and National Security." *Natural Resources Forum* 34 (4): 280–289.

———. 2008b. "Capturing the Nature of Cooperation, Unstable Cooperation, and Conflict over International Rivers." *International Journal of Global Environmental Issues* 8 (3): 286–310.

———. 2009. "Mediating International River Disputes: Lessons from the Indus River." *International Negotiation* 14: 281–310.

———. 2012. "Popular Protests and the Governance of Scarce Freshwater in Jordan." *Arab World Geographer* 15 (4): 265–299.

Zawahri, Neda, and Erika Weinthal. 2014. "The World Bank and Negotiating the Red Sea and Dead Sea Water Conveyance Project." *Global Environmental Politics* 14 (4): 55–74.

Zhang, Xuebin et al. 2005. "Trends in Middle East Climate Indices from 1950 to 2003." *Journal of Geophysical Research* 110: D22104 1–12.

Chapter 7

WATER AND POLITICS IN THE TIGRIS–EUPHRATES BASIN: HOPE FOR NEGATIVE LEARNING?

David P. Forsythe

This chapter examines the role of transboundary river flows in the complex and conflicted relations between states, primarily among Turkey, Syria and Iraq, with passing reference to other countries. The introduction reviews some fundamentals of transboundary surface waters in this area. A second section reviews the international legal framework for management of these water issues, but expresses considerable doubt about the practical impact of this law in this region. The chapter then analyzes the politics of water among all three countries, noting the prevalence of conflict despite some diplomatic agreements on transboundary river flows. In particular it notes the deterioration of water security from 2003 and the US invasion of Iraq, and especially from 2011 and the start of the internationalized Syrian civil war. In this time frame, water continued to be a politicized and securitized subject, and even part of violent politics. Water continued to be manipulated for strategic political purposes, often to the detriment of basic human needs. In this often violent context, efforts to consider access to safe water as a human right, effectively protected by general international law and the laws of war, faded into oblivion. The chapter concludes by asking whether declining water security in the Tigris–Euphrates basin might eventually lead to negative learning, through which major actors might learn from the errors of past policies and discover the need for improved water management in the future.

Introduction

After World War I the gradual emergence of the contemporary states of Turkey, Syria and Iraq resulted in all three legally independent states being inherently interconnected on water issues. About 50 percent of the Tigris River and about 90 percent of the Euphrates River originate in Turkey. While this situation gives Turkey certain advantages in regional water disputes (only about 1 percent of its freshwater originates in foreign areas), it guarantees that Turkey will be subject to demands by others that it be sensitive to equitable water-use and humanitarian considerations in downstream countries. In other words, natural resources in this river basin show a prevalent condition and indicate the probability of disappointment for efforts at multilateral riparian management: Turkey can project more power in hydropolitics than others, making mutually agreed river management difficult or impossible (for the general pattern see Allan and Mirumachi 2010).

The Euphrates passes through first Syria and then Iraq and comprises essential amounts of in-stream flows for both countries, each downstream state being highly susceptible to water shortages. (For a concise overview, see http://www.futuredirections.org.au/publications/food-and-water-crises/678-water-shortage-crisis-escalating-in-the-tigris-euphrates-basin.html.) "Both Iraq and Syria are highly reliant on the Tigris–Euphrates for their water supplies. Iraq's 'dependency ratio' on external water flows is 53.5 percent and Syria's is 72.3 percent. Turkey's dependency ratio, by contrast, is 1 percent" (Michel et al. 2012, 11). Given climate change and global warming, some experts predict continued declining rainfall and snowfall in Turkey's highlands. Some computer models predict a future reduction of river flows in the Tigris–Euphrates basin of some 30–70 percent.

Much of the Syrian northeast and virtually all of Iraq beyond the Kurdish region are desert areas with negligible annual rainfall. Much of Iraq, for example, gets only 4–7 inches of rainfall annually. The Iraqi Kurdish mountain area, by comparison, averages about 24 inches of annual rain. These figures have been negatively affected by a long-running drought in recent years.

The Tigris is also important for Iraqi water resources but does not directly affect Syria. The Iraqi capital of Baghdad, home to almost four million people, is greatly dependent on water flows in the Tigris river basin. South of Baghdad, the culture of the marsh Arabs, who are mainly Shia, was threatened by the intentional diversion of the Tigris by the Saddam Hussein regime in the early 1990s as he used water as a political weapon to force an end to their insurrection. Subsequent Shia authorities in Baghdad since 2003 have not been able to fully repair the damage caused by Hussein, and the Iraqi marsh Arabs remain threatened by past changes in the Tigris.

Even absent recent environmental and political factors, Iraq and Syria—like most nations in the Middle East and North Africa—can never be fully secure concerning water from natural resources. Even Turkey may face future problems in this regard, as suggested above. Iraq and Syria can reasonably expect to have enough water for drinking, sanitation and industrial purposes but never self-sufficiency in water for food. The rapid population growth in these two states, projected to continue, also rules out any total water security.

International Legal Framework for Water Disputes

There is an international legal framework for the management of various water conflicts, both in peace and war. But one cannot be optimistic about the effectiveness of this normative framework in the present and near future given certain evident political factors in play in the Tigris–Euphrates river basin.

In 1997, states negotiated the Convention on the Law of the Non-Navigational Uses of International Watercourses (hereafter, the Water Convention). This multilateral framework treaty came into legal force in 2014 for consenting states. Currently, 35 states are parties to the treaty. Another 16 have signed but not completed the ratification process. Turkey not only has not ratified but also has voted against approval in the diplomatic conference that opened it for signature. Around the world, almost no upstream state has signed on. Only downstream states have done so. This is particularly the case outside of Europe (which also had its own regional treaty on transboundary water). Iraq and Syria ratified the Water Convention shortly after it was approved.

The Water Convention established general principles for transboundary water use apart from navigation issues, to which states might add whatever compatible particulars they desired in subsequent agreements. A central norm was "equitable and reasonable utilization and participation" with regard to relevant water issues. What was equitable and reasonable was to be defined in particular contexts by reference to multiple factors as listed in the document. It was indeed a framework treaty, designed to encourage further specific agreements later. The treaty established a general obligation for upstream states not to cause significant harm to others and to "discuss" compensation matters in the event of such harm. There was also a complex procedure laid out regarding notification of and response to water shortages. Further complexities could be found in an elaborate process for the peaceful settlement of disputes.

Article 29 in the Water Convention made reference to the international law of armed conflict (also known as international humanitarian law or the laws of war). In the event of international or internal armed conflict, specialized international law became relevant. Here too one found several general principles relevant to our present subject—for example, the military options for fighting parties were not unlimited but were bounded by such considerations as protecting the environment and minimizing damage in forceful operations. (For a brief overview, see https://www.icrc.org/eng/resources/documents/misc/57jmau.htm.)

Without reviewing all the details of this large and complicated body of law, one can note 1977 Additional Protocol I (API) to the 1949 Geneva Conventions (GCs) for victims of war, applicable in international wars and in occupation resulting from such wars. In addition to a series of articles designed to protect the civilian population, article 35(3) prohibits means and methods of war producing long-term damage to the environment, and article 55 prohibits actions that call into question the future survival of the civilian population.

Additional Protocol II (APII), applicable in certain internal wars (also known as civil wars), prohibits in article 14 attacks on resources "essential to the survival of the civilian population" and makes specific reference to "drinking water installations and supplies" and "irrigation networks." Article 15 prohibits attacks on "dangerous [ecological] forces." These particular articles represented a reaction to US bombing policies in (North) Vietnam in the 1960s.

All states have consented to be bound by the four 1949 Geneva Conventions for victims of war. At the time of this writing, 174 states had accepted API, while 167 had accepted APII. Turkey had consented only to the 1949 GCs. Syria and Iraq had accepted API but not APII.

The rejection of APII by all three states under discussion in this chapter is understandable in the realist sense that all three faced the prospect or actuality of internal armed movements and did not want to be further bound by law that restricted their freedom of policy choice in such situations. They remained bound by common article 3 from the 1949 GCs, a set of basic humanitarian norms pertaining to internal war, but that article made no explicit reference to ecological matters.

Turkey rejected API for international armed conflicts for the same reasons as the United States and Israel. Article 1(4) of API includes wars of "self-determination" in its jurisdiction. The intent of those who supported the final wording was to place such wars and those who fought in their behalf on the same legal plane as traditional interstate war and regular military personnel in uniform. If one assumes it is possible to objectively identify such wars, then a state detaining such fighters is obligated to treat them comparable to prisoners of war. Just as Turkey did not want to be bound by APII when jousting with the armed wing of the Kurdish Workers Party (PKK) and any other armed nonstate actor, so did it also not want API to be said to apply to any such confrontation. Was the PKK fighting a war of Kurdish self-determination? Turkey did not want third parties saying it was bound by API in its response.

To state the obvious, accepting to be bound by the law in principle is not the same as actually implementing the law in concrete situations. In Syria in 2011, the Bashar al-Assad government, which was legally bound by 1949 common article 3 for internal war, denied logic as well as much expert opinion when it said that it did not face an internal armed conflict but only violence carried out by terrorists. (Once outside parties began to participate in the violence, whether the Hezbollah militia from Lebanon or US and Israeli air forces, it could be argued that the situation had become an international armed conflict—at least in part or at certain times.)

It is also relevant that in 2010 the United Nations General Assembly passed a resolution recognizing a human right to safe water (A/Res/292, July 28, 2010). The vote was 122 in favor, none in opposition and 41 abstaining. This resolution, not immediately binding but in law a recommendation, made clear what could be logically deduced from other norms. Building on the 1948 Universal Declaration of Human Rights, the 1966 International Covenant on Economic, Social and Cultural Rights recognized a human right to life, to adequate health and health care and to adequate food, inter alia. All of these recognized rights required adequate access to clean water, as the Brazilian delegation noted in explanation of its vote in 2010 (http://www.un.org/press/en/2010/ga10967.doc.htm). A General Assembly resolution such as A/Res/292 may be an authoritative statement of the meaning of other legal norms, such as found in the socioeconomic covenant, which *are* legally binding. Presently there are 162 states that have fully consented to the 1966 socioeconomic covenant. Iraq, Syria and Turkey are full parties to this multilateral treaty. Thus, according to the logic explained above, they have accepted a legal obligation to treat adequate access to safe water as a fundamental human right. Furthermore, Iraq and Syria voted for A/Res/292, while Turkey abstained. (Parts of the 1948 Universal Declaration, as well as parts of some treaties, may have passed into customary international law, binding even on those states that have not explicitly consented to be so bound. But that complicated subject need not detain us here.)

The summary point for present purposes is that there are many international norms from international law—as well as authoritative diplomatic statements—emphasizing that public authorities have an obligation to guarantee individual access to adequate safe water. This obligation remains even during armed conflict. Legal logic and the notion of legal obligation, however, do not always control policy making, to understate the problem. This is certainly so for dictatorial regimes not characterized by a humane rule of law and for radical movements dedicated to overthrow of the legal and political status quo.

As will be shown below, all three states under discussion usually saw water resources as leverage in various disputes (Scheller 2014). This has been true for a long time (see Woertz 2013 regarding politicized oil and water). Syria and Iraq—and to a lesser extent Turkey—also manipulated water resources in various militarized disputes, as did various armed nonstate actors such as the Islamic State (ISIL or ISIS). Whereas international law in both peace and war sought to guarantee to individuals a certain minimum degree of water security based on equitable use and adequate protection, the three governments considered here and other political actors were opposed to taking water out of play in contentious political maneuvers. All political operatives in the Tigris–Euphrates basin saw water resources as something to be manipulated for purposes of gaining or exercising power, and hence controlling contested policy outcomes. As a matter of politics unchecked by law, they did not agree to limit their political struggles with an eye to water security for all civilians without discrimination, or even with regard to the viability of the region for human development in the future. Particularly in Iraq and Syria, political actors were so consumed in struggles for power that water resources suffered greatly, despite dire predictions about the fate of water there in the future.

Whether or not a given state had voted for a particular norm, or had deposited a certain legal instrument of ratification, seemed to be a fact of marginal importance in the water politics of the Tigris–Euphrates basin. The role of radical armed nonstate actors only made the situation worse from the standpoint of water security. As Allan and Mirumachi have concluded in general (2010), international law has had a very modest impact on most water disputes. This is clearly true for the Tigris–Euphrates basin.

Water and Conflict: The Tigris and Euphrates

Turkey, Syria and Iraq have long negotiated over water issues, engaged in various forms of conflict over water issues and from time to time reached diplomatic agreements on water issues (http://www1.american.edu/ted/ice/tigris.htm). One can find water agreements between Ottoman Turkey and French Syria in addition to even earlier examples. More than one author writing on this general subject has mentioned a development much earlier indeed: "the history of international water treaties dates as far back as 2500 BC, when the two Sumerian city-states of Lagash and Umma crafted an agreement ending a water dispute along the Tigris River—often said to be the first treaty of any kind" (http://www.ejolt.org/2013/08/declaration-of-the-ekopotamya-network-turkey-iran-iraq/). Two contemporary developments are of special importance for this area's transboundary water politics.

First, Turkey undertook the Southeastern Anatolia Development Project (GAP in Turkish) in its southeastern region from the mid-1980s. This scheme consisted of multiple dams on the Tigris and Euphrates Rivers, mainly in order to improve irrigation and energy production for the area. Turkey's southeastern region had historically been impoverished and was also the locus of much discontent and even a Kurdish secession movement. Inherently the

GAP development scheme, seen as reasonable from Ankara's point of view as a means to agricultural development in its southeast region, raised concerns in the two downstream states as Turkey improved its control over transboundary river flows. For example, Turkish temporary interruption of river flows while dams were being built negatively impacted both Syria and Iraq. Some research projects that Turkey's GAP, when finished, will delay 50 percent of the flow in the two rivers and pollute 40 percent of the remaining flow as irrigated water into agricultural fields drains back into the river basins. Other researchers estimate that if the GAP is fully developed, that scheme will reduce the Euphrates flow by 25 percent and the Tigris flow by 30 percent.

Turkey, being aware of certain critical views of its development policies, did promise equitable sharing of transboundary flows—but without pinning itself down clearly and specifically as to what "equitable" meant. Earlier diplomatic agreements during the 1980s had been reached among the three states, and especially between Turkey and Syria, regarding river resources. But these were superseded and thus dated with the development of the GAP project.

The central Turkish view of these matters was reflected in the statement, oft quoted, by then-Prime Minister Suleyman Demirel, with regard especially to Iraq: "Water resources are Turkey's and oil is theirs. Since we do not tell them, 'Look, we have a right to half your oil,' they cannot lay claim to what is ours" (quoted in Michel et al.). Hence, Turkey manifests a view of absolute state sovereignty over its natural resources. (For a clear statement of the Turkish water principles, see http://www.mfa.gov.tr/turkey_s-policy-on-water-issues.en.mfa.) This is reflected in its position on diplomatic and legal matters discussed above.

Turkey and Syria have engaged in sharp disputes from time to time over access to river flows on the Euphrates (Wolf and Newton 2008). GAP was broadly relevant as a fundamental background condition. Turkey sometimes made its cooperation with Syria on water issues dependent on Syria's not providing sanctuary or other support to Turkish Kurdish militants like the PKK (under the leadership of Abdullah Ocalan). Transboundary water flows thus got caught up in strategic political bargaining over a broad range of issues. On most of these issues Turkey held a strong position, being able to either increase or decrease vital river flows. Water disputes between Turkey and Syria were certainly politicized in a broad sense.

Syria tried to use the issue of Ocalan and the PKK to pry more water out of Turkey, providing support to what Turkey considered a terrorist organization (Kibaroglu et al., 2011). Thus water disputes became securitized—namely, made part of contestations over perceived national security. But Syria yielded on that issue in 1998 when faced with Turkish pressure based on threats to manipulate river flows along with the massing of Turkish troops on their common border. Water disputes, already politicized, became securitized and even militarized. (On disputes becoming politicized, securitized and militarized, see Buzan 1995.) Syria forced the fugitive Ocalan to abandon sanctuary in Syria and seek another safe haven in his then-violent campaign to get the Kurdish southeastern region of Turkey to secede (http://www.washingtonpost.com/wp-srv/inatl/daily/feb99/ocalanturkey18.htm). The ebb and flow of Turkish–Syrian relations can be seen in the fact that in the wake of the shift in Syrian policy in 1998, bilateral relations were again good for a time. The Assad family vacationed in Turkey occasionally. And there were new river agreements in the first decade of the new century. By 2011, however, Turkey gave support to various rebel factions trying to force the overthrow of the Assad government. Turkey favored the Arab Spring of democratic reform and became disenchanted with Assad when he resisted democratic change and cracked down hard on protesters.

It was also the case that Syria and Iraq almost engaged in armed conflict over Euphrates River flows in 1975. As Syria diverted the Euphrates during the building of the Taqba Dam forming Lake Assad, Iraq was severely affected and threatened a military response. Violence was averted by regional mediation and a diplomatic accord under which Syria agreed to guarantee that 60 percent of the Euphrates River flow in its territory continued into Iraq.

In addition to the GAP project, the second broad development was the deterioration of stability in Iraq and Syria. The US invasion of Iraq in the spring of 2003 led to pronounced and prolonged violence after the Hussein regime was toppled. A bungled US occupation during 2003 and 2004 was followed by vicious sectarian violence from 2004–2009 as Iraqi Shia and Sunni struggled for power in postoccupation Iraq. Fragile stability during 2009–2011 then disintegrated when the United States pulled out its military forces. The United States had been mediating among various Iraqi factions and thus helping maintain what stability existed. Even before the rise of the Islamic State armed movement, some experts predicted that by 2015 Iraq would be about one-third short of its water needs due to war, neglect, looting and other elements of the chaos and instability there. Because of chronic mismanagement by various authorities, the Iraqi economy was disrupted.

Complicating matters was the fact that the equally vicious Syrian civil war that had erupted in 2011 eventually spilled over into Iraq. Radical Sunni militants who had been focused on removing the Assad regime in Syria also seized upon the Iraqi instability, Sunni disenchantment and governmental defects to expand their operations across great stretches of Iraq. Principally the Sunni movement calling itself the Islamic State (ISIS or ISIL), and mostly led by disgruntled Iraqi Sunnis, sought to build on Sunni discontent in both Syria and Iraq. It therefore sought not only the overthrow of the Alawite Syrian government (a spin-off of Shia Islam) but also the removal of the Shia-dominated and Iran-supported governments in Iraq (the al-Malaki government and its successors).

These developments in Iraq and Syria made a reasonable policy impossible concerning the Tigris and Euphrates Rivers as energies were consumed in struggles for power, control and governance. The very existence of Iraq and Syria, their future boundaries, the nature of their governments and whether an independent Kurdistan would emerge from northern Iraq and northeast Syria were all at stake. The creation of a new Islamic caliphate, in effect a new multinational and theocratic empire featuring an extreme and bloody-minded interpretation of the Koran, was at least temporarily a possibility. The details of these developments will be addressed further below.

In Syria, the Assad government lost control of various portions of the country. It should be noted that water problems constituted one factor contributing to the outbreak of instability in 2011 (de Chatel 2014). In previous years the Assad regime has pushed for food security by developing water-intensive crops such as cotton and wheat. This was a dubious decision given the lack of annual rainfall and dependence on Turkish cooperation in water matters. Then from roughly 2005–2010 a prolonged drought kicked in. The result was much agricultural failure, the collapse of many farms and even entire villages and the failure of the central government to respond in a timely and supportive fashion. The further result was a mass movement of rural citizens into urban areas in search of income. When the Arab Spring democratic movement spilled over from Tunisia and Egypt into Syria in the first part of 2011, many Syrian males of rural origin were uprooted and alienated in urban areas and thus ripe for mobilization into various rebel movements. Thus it can be said that misguided agricultural and water policies by the Assad government contributed to demands that it should go (http://www.smithsonianmag.com/innovation/is-a-lack-of-water-to-blame-for-the-conflict-in-syria-72513729/?no-ist). Of course, water/food policies were only one factor at play. The repressive and brutal policies of the Assad regime were another. Eventually the central government was increasingly seen as benefitting only the Alawites and their political allies mainly in and around Damascus, as many Syrian Sunnis moved into violent opposition (http://climateandsecurity.org/2012/02/29/syria-climate-change-drought-and-social-unrest/).

A persuasive view held that in Syria as in certain other states, since local water security was impossible due to natural resource and demographic factors, the agricultural policies chosen were greatly in error. In this view, the route to security in water-for-food was through development of a vibrant and diversified economy leading to national economic growth. Such a situation would allow "virtual water" through trade (Allan 2001). That is, the well-developed and well-managed state could trade for its food needs, thereby importing "virtual water" inherent in such commodities as wheat, etc. But the Assad regime did not pursue this path. The key to security in water-for-food lay in wise political leadership. Unfortunately, Syria was not Singapore when it came to utilizing a well-considered and broadly beneficial economy to guarantee adequate food and water.

By 2014, ISIS, the radical and bloody Sunni militant movement, came to control parts of north Syria. If one looks at a map of ISIS's ribbons of territorial control, it was clear that the movement sought strategic domination over waterways and roads (http://www.theguardian.com/environment/2014/jul/02/water-key-conflict-iraq-syria-isis). The ISIS de facto capital was the city of Raqqa, which sits astride the Euphrates River. From this and other positions ISIS used water both in a positive and a negative exercise of power. In some cases it released water to win the hearts and minds of locals, or at least to try to secure their temporary deference. In other cases it denied water deliveries to pressure enemies or delayed water delivery to secure payment of "taxes" to enrich its coffers. (It also controlled roads to raise money.) Where it lacked the technical expertise to operate dams and other complex water facilities, it secured the cooperation of skilled managers in return for release of water. In some situations officials of the Assad regime wound up operating waterworks for ISIS, with the knowledge of the central government, as the price of securing water in government-controlled areas. Thus ISIS allowed some water to flow to government-controlled areas in order to "govern" its own areas despite a lack of technical expertise. It was obvious that ISIS considered water resources an important part of power politics (http://www.aljazeera.com/news/middleeast/2014/07/water-war-syria-euphrates-2014757640320663.html).

Over time this situation combined with continuing drought to seriously deplete Syrian water reserves in the Euphrates basin. The Syrian underground water table dropped as government neglect, ISIS manipulation and the wildcat digging of multiple unauthorized wells seriously impacted water reserves. Some experts predicted disastrous consequences for Syria unless order and at least a modicum of wise water management could be restored.

More or less the same political dynamics played out in Iraq next door. The incompetence of the al-Malaki central government, and in particular its narrow sectarian approach to governing, which favored certain Shia factions as well as the prime minister himself (who also held other cabinet positions), led to disaffection, especially among Sunni elements. When ISIS consolidated its position in northern Syria, it then moved into western Iraq all the way to the outskirts of Baghdad (where its advance was halted by local Shia militias strongly supported by Iran). Sunni personnel in the Iraqi army deserted and fled, leaving their weapons and equipment to fall into ISIS hands. ISIS also took temporary control of various Iraqi Kurdish areas such as the major city of Mosul, along with its banks and their financial contents.

Due to the presence of Hussein, United Nations sanctions during his rule, US invaders and occupiers and then the al-Malaki government, the Iraqi economy was characterized by low and erratic growth in gross national product (GNP) per capita. Political instability and infighting plus perpetual mismanagement prevented the emergence of a dynamic and diversified economy in which food needs (and hence virtual water) could be imported. Iraq, like Syria, became a failed state. (On the 2014 Failed State Index, where #1, South Sudan, is the worst, Iraq ranked #13 and Syria #15 out of 178 states analyzed. Finland was the best). If ISIS could be forced into retreat, Iraq had the potential to secure its minimal water needs for drinking, sanitation and industry. But without a proper economy it could not eventually be secure in water for food. Also, it manifested a population that grew too fast for its natural resources. For a good overview of this situation, with much attention to water, see http://www.trust.org/item/20140127121610-cdrqu/?source=spotlight by the Reuters Foundation.

Again in Iraq as in Syria, ISIS tried to control certain key roads and waterways (http://www.washingtonpost.com/world/middle_east/islamic-state-jihadists-are-using-water-as-a-weapon-in-iraq/2014/10/06/aead6792-79ec-4c7c-8f2f-fd7b95765d09_story.htmls). Just as the United States had paid great attention to dams and other water facilities when it invaded Iraq in the spring of 2003, so ISIS likewise knew that water was politically important. Again it used water as a tool of power, flooding out some Shia villages (displacing some 40,000 Shia after it took control of the Fallujah Dam) or manipulating water disbursements to collect "taxes" from those who found they had few alternatives but to pay if they wanted to stay on the land. For a time, ISIS took control of the major dam at Mosul on the Tigris River. This facility, built in 1980, and fragile because of neglect and wear and tear, was vital for Baghdad water supplies. ISIS was forced to retreat from this area only when the United States began air strikes in conjunction with the operation of determined Kurdish fighters on the ground. Other fighting centered on the Haditha Dam on the Euphrates, and on the Fallujah Dam further south. Once again, water issues were politicized, securitized and even militarized (http://news.nationalgeographic.com/news/2014/11/141104-iraq-water-crisis-turkey-iran-isis/).

At present, ISIS remains a major player in the violent politics of both Syria and Iraq. It continues to manipulate water resources for political purposes (http://e360.yale.edu/feature/mideast_water_wars_in_iraq_a_battle_for_control_of_water/2796/). On the one hand, it is supported by no government anywhere, and its offensive success has been stalemated by a combination of outside air strikes (by both Iran and the United States) and Kurdish and a few Iraqi fighting forces (supplemented by Shia militias) on the ground. On the other hand, there are many alienated persons, both male and female, in various Islamic circles around the world who rally to the ISIS cause and provide fighters for its extremely brutal actions.

Related Issues

We should note briefly that Iraqi water supplies are also affected by Iranian water policies to a considerable extent, as dam building on Iranian tributaries of the Tigris River in particular results in less stream flow to Iraq. Iran is the source of about 10 percent of the water flow in the Tigris basin, on average. In addition to Iranian–Iraqi contentious discussions about various water issues along common waterways in the Iraqi south, there has been a long-running dispute between the two countries over the Karun and Karkha Rivers, both of which have been diverted by Iran away from southern Iraq, depriving Basra of important supplies of freshwater. There was also a dispute between the two countries about Iran's diversion of the Wand River (or Alwand River, in some translations). According to some reports, in 2012 Iran had shut off the river for four years, leading to damage to 10 percent of Iraq's arable land as well as the depopulation of several rural villages. From such reports it seemed that Iranian water policies were a significant factor in Iraq's shrinking supplies of safe water, mainly through the building of dams but also through the dumping of waste water into transboundary rivers (http://www.alarabiya.net/articles/2012/07/17/226887.html). Still further, other reports covered the Iranian–Iraqi dispute over the Diyala River, where Iranian policies had reduced the water flow in Iraq by up to 80 percent in some years. As with the other riparian conflicts mentioned above, researchers predicted the Diyala effects to worsen in Iraq in future years (http://www.salford.ac.uk/news/university-of-salford-researchers-call-for-iran-iraq-water-treaty).

Even though the central governments in Baghdad and Tehran were both dominated by Shia political circles, this fact did not prevent serious water disputes between them. National differences sometimes trumped sectarian commonalities. (At the same time, Shia Iran lent direct support to Shia Iraq as both sought to resist advancing Sunni power in the form of ISIS.) Most sources predicted a catastrophic water situation in Iraq in future decades if water policies in Iran (and Turkey) were not changed. There was also the matter of climate change, declining rainfall, increased population and growing desertification in much of Iraq.

Moreover, in the future, should what is now Iraqi Kurdistan become even more autonomous or even independent, that kind of Kurdistan would also become a major consideration for the Iraqi water situation. As noted, the present Kurdish region of Iraq receives most of the Iraqi rainfall (Mosul receives roughly the same amount as Lincoln, Nebraska). Moreover, the Tigris passes through this region, as do several other Iranian small downstream flows. Iraq would definitely need to work out a cooperative arrangement with an independent Kurdistan regarding water flows. An independent Kurdistan might try to hold Iraq hostage with regard to both water and oil.

Whereas Iraq was definitely affected by Iran's water policies, Syria was definitely affected by Israel's, but to a lesser extent, relatively speaking (http://electronicintifada.net/content/shebaa-farms-real-issue-water/8438). Syria was negatively affected when Israel took possession of the Golan Heights and an area called Shebba Farms from 1967, as this political development led to Israel controlling the Lake Tiberias–Lake Kinneret–Sea of Galilee catchment basin—the major runoff area from Mount Hermon and the source of the Jordan River. (Different parties use different names to refer water resources in this area.) As Israel took control of certain water flows for the benefit of itself and some others, such as Jordan and the Palestinians in the West Bank area, water resources were depleted in Syria. (Previously, in 1965, when Syria and Lebanon started to divert several rivers that ran into Israel, the latter attacked the construction sites of the former, which was one issue that contributed to the 1967 war.)

Israel has invested significantly in developing the water resources of the Lake Tiberias–Lake Kinneret–Sea of Galilee catchment since 1967. These water resources are now estimated to provide about a third of Israel's freshwater. To say the least, it would take major political developments between Israel and Syria, or whatever is left of Syria after its contemporary civil war, for Israel to return the Golan Heights, which it formally annexed in 1981. Water issues in this area are intertwined with security issues, as the Golan Heights also have military significance.

From the Lake Tiberias–Lake Kinneret–Sea of Galilee water resources, Israel guarantees a certain water flow to Jordan, as per their 1994 peace accord. This arrangement is highly important for Jordan, which has meager water supplies. Some disputes have arisen over this arrangement, but in general it is clear that Israel has intended to cooperate with Jordan on water matters in return for Jordan's willingness to make peace with the Jewish state.

Moreover, the Jordan River is also crucial to water supplies in the West Bank area of Palestinian territory. There have been numerous disputes about this latter subject, with critics charging that Israel diverts too much of the Jordan River to itself and not enough to Palestinian territory, especially in drought years (B'Tselem 2008; Amnesty International 2009; Human Rights Watch 2010). Any future peace accord between Israel and the Palestinians based on a two-state solution would necessarily have to contain provisions on shared water resources, as was true of the peace accord between Israel and Jordan.

Conclusion: Negative Learning in the Future?

Water politics in the Tigris–Euphrates basin since 1919, and especially since about 1980 indicates several fundamental points: (1) the persistent politicization of water as a scare resource useful in power struggles, regarding both who rules and for what purpose; (2) the weakness of various parts of international law in pursuit of principled regulation of this subject; (3) the existence of a few interstate water agreements here and there, usually of short duration; (4) the deterioration of water security—especially in Iraq and Syria—in recent decades; and finally (5) the prospect of continuing problems along with pessimism about effective multilateral management of riparian issues.

Paradoxically, an improvement in water security is not out of the question for this region. This would require negative learning, however, as political leaders would need to recognize the errors of the past and be willing to adopt new policies in the future (http://www.merip.org/mer/mer254/turkeys-rivers-dispute; http://www.huffingtonpost.com/peter-h-gleick/water-and-conflict-in-syr_b_5404774.html).

Larry Diamond, looking at Iraq after the US invasion, wrote that one cannot get to Madison except by way of Hobbes (Diamond 2005). That is, in his view, first, one has to solve the security dilemma featured in the writings of Thomas Hobbes, as explained in his magnum opus, *Leviathan*. The first order of business is to establish secure territorial states whose governments have the ability to provide physical security within their jurisdictions. He has a point, but I would say that in contemporary times one has to deal with Hobbes and James Madison at the same time, since major threats to physical security often come at least in part from domestic causes. The security of the modern state usually depends not only on the capability to resist outside incursions through effective security policies but also on the wisdom to govern wisely so as to avoid internal uprisings. Hence Madison is as relevant to contemporary security concerns as Hobbes.

State security is now no small matter in this riparian basin, involving (1) the suppression and eventual elimination of ISIS and similar radical armed movements with destabilizing, expansive and bloody agendas; (2) the creation of responsible and sensitive governments in Iraq and Syria actually committed to ruling for the benefit of the nation; and (3) resisting tendencies toward authoritarian, insensitive and repressive rule in Turkey that might trigger a return to coups and internal instability. Under the best of circumstances, learning from Hobbes and Madison will take years to achieve. The first step is to recognize why the al-Malaki and Assad policies led to failed states, ripe for internal violence and external penetration. No sustainable water policies can be developed in contemporary Iraq and Syria given the present level of violence and disarray. Basic physical security must be established as per Hobbes, requiring effective security forces. Diamond is right in this regard.

Equally important, if and when basic order can be restored (and it might be recalled that the Lebanese civil war lasted some 15 years, from more or less 1975 to 1990, and was ended by negotiated power sharing), then one can emphasize the concerns of Madison and the making of a well-ordered and constitutional state. Such a state controls factionalism through the sharing of power, checks and balances and other constitutional arrangements leading to stability based on satisfaction of a variety of interests. In most cases Madisonian concerns, properly understood and applied, reinforce the Hobbesian focus on the state as provider of security. A constitutional republic with proper checks and balances usually contributes to domestic stability and security in addition to other desired values. The Madisonian state in its pursuit of citizens' freedom and development can in most cases contribute to internal security. In contemporary times, violence threatening civilians' security is more likely to come from civil rather than international wars (Mueller 1989; Pinker 2011).

As for our concern here with water, the future well-considered state of the Tigris–Euphrates basin would recognize the broad benefits of a strong and diversified economy allowing the sustained importation of many food stuffs, particularly as a substitute for water-intensive local crops. For this, one needs a well-trained and productive work force operating within the proper regulatory framework capable of producing goods and services desired at home and abroad, and which thus provides the marginal economic gains to pay for food imports, also known as virtual water. This strategy might even pertain to Turkey if climate change or another factor reduces the prospects of agricultural bounty in its southeastern highlands. This kind of economic development, like the creation of stable constitutional republics, will certainly not happen overnight. But the more the three states of concern here move in this direction (or in Turkey's case resists backsliding), the less there will be intensive conflict over various river flows. No doubt some water conflicts will remain, but the intensity of the disagreements should be reduced. As in some other cases, the pacification of transnational water disputes and the pursuit of greatly improved water security within nations is to be found primarily in other domains, like economic development and trade.

In the meantime, which may last several decades, as soon as minimal order can be restored in Iraq and Syria, one should still pursue whatever riparian agreements can be negotiated, even if marginal in the big picture of hydropolitics. Basic water supplies for drinking, sanitation and industry need to be guaranteed and protected. Diversions and pollution need to be minimized. Droughts need to be planned for. Even Turkey, at present rather water sufficient, needs peace on its borders and an absence of disruptions from both internal and foreign discontents.

A look at evident problems in the past should help in moving toward better water security in the future for the Tigris–Euphrates basin. Unfortunately, it often seems to take negative learning from past disasters to get both leaders and followers to change course (Stoessinger 1990).

Finally, space does not permit exploration of, but future research might focus on, three related points. (1) Even in certain constitutional democracies there is instability because of poorly chosen public policies, as in Greece and Argentina, inter alia. A stable Madisonian state must also be effective not only in its constitutional arrangements but also in its socioeconomic policies. (2) Many Middle East nations are a mosaic of ethnic and sectarian identities, making a stable balancing of interests difficult. That is why I used the term "constitutional republic" rather than "liberal democracy." The former is more likely in the Middle East than the latter, as per Jordan and Morocco. We do not know yet about Tunisia. For those inclined to cite Singapore as a model of proper water policies, one might recall that Singapore is often referred to as a soft authoritarian state since the same political faction has ruled for about five decades and challengers are often harassed. The NGO Freedom House correctly concludes that Singapore is not an electoral democracy and does not rate it in the first tier of states regarding civil and political rights. (3) States outside the Tigris–Euphrates basin can help or hinder positive developments. The United States, Europe, Russia, China, Iran and Israel all have important roles to play, directly or indirectly, in the future of water politics in this area.

References

Allan, J. A. 2001. *The Middle East Water Question: Hydropolitics and the Global Economy*. London and New York: I. B. Tauris.

Allan, J. A., and N. Mirumachi. 2010. "Why Negotiate? Asymmetric Endowments, Asymmetric Power and the Invisible Nexus of Water, Trade and Power That Brings Apparent Water Security." In *Transboundary Water Management: Principles and Practice*, edited by A. Earle, A. Jägerskogand and J. Öjendal, 13–26. London and Washington, DC: Earthscan.

Amnesty International. 2009. *Troubled Waters: Palestinians Denied Fair Access to Water*. London: Amnesty International.

B'Tselem. 2008. "Israeli's Discriminatory Water Policies Leave West Bank Dry," July 1. Accessed July 2008, http://electronicintifada.net/content/israels-discriminatory-water-policies-leave-west-bank-dry/3371.

Buzan, Barry. 1995. "Security, the State, the 'New World Order,' and Beyond." In *On Security*, edited by Ronnie D. Lipschutz, 187–211. New York: Columbia University Press.

De Chatel, Francesca. 2014. "The Role of Drought and Climate Change in the Syrian Uprising." *Middle East Studies* 50 (4): 521–535.

Diamond, Larry. 2005. *Squandered Victory*. New York: Henry Holt.

Human Rights Watch. 2010. *Israel/West Bank: Separate and Unequal*. New York: Human Rights Watch.

Michel, David, Amit Pandya, Syed Iqbal Hasnain, Russell Sticklor and Sreya Panuganti. 2012. *Water Challenges and Cooperative Response in the Middle East and North Africa*. Washington, DC: Brookings Institution Press.

Mueller, John 1989. *Retreat from Doomsday: The Obsolescence of Major War*. New York: Basic Books.

Pinker, Steven. 2011. *The Better Angels of Our Nature*. New York: Viking Penguin.

Scheller, Bente. 2014. *The Wisdom of Syria's Waiting Game*. New York and Oxford: Oxford University Press.

Stoessinger, John. 1990. *Nations in Darkness, Nations at Dawn*. New York: McGraw-Hill.

Woertz, Eckart. 2013. *Oil for Food*. New York and Oxford: Oxford University Press.

Wolf, Aaron, and Joshua T. Newton. 2009. *Managing and Transforming Water Conflicts*. Cambridge: Cambridge University Press.

Chapter 8

THE POLITICAL AND CULTURAL DIMENSIONS OF WATER DIPLOMACY IN THE MIDDLE EAST

Lawrence E. Susskind

My overall interest is in identifying new and better ways of managing trans-boundary water resources. Better, in my view, means maximizing the sustainable use of water at a reasonable cost while ensuring that the urgent water needs of all water users (that is, city residents, farmers and industrial developers) are met simultaneously. This has to happen while ecosystem services are maintained. In most parts of the world, efforts inspired by Integrated Water Resource Management (IWRM) do not meet these objectives.

Within each country, national and state governments set water-management goals and provide the infrastructure needed to meet them. They fund these efforts with general tax revenues or rely on dedicated water tariffs and fees to do so. Government agencies try to coordinate public and private efforts to deliver water to urban dwellers, manage wastewater, provide water for food production and manage the water necessary to produce and distribute energy. They must have the capacity to get bureaucrats at multiple levels to work together, either by offering them financial incentives or by exercising the authority required to ensure compliance. In most instances, they have trouble doing both.

Managing waters that cross international boundaries is even more difficult. Nations are sovereign. While international laws call for the sharing of transboundary waters, it is sometimes difficult to force countries to comply. However, most governments comply, most of the time, with most transboundary agreements because they do not want to lose their credibility (and they do not want to be forced out of other international regimes that are important to them). This is generally referred to as "compliance without enforcement" (Chayes and Chayes 1991). The water-sharing agreements that work best are those that meet the interests of the (people in the) states involved and do not require much enforcement.

Water management within a country and water diplomacy across international borders depend on the problem-solving capabilities of the political entities involved, especially when the self-interests of the parties are not aligned. Water management (that is, operational efforts to implement laws, policies and programs that water diplomacy generates) is only effective when allocation and investment decisions are made in a timely fashion, parties who stand to be affected by decisions are engaged in monitoring the results and helping revise decisions, staff capacity is sufficient and long-term relationships (especially trust) among relevant stakeholders are maintained or enhanced. Water diplomacy, in contrast, is usually judged to be successful when the actions of institutional actors are viewed as legitimate by those affected by them, decisions take account of local knowledge and agency discretion (in the face of unanticipated events) is exercised wisely. Let us examine two hypothetical cases to understand why and how water diplomacy and water management often fall short.

Two Hypothetical Cases

When I look at the water conflicts described in the AquaPedia, I see that many of the same disputes occur repeatedly: (1) water supplies are not allocated fairly (in the eyes of at least some of the relevant parties); (2) even as short-term water demands are met, the long-term sustainability and increasing variability of water supplies are ignored; (3) decisions about urban land use, industrial development, investment in infrastructure and agricultural and energy programs are not well coordinated with regard to their impact on water resources; (4) institutions with transboundary water-management responsibilities engage their constituents or stakeholders only after decisions are made (often on the grounds that water management should be left to experts); and (5) water supplies are wasted because conservation efforts, water-quality improvements and water reuse are insufficient, water is priced inappropriately and water tariffs go uncollected ("AquaPedia Case Study Database"). The only way to do better is to enhance the ongoing problem-solving capabilities of the agencies and stakeholders involved.

Imagine two hypothetical situations in which these difficulties are playing out. The first involves a growing metropolitan area in the developing world with a burgeoning population. The demand for potable water has outstripped the available supply, even though pipes have been extended great distances to tap an outlying lake. Groundwater in some parts of the region (all within the same country) has been contaminated by poorly managed industrial sites.

More than 70 percent of the available water in the region is used for agricultural purposes, particularly in outlying areas, leaving many city residents feeling shortchanged. Traditional agricultural practices are quite water intensive, and farming technologies and methods have not changed for a long time. A significant share of the water has been diverted for hydroelectricity. All in all, it seems as if there is not enough water to meet the needs of a growing number of urban dwellers as well as the needs of farmers in outlying areas. This is just an assumption, though, and there is no forum in which all the parties can put their heads together to work out possible solutions. There is no history at all of face-to-face problem solving. Yet, when asked, regional officials claim they are committed to IWRM. They emphasize that they have produced a basin-wide plan that calls for more efficient use of water. They claim to be committed to collecting water tariffs more efficiently, and they promise to invest in improved infrastructure when they have additional funds. Above all, they claim to be listening quite carefully to the concerns of stakeholders.

The regional water commission in this hypothetical basin has most of the management responsibility. It is supposed to coordinate infrastructure investment, set water rates, ensure water quality and generate long-term plans to satisfy competing water needs. Unfortunately, the commission is shorthanded. It has relied heavily on international consultants to produce supply and demand forecasts. Indeed, the consultants have produced a "scorecard" showing that progress is being made on ensuring environmental sustainability, improving the efficiency of water-delivery systems, collecting more water tariffs, monitoring water quality and engaging governmental and nongovernmental stakeholders. Two highly publicized public consultation sessions have been held over the past 18 months. New water legislation has been submitted, calling for increased privatization of distribution and wastewater management systems. The legislation also calls for higher water prices and tariffs. Parliament, however, has refused to consider these bills. Many groups in the region claim that no one is listening and nothing is changing. The need for potable water is increasing (with a growing population and new industrial development), while supplies appear to be shrinking because of leaks in the system, illegal withdrawals and the effects of an extended drought. No one has definitive information on any of these trends.

Some regional leaders think the drought is a harbinger of things to come. They worry that climate change will reduce water supplies even further. Water rates continue to go uncollected in several parts of the city, while illegal withdrawals are quite common, especially in rural areas. Efforts to inaugurate a public-private partnership to finance a new wastewater treatment facility as well as a small-scale hydroelectricity plant have not attracted private investors. Poorer groups and areas in the region have been waiting for new water lines to reach them. While some outspoken advocates think the country's constitution guarantees everyone a right to water and sanitation, the courts have not supported this interpretation. Successive rounds of politicians have promised to "do something" about all these problems, but nothing has changed. The stated commitment to IWRM has not made much of a difference in anyone's life.

The second hypothetical involves a major river shared by several countries in a different part of the world. The upstream nations are less developed, while the downstream countries are highly urbanized. Megacities in the transnational river basin add millions of new inhabitants every decade. At the moment, there is no treaty governing the use of the river's waters, although there are a number of bilateral "understandings" in place among pairs of adjacent countries. Historically, there has been sufficient rainfall to allow every country to withdraw the water it needed to meet agricultural, industrial and urban requirements. Population growth and reductions in water supply have changed all of that. In addition, the unilateral building of dams by one upstream country has interfered with the ability of several downstream countries to withdraw the water they need in the dry season. If downstream countries allocate the water farmers are demanding, there will not be enough to run their hydroelectric turbines. Additionally, another upstream country has been steadily depleting a key aquifer. In narrower stretches of the river, increasing salinization is a new worry. Some of the national leaders have threatened their neighbors, whom they blame for their growing water difficulties. These threats play well at home, but they increase water insecurity in the entire region. There is no problem-solving conversation taking place among the countries involved.

Continuing the second hypothetical situation, we may imagine that international agencies have offered to underwrite a partial expansion of water infrastructure in one or two countries (including a major desalination plant), but this has just exacerbated the disagreement among the countries involved. The motives of the outside agencies are also very much in question. Because there is no established regional forum in which to discuss basin-wide priorities, there is no hope of producing a unified water allocation plan. International environmental nongovernmental organizations (NGOs) are supporting activists in the region who are increasingly vociferous about the possibility that climate change might cause a permanent drought. They want to see more of an emphasis on water reuse, recycling and repair of both urban and rural water systems.

In this second situation, national leaders claim that they too are implementing IWRM. In a status report prepared by a multilateral development banks, almost all of the countries received pretty high marks for trying to improve environmental sustainability, enhance the efficiency of water allocation, repair infrastructure, enhance stakeholder engagement, improve revenue collection and ensure adequate financing for infrastructure development. It seems they can show progress on all these fronts without actually increasing water supplies, reducing demand or implementing more efficient technologies. In situations like these, political leaders say they are committed to further cooperation, but they appear to be interested only in their own country's (rather than basin-wide) interests. No real-time problem solving is going on.

The leaders involved remain silent about the adverse effects of rapid population growth. They do not mention worsening income inequality or the ways in which their governments are undermining the viability of informal settlements. In practice, environmental issues get almost no attention on the grounds that urgent economic development needs are more important. This mirrors the tendency of government agencies to present everything in zero-sum terms. That is, any proposal to allocate more water for one use is presumed to require cutbacks in another. The more water (and money) used to meet the needs of a growing urban population, the argument goes, the less money there will be for farmers in rural areas. This zero-sum logic is at the heart of IWRM.

Integrated Water Resource Management

Historically, IWRM has focused on optimization: how to use existing water supplies in the most efficient way. IWRM began with the Dublin Statement on Water and Sustainable Development (Dublin Principles) in 1992: (1) Freshwater is a finite and vulnerable resource essential to sustain life, development and the environment. (2) Water development and management should be based on a participatory approach, involving users, planners and policy makers at all levels. (3) Women play a central part in the provision, management and safeguarding of water. (4) Water has an economic value in all its competing uses and should be recognized as an economic good (Salman and Bradlow 2006).

In the United States, the US Army Corps of Engineers has expanded on these ideas, arguing (1) effective water allocation requires cooperation among industry, governmental agencies, private institutions and academic organizations; (2) technical solutions must include increased habitat protection and preservation of fundamental components of long-term watershed vitality; (3) the complexity of information management and the scope of experimental manipulation needed to ensure the efficient allocation of water often exceed the capacity of individual water-management institutions; (4) the tendency to seek conceptualized solutions at the expenses of data-driven decisions must be reversed; (5) intra- and interagency inconsistencies in environmental regulations must be corrected; and (6) human activities are a key element of ecosystem vitality and must be integrated with environmental considerations before long-term sustainability can be achieved (US Army Corps of Engineers, 2014).

If we consider both sets of principles and statements, it is clear that integrated water-resource management depends on reconciling conflicting interests, values, demands and interpretations. But, how can this be done? It is one thing to say that decisions should be coordinated and data driven and account for the concerns of multiple agencies and constituencies at multiple scales simultaneously, and it is quite another to make specific trade-offs when they have to be made. IWRM is surprisingly silent on how competing claims should be adjudicated. And, surprisingly, IWRM does not emphasize the need to "create" more water by facilitating the reuse of gray water, the acquisition of green water and the creation of more blue water (Allan 2011). Nor does it create more value by linking water-allocation decisions to other important needs that must be met (Islam and Susskind 2012).

Buried within the many hundreds of articles and books about IWRM is a presumption that competing claims on limited resources can be resolved through analysis, that is, a process of optimization. The analyst should specify what the most efficient use of limited water resources should be. And the presumption is that this can be determined, in any situation, by taking account of supply estimates, demand forecasts (assuming correct prices) and a ranking of competing needs. Technical analysis by experts will supposedly reveal the best use of limited resources (that is, the most efficient way of achieving multiple objectives simultaneously). In practice, this does not work. There is no technical basis for specifying which user group's needs ought to be given priority. Forecasts of supply are suspect because of the uncertainty created by climate change. Demand estimates are unreliable because, in many instances, water is not priced consistently or appropriately. Every allocation decision, therefore, depends on political and cultural considerations, not technical analysis. Trade-offs often have to be made on the spur of the moment and, when there are no trusted problem-solving arrangements in place, each interest group or each country seeks to maximize its own advantage. Greater involvement of stakeholders in the form that IWRM typically elicits only deepens the distrust of decision makers and sharpens competing claims.

The American Water Resources Association (AWRA) says that IWRM ought to involve four phases of work, each building on technical analyses of various kinds:

Phase I: Assess the current situation, recognize problems, build governmental and public awareness, and generate the incentives and capacity for action. Recognize and identify problems, threats, opportunities and needs.

Phase II: Assess problems and identify potential solutions. Conceptualize at a broad scale so as to include all relevant participants and variables.

Phase III: Evaluate options in order to identify a plan. Coordinate and plan in detail.

Phase IV: Implement, monitor, and evaluate IWRM actions and results so as to start the cycle again with forethought and hindsight generated by evaluation and feedback (UNESCO 2009).

Who is supposed to be doing each of these things (and on whose behalf) is not clear. How to move from phase II to phase III is not explained. Once options have been identified, the task of "making a plan" requires taking a "normative leap," that is, advocating a move from the status quo to some alternative future. Given that data are always limited and the interests of the stakeholders are usually in conflict, this is not an optimization task that can be entrusted to engineers. Some other mode of problem solving is required in which the need to make political trade-offs is acknowledged. Only if the proper problem-solving procedures are followed is it possible to meet the most important and conflicting interests of all the relevant stakeholders.

In the end, the analyses described by the AWARA must yield to political and cultural considerations. The credibility and legitimacy of each choice in water management and water diplomacy, more than their correctness or the efficiencies they can achieve, are paramount.

The conventional wisdom about integrated water-resource management assumes that allocating water supplies in a way (and at prices) that match supply and demand is of the utmost importance. IWRM assumes that scientific information will provide a basis for making optimal decisions, even when substantial uncertainty abounds and past patterns of water supply do not enable trustworthy predictions. While it is true that the practice of IWRM continues to evolve, it begins and ends with a win-lose focus: how to allocate water in an optimal fashion given limited supplies. Emphasis is on trying to "get the prices right" so that optimal allocations can be justified on economic grounds. A few places have moved away from IWRM and the logic of optimization to what I call the Water Diplomacy Framework (WDF). WDF assumes water allocations are primarily a political and cultural task rather than a technical one. WDF also assumes that water users need to be involved in both water-management and water-diplomacy decisions from beginning to end.

The Water Diplomacy Framework:
A Mutual-Gains Approach

WDF assumes that water is a flexible rather than finite resource. That is, if the same water is used multiple times (perhaps for different purposes), the amount of available water increases. It assumes that the interests of stake-holders rather than past volumes of water should be the starting point for water-allocation decisions and that negotiations, not technical or economic analyses aimed at maximizing efficiency, are vital. WDF assumes that water networks are open and constantly evolving as opposed to bounded and fixed. WDF also assumes that perceptions of fairness and trust are more important than easily monetized costs and benefits. Finally, WDF favors a mutual gains approach to water negotiations (that is, an effort to meet the basic interests of all sides simultaneously) rather than a zero-sum approach to water allocation that allows only the most powerful to get what they want. The key to achieving mutual gains is value creation through multiple uses of the same water and trades that are simultaneously advantageous to all parties.

It is my objective in this paper to describe what water management and water diplomacy entail if a WDF approach is used. I do this by comparing the difficult water situation in Gaza with the recent agreement reached by Jordan, Israel and Palestine regarding a water-sharing arrangement that will move water from the Red Sea to the Dead Sea and generate much-needed water for Jordan in the process. Sharon Usdain (2015) writes that in Gaza, following the destruction of a substantial portion of Gaza's water supply and delivery system in the summer of 2014, water supplies are inadequate (even after the Israeli government recently increased the amount of water it supplies to Gaza from 5 million cubic meters per year to 10 million cubic meters per year. There is no joint fact finding underway, and very few steps are being taken by Israel or the international community to ensure that the residents of Gaza get the water they need. In the south of Israel, though, the Red Sea–Dead Sea project (Red–Dead, as it is known) will provide additional water for Jordan and the West Bank. (Palestinians in the West Bank will also have the option of buying additional water each year as part of this arrangement.)

In Gaza, stakeholders are not working together or exploring incremental efforts to resolve the current water crisis. In the case of Jordan–Israel–Palestine Red–Dead negotiations, the leaders managed to generate an elaborate (albeit controversial) agreement that will involve the investment of as much as $10 billion (US) (Josephs 2013). I will examine the political and the cultural dimensions of the negotiations that took place in both situations.

The Politics of Water Diplomacy: A Focus on Gaza, Israel and Jordan

Water insecurity is the cause of many disagreements in the Middle East (Susskind and Islam 2012). While there are numerous ways a country can,

Table 8.1 The Water Diplomacy Framework (WDF) and the Integrated Water Resources Management (IWRM)

	Water Diplomacy Framework (WDF)	Integrated Water Resources Management (IWRM)
Water availability	Water is a flexible resource. Embedded water, blue and green water, virtual water, new technology that allows for water sharing and even water production can create flexibility in responding to competing demands for water. Disputes can be negotiated.	Water is a finite and vulnerable resource. Competing claims on finite resources usually lead to conflicts. Expert analysis should be given top priority in resolving water disputes.
Values, principles and interests	Values, principles and the interests of stakeholders, more than technocratic concerns, are central to characterizing water-management problems.	Water-management problems are defined in highly technocratic terms, although IWRM has begun to take the interests of stakeholders more seriously.
Domains and scales (i.e., unit of analysis)	Multiple domains and scales (e.g., space, time, jurisdictional, institutional) are all possible network boundaries. A distinction is made among watersheds, problem-sheds, and policy-sheds.	Watersheds or river basins are bounded systems and should be the focus of water management.
Integration	Integration of natural and societal variables within a political context. Emphasis on achieving multiple dimensions of sustainability.	Integration of natural and societal variables using "pricing" (of costs and benefits) as a key consideration.
Negotiation theory	The Mutual Gains Approach (MGA) to value creation; multiparty negotiation keyed to coalitional behavior; mediation as informal problem solving.	Hard bargaining informed by Prisoner's Dilemma–style game theory; principal-agent theory; decision analysis (Pareto Optimality).

Source: Islam and Susskind, *Water Diplomacy*.

on its own, address its water needs (that is, by building or improving its water-distribution systems, modernizing farming practices, collecting water tariffs more efficiently, investing in desalination or wastewater-management facilities and so on), many countries require the cooperation, if not the active participation, of neighboring countries. The Palestinian territories, for example, have no choice but to rely on Israel to meet their water needs, since Israel has complete control over the movement of water and electricity (and other necessities) into Gaza and the West Bank. Similarly, because Jordan has no surface water-storage capacity, it depends on Israel to store water on its behalf during the rainy season and release that excess during the dry season. Jordan is also is looking to draw on Israel's desalination expertise. With Israel's help, Jordan is planning to move desalinized water from the Red Sea to its capital region in Amman (at the same time that brine from the desalination facility is delivered to the Dead Sea in Israel). Thus, water sharing is very important throughout the Jordan River valley. In the case of Gaza, though, the politics of water diplomacy have not yielded workable agreements. In the Jordan–Israel case, they have. Let us try to understand why.

The Scope of the Water Problem in Gaza

Gaza is a dry area. Its coastal aquifer can supply about 55–60 MCM/year through natural recharge (Wikipedia 2015). Yet, because of increasing population pressures (that is, an annual growth rate of 3.5 percent) and limits imposed by Israel on the operation of desalination plants, reuse of gray water and access to area-wide water supplies, Palestine is drawing more than 180 MCM/year from the coastal aquifer (Wikipedia 2015). This is unsustainable. Indeed, the coastal aquifer is almost depleted and is currently experiencing seawater intrusion (Wikipedia 2015). The total amount of water reaching residents of Gaza is less than 100 liters per capita per day, the absolute minimum established by the World Health Organization. Moreover, as much as 95 percent of this water is of "unacceptable quality" (Wikipedia 2015). The Palestinian Water Authority (PWA) hopes to provide 120 liters per capita per day by 2030 to meet the domestic and industrial needs of the more than 2.3 million Gaza inhabitants expected by then (Wikipedia 2015). This will require (1) Israel increasing the amount of water it sells to Palestine (and the Gaza administration increasing the efficiency of its urban water infrastructure beyond its current 60 percent rate) (Wikipedia 2015); (2) additional investment in reliable energy production to support continuous water delivery; (3) reconstruction of the parts of the water system destroyed by Israel's most recent military action (ICRC 2014); (4) improvements in the efficiency of agricultural irrigation; and (5) reductions in unaccounted for water (Wikipedia 2015).

While there are numerous steps that the PWA can take on its own to address these requirements, continued interaction with Israel—even after an independent Palestinian state is created—is essential. So, even if Palestine finds a way to reduce population growth in Gaza, and the PWA collects water tariffs more efficiently, restricts the rate of abstraction from the coastal aquifer, encourages more efficient farming practices and invests in new desalination plants, it will still need to purchase substantial amounts of water from Israel. And, until it is an independent state, Palestine will depend on Israel to (1) meet the terms of the Oslo II agreement (which call on the Israeli water company to provide 10 MCM a day); (2) lift the blockade on construction materials going into Gaza; (3) provide electricity on a regular basis at affordable rates; and (4) provide the technical assistance required to reuse treated wastewater.

From a political standpoint, Gaza needs Israel's assistance in the short term and its cooperation in the long run. Israel, however, appears unwilling to help until long-term political and security questions are resolved. This makes it difficult to address short-term water needs. Problem solving is impossible if water is going to be "held hostage" to other political agendas. Institutions like the Joint (Israel–Palestine) Water Committee need the authority and resources to act as short-term problem solvers, even as longer-term political arrangements are worked out. This is not happening.

The Scope of the Water Problem in Jordan (and Israel's Dead Sea Problem)

Jordan and Israel signed a peace treaty in 1994 (IMFA 1994). It is only the second peace treaty signed by Israel and its Arab neighbors, and it is the only treaty that addresses water sharing directly. The treaty includes an annex dealing specifically with ways of increasing the available supply of water available to both Jordan and Israel. One of the most important elements of the treaty is a provision that allows Israel to draw water from the Yarmouk River, store it in Lake Tiberius during the wet season and enable Jordan to pump more than 50 million cubic meters (through pipes that Jordan built, partly on land in Israel) in the dry season. In effect, the treaty allows Jordan to store winter runoff in Lake Tiberius in Israel, the only major surface reservoir in the region, while Israel is allowed to use land located in Jordan for groundwater wells and conveyance systems (Meisen and Tatum 2011). This arrangement has worked for more than a decade, although water shortages continue to increase in Jordan.

The treaty also created a Joint (Israel–Jordan) Water Commission (JWC) to oversee water-sharing obligations and to identify additional water resources for Jordan, particularly through Jordanian investment in dams and other infrastructure and Israeli investment in desalination ("Benefit Sharing, Water Cooperation," *Turkish Review*, May 1, 2014). The JWC has continued to meet and engage in problem solving of various kinds, even as Israel's relationships with its Arab neighbors have continued to deteriorate.

In the past three years, more than 620,000 Syrian refugees have arrived in Jordan (Farishta 2014). They live mostly in urban areas in the north of Jordan and in refugee camps. The refugees represent almost a 10 percent increase in Jordan's population since 2010. Jordan has been dealing with water shortages for a long time, but the arrival of so many refugees in camps and in cities that are woefully ill-equipped to meet their needs has made matters much worse. Urban water delivery systems desperately need upgrading. According to one report, 7.6 billion liters a year are lost through poorly maintained systems. Keith Proctor (2014) asserts that is enough to meet the water needs of almost one-third of Jordan's population.

As early as 2006, Jordan faced an annual deficit of 600 million cubic meters (Alfarra et al. 2012). The Jordan River is now reduced to just 2 percent of its original flow (Gafny et al. 2015). Climate change, inefficient water distribution systems (that is, Jordan loses almost 50 percent of its water to aging infrastructure) and continued population growth increase water shortages still further.

Israel, in the meantime, is concerned about the loss of the Dead Sea. Gwen Ackerman (2012) reports the Dead Sea shrinking at a rapid rate, down to 600 km2, almost a 15 percent reduction in scale since 1980. The flow of water into the Dead Sea from the Jordan River is affected by increases in large-scale irrigation and very low rainfall levels. At what may be the lowest spot on earth (more than fourteen hundred feet below sea level), the Dead Sea is one of the world's saltiest bodies of water. Israel would like to find a way to add the right amount and mix of saltwater to the Dead Sea on a regular basis to reestablish its original size and maintain its ecological balance.

One way of doing this is the Red Sea–Dead Sea Water Conveyance Project (Meisen and Tatum 2011, 17–18). The proposed canal would pump seawater from the Red Sea through the Gulf of Aqaba (where a desalination plant would generate 800–1,000 cubic meters of water per year) to the Dead Sea. The potable water would be shared between Israel, Jordan and Palestine, while the brine would be pumped to the Dead Sea 110 miles to the north. The intention is to replenish the declining Dead Sea, and along the way, generate hydroelectricity and provide freshwater through desalination for both Jordan and Israel. The project may take to decades to complete and cost $4–$5 billion (US). Significant environmental concerns have been raised over the project, however, including questions about its effect on fragile coral reefs in the Gulf of Aqaba, the impact of discharging brine from desalination into the Dead Sea and overall energy costs (Meisen and Tatum 2011, 18).

Political Obstacles to Solving These Problems

As in other parts of the world, the key to dealing with water shortages, water-quality concerns and disagreements about how existing water supplies should be shared, is trust. Joint management of transboundary water resources depends on the willingness of the people in one country to believe that the people in neighboring countries will do what they promise. Jordan and Israel have reached a point where, for the most part, Jordan counts on Israel to store a certain amount of water and release it when Jordan needs it. Israel expects Jordan to pump only a certain amount of water from the Jordan River and underground sources. The JWC meets regularly and, while negotiations over the Red Sea–Dead Sea Project have been contentious, and there are many critics of the plan, an agreement was reached that will, in theory, meet the most important interests on all sides. While Palestine was a party to the agreement, Jordan apparently handled most of the negotiations on Palestine's behalf (Namrouqa 2013).

There is no trust between Israel and Gaza. The Israel–Palestine JWC has a very restricted agenda (at Israel's insistence). When the JWC does meet, the participants are consumed by disagreements. They do not trust each other. They have not been able to agree on exactly when and how the terms of Oslo II will be met (Shamir 1998, 103). Part of the problem is that since the treaty and its various annexes were signed, the government of Gaza has changed hands. Hamas is now in charge, and even relations between Gaza and the Palestinian Authority in the West Bank are filled with suspicion and tension. In Gaza, water always seems to be held hostage to other concerns. For instance, the construction materials Gaza needs to repair damage to existing water systems (caused in part by Israel's most recent military action) have been embargoed by Israel, which is worried that the supplies will be used to rebuild secret tunnels that threaten Israel's security. Trust and institutional problem-solving capabilities are in place in Israel–Jordan, but not in Israel–Gaza. This appears to reinforce the long-held assumption that water shortages are not what lead to conflict; rather, it is the way they are handled that triggers conflict.

Summary of the Politics of Water Diplomacy

Water-allocation decisions (especially across national boundaries) always take place in a political context. While some water professionals would like to believe that their job is to focus exclusively on technical considerations (and the allocation of funds for building water infrastructure), there is almost always more at stake. Water professionals usually report to politicians, who must juggle a whole range of political and cultural factors in determining who gets what water, when, how and at what cost. Decisions along these lines invariably reflect the pressures exerted by a wide range of stakeholders from numerous policy arenas.

Here are five determinants of the politics of water diplomacy. First, is the issue of voice, that is, who speaks for which stake-holding interests. Voices that are not heard are not likely to have their interests met. Water diplomacy hinges on negotiation, which, in turn, is a function of who is "at the table." Leaders in different parts of the world hold very different views about what democracy requires by way of ensuring stakeholders an opportunity to participate directly in decision making. In many countries there is a belief that elected officials speak for everyone. In other countries, like the United States, stakeholders often have an opportunity to participate directly in water-management decisions, either through standing advisory committees or public consultations.

Elections rarely yield definitive statements of public concern regarding specific water-allocation choices. People support candidates for many different reasons. Thus, it is difficult to infer from elections what the various segments of the public prefer with regard to specific water-allocation options. Furthermore, it is entirely unclear who speaks for ecological interests, future generations or the disenfranchised. Nongovernmental groups (that is, civil society) can sometimes help ensure that these hard-to-represent interests are heard. In the Middle East, groups such as Friends of the Earth (with its separate operations in Israel, Palestine and Jordan) have been increasingly effective in making sure that environmental interests are heard. Unfortunately, other parts of civil society are not well organized or are not invited to the table in the Middle East with a right to speak. Unless and until all stakeholder voices are represented at the table when water decisions are made, the politics of water diplomacy will always be less than fully democratic.

Second, is the issue of so-called back table pressure. As is the case with every other kind of diplomacy, water diplomacy often involves spokespeople who sit at the formal decision-making table, but have a back table to which they are accountable. The back table problem, as I call it (Susskind 2014), or the "two-level game," as it was named by Robert Putnam (1988), often means that the "solution space" in various problem-solving situations (that is, the zone of possible agreement given the key interests of all the parties) is even more limited than it might otherwise be. The parties at the first table (or the international table in Putnam's case) have to reach agreement, and that is hard enough. But, when each negotiator must also take account of the mandate they have been given by their second table, the negotiations are even more difficult. The back tables must concur, or whatever is agreed to at the negotiating table will be rejected later when it comes time for ratification or implementation.

Third, is the issue of time frame. The time frame that political leaders work with is usually shorter than the multigenerational time frame required for sustainable management of water and other natural resources. This means that the politics of water diplomacy often discount the needs of future generations. Even if they have proxies representing them at the table, the pressures on elected officials to focus on reelection or reappointment in the next few years always seems to take precedence over the long-term interests of future generations.

Fourth, is the issue of uncertainty. Uncertainty calls for tentative, or stepby-step rather than definitive, decision-making. When the future is uncertain, it makes sense to take provisional actions, monitor what happens and make adjustments. Political leaders, however, prefer to take definitive action so they can claim credit for having solved the problem. When some voices in political decision-making argue that more information is needed, or that smallscale experiments would be most appropriate, political actors tend to disagree. They prefer the symbolism of definitive political gestures or, at the very least, they want to look as if they are not afraid to take action.

The fifth determinant of the politics of water diplomacy is the emergence of coalitions. In multiparty negotiations, decisions are often a byproduct of the emergence of winning and blocking coalitions (Susskind and Crump 2008). Efforts to predict the outcome of political confrontations are often wrong because they overlook the possibility that less powerful parties will ally with more powerful parties, altering the relative levels of power of the parties (Fisher 1983). Coalitions emerge when parties see a chance to build alliances that will enhance their decision-making power. So, water diplomacy often yields surprising results because coalitional dynamics distort what would otherwise have happened.

The Cultural Dimensions of Water Diplomacy: A Focus on Gaza, Israel and Jordan

To understand water conflicts and what can be done to resolve them, it is necessary to look not just at the political forces at work (and the way power is exercised), but at the cultural assumptions underlying the politics of water diplomacy. The cultural dimensions of water policy making include prevailing assumptions about the (legal or moral) rights of individuals to clean water; the significance of water in sacred practices and important everyday rituals; general attitudes toward the prospect of science and technology yielding solutions to social and environmental problems; and, finally, philosophical assumptions about fairness, efficiency and the responsibilities of government.

There are long-standing religious, ethnic and cultural traditions that postulate very different answers to the question "Whose water is it?" Some religious traditions assume that water is part of the heritage of humankind and that all of us are merely custodians of the natural environment. Others operate on the assumption that humans are expected to flourish, using their hands and their minds to exploit the natural resources available to them. These two different views are diametrically opposed. Regardless of who has the political power (the hydrohegemon) (Zeitoun 2011), underlying cultural assumptions shape the way power is used.

There is growing international agreement that citizens have moral or legal (Murthy 2013). Such rights are rarely enumerated in national constitutions or national water law (although there are exceptions), but some legal scholars and political philosophers believe nonetheless that there is a natural human right to water. Cultural assumptions (even in the absence of enforceable legal requirements) are a second factor shaping the politics of water diplomacy.

Some groups see water as part of their cultural heritage (that is, water is central to both their sacred practices and the way everyday life is lived) (Susskind and Anguelovski 2008). There are many aboriginal groups (or First Peoples) whose creation stories have at their core, legends about Mother Nature and the spirit of life that resides in the water (Groenfeldt 2007). While these may not be spoken about explicitly in policy-making situations, it is reasonable to assume that they are in the back of the mind of those who exercise power in water diplomacy.

Because of long-standing engagement with and intimate knowledge of the dynamics of water systems, some groups have local environmental knowledge (LEK) that they believe should be incorporated into all scientific or technical efforts to model water systems or make predictions about water availability (Schulman 2007). To the extent that there are historical and site-specific insights into the way water resources operate in real time, arguments for stakeholder involvement in water policy making and water-management decisions take on a functional importance that is entirely separate from philosophical arguments about the importance of giving those affected by decisions a chance to participate in making them.

Some cultures are technologically optimistic, that is, they assume that technology innovation (for example, desalination) will allow them to escape whatever resource allocation constraints they may be facing (Marx and Smith 1994).[1]

---

1   Leo Marx and Merritt Roe Smith, *Does Technology Drive History?: The Dilemma of Technological Determinism*, editors Leo Marx and Merritt Roe Smith (Cambridge: MIT Press, 1994).

Others worry that each new technology innovation (genetically modified organisms, for example) carries with it inherent and unforeseen dangers (Hochschild, Crabill and Sen 2012). It is not hard to see that these assumptions are in play when the politics of water diplomacy unfold.

At the nexus of water, energy, food and land use, public and private decisions are often influenced by assumptions about the responsibilities of government and the responsibilities of the individual. Whatever the law requires with regard to the process and outcome of government decision-making or the appropriate role of government, cultural assumptions (often informed by religious beliefs) come into play in water diplomacy. Mandates to maximize efficiency (and rely more heavily on market mechanisms) are often countermanded by cultural beliefs. For example, in Islamic cultures, according to some scholars, it is forbidden to charge poor residents for water (Faruqui, Biswas and Bino 2000). Whenever Israel presses Palestine to do a better job of collecting water tariffs, the Palestinian response, in part, reflects Islamic beliefs with regard to water pricing, water tariffs, the sale of excess water and the needs of the poor. I gather it is permissible to ask people to pay their fair share for the construction and maintenance of water infrastructure, but not for public water itself. Sometimes the politics of water diplomacy supersede cultural assumptions, but in other instances political and cultural forces must be reconciled (Haddad 2005).

The Implications of Political and Cultural Considerations for the Practice of Water Diplomacy

There is an ongoing debate among scholars of water diplomacy about whether peace must precede stability or whether the opposite is true—stability must be established before peace can be negotiated (Abukhater 2013). Some analysts have reached the conclusion, and I concur, that it is not the scarcity of water that leads to conflict, but rather the way scarcity or water insecurity is addressed that causes destabilizing conflicts. Neither peace nor stability is a prerequisite for effective problem solving; rather, it is the way the parties, governments and institutions involved deal with each other, even in the face of mistrust or terrible past relationships.

Given the growing uncertainties in the world, particularly the hard-to-predict impacts of climate change, water agreements need above all to be adaptable. Adaptability was not a priority in the past. Predictions about water supply and demand were made for some point in the future, and agreements reflected substantial confidence in the accuracy of those forecasts. Institutional arrangements, or regimes, were put in place on the assumption that they would remain indefinitely. In recent years, it has become clear that not only are forecasts about supply and demand likely to be wrong but also the political entities and the "rules of the game" are likely to evolve quickly. So, those affected by water policy and water-management agreements need to pay attention to what is happening around them and make adjustments of many kinds. Someone needs to have responsibility for close monitoring of socioecological changes and reconvening the appropriate parties to modify whatever they agreed to previously. Authority to improvise and make adjustments in water allocation arrangements cannot be too centralized, or modifications will not be accepted by all the stakeholders involved. A wide range of stakeholders can participate directly in formulating agreements (even contingent elements of agreements), but it is impractical to assume that all the relevant stakeholders can play an ongoing role in making the necessary adjustments. Instead, what is needed is some form of collaborative adaptive management (CAM) (Susskind, Camacho and Schenk 2012). When uncertainty (and complexity) overwhelm the ability to predict what is going to happen, we need to put in place institutional arrangements that place a premium on improvisation and problem-solving capabilities. As these institutions respond, presuming that they do a good job, trust (and adaptive capacity) can be built over time. IWRM has never put a premium on building such institutional capacity. WDF makes it a priority.

Thus, we need to legitimize more widespread stakeholder engagement in making initial water-management and water-diplomacy decisions, and incorporating into these agreements clear provisions for collaborative adaptive management. If this is done correctly, it should lead to increased trust in the problem-solving or adaptive capacity of the institutions and water professionals involved. It may be that "neutral facilitators" need to be added to the mix (Islam and Susskind 2012). When trust has not already been established, efforts to modify earlier agreements are sometimes viewed with alarm by parties who feel that the existing agreement is serving them reasonably well. They often assume that anyone proposing modifications is trying to manipulate the situation to "get more" for themselves. The involvement of professional neutrals, who are not stakeholders, is often the way to assure all the parties that agreement modification must be the product of a consensus-building process (Susskind and Cruikshank 1989).

It may also be desirable for the parties to commit to a procedure called joint fact finding (sometimes known as mediated modeling). This is a form of joint problem solving involving collaborative efforts to collect and interpret technical data. It allows all the parties to draw on shared expert advice (Matsuura and Schenk 2016). Joint fact finding can avoid adversarial confrontations in which each side acquires its own technical adviser and uses scientific information to advance its own interests rather than as a tool for collaborative problem solving. When the parties have access to a shared database or a common set of forecasts, it is much more likely that scientific information will be taken into account when water-allocation decisions are made.

Often it helps to link water-management decisions more closely to policy making about energy, food, urban development or other development concerns. This may seem counterintuitive at first, since adding more issues to a negotiation obviously increases the complexity of the task. However, the more issues that are on the table, the easier it is to find mutually beneficial trades that create value for all sides (Susskind 2014). The best way to escape the difficulties of zero-sum bargaining is to find the nexus between water and other resource management and economic development considerations.

Instead of focusing on optimization, the way IWRM suggests, water management and water-diplomacy organizations should focus on "super-optimization" (Nagel 2001). This is an approach to collaborative decision-making that allows water negotiators to achieve more than they thought possible by altering their underlying assumptions about how much value they can create. By adding parties (that is, new voices) and engaging in joint fact finding—particularly tapping local knowledge, enriching the agenda of issues across which trades can be made, acknowledging underlying cultural concerns and agreeing to move on a contingent basis—water negotiators in countries and between countries can achieve more than they thought possible. In Gaza, none of these options is being explored effectively. In the case of the Red Sea–Dead Sea proposal, sufficient trust was built over time to allow at least some features of superoptimization to be achieved.

References

Abukhater, Ahmed. 2013. *Water as a Catalyst for Peace: Transboundary Water Management and Conflict Resolution*. New York: Routledge.Ackerman, Gwen. 2012.

Alfarra, Amani, Eric Kemp-Benedict, Heinz Hotzl, Nayif Sader and Ben Sonneveld. 2012. "Modeling Water Supply and Demand for Effective Water Management Allocation in the Jordan Valley." *Journal of Agricultural Science and Applications* 1 (1): 1–7.

Allan, Tony. 2011. *Virtual Water: Tackling the Threat to Our Planet's Most Precious Resource*. New York: I. B. Tauris.

AquaPedia. 2015. "AquaPedia Case Study Database." Accessed June 1, 2015, http://aquapedia.waterdiplomacy.org.

Chayes, Abram, and Antonia Chayes. 1991. "Compliance without Enforcement: State Behavior under Regulatory Treaties." *Negotiation Journal* 7 (3): 311–330.

Farishta, Aleena. 2014. "The Impact of Syrian Refugees on Jordan's Water Resources and Water Management Planning." Master's thesis, Columbia University.

Faruqui, Naser I., Asit K. Biswas and Murad J. Bino, eds. 2000. *Water Management in Islam*. Tokyo: United Nations University Press.

Fisher, Roger. 1983. "Negotiating Power: Getting and Using Influence." *American Behavioral Scientist* 27 (2): 149–166.

Gafny, Sarig, Saner Talozi, Banan Al Sheikh and Elizabeth Ya'ari. 2010. "Towards a Living Jordan River: An Environmental Flows Report on the Rehabilitation of the Lower Jordan River." *Friends of the Earth Middle East*. Accessed on June 1, 2015, http://foeme. org/www/?module=publications&project_id=23.

Groenfeldt, David. 2007. "Water Development and Spiritual Values in Western and Indigenous Societies." *Water-Culture Institute*. Accessed June 2, 2015, http://www. waterculture.org/uploads/Groenfeldt_-_Wate_Spirituality.pdf.

Haddad, Marwan. 2005. "Public Attitudes towards Socio-Cultural Aspects of Water Supply and Sanitation Services: Palestine as a Case Study." *Canadian Journal of Environmental Education* 10: 195–211.

Hochschild, Jennifer, Alex Crabill and Maya Sen. 2012. "Technology Optimism or Pessimism: How Trust in Science Shapes Policy Attitudes about Genomic Science." *Issues in Technology Innovation* no. 21. Accessed on June 2, 2015, http://scholar.harvard. edu/files/msen/files/hochschild_crabill_sen.pdf.

International Committee of the Red Cross (ICRC). 2014. "Gaza: Water in the Line of Fire." *ICRC Blog*. Last modified July 15, http://blogs.icrc.org/ilot/2014/07/15/gaza-water-in-the-line-of-fire/.

Islam, Shafiqul, and Lawrence Susskind. 2012. *Water Diplomacy: A Negotiated Approach to Managing Complex Water Networks*. New York: Routledge.

Israel Ministry of Foreign Affairs (IMFA). 1994. "Israel–Jordan Peace Treaty." Accessed June 1, 2015, http://mfa.gov.il/MFA/ForeignPolicy/Peace/Guide/Pages/Israel-Jordan%20Peace%20Treaty.aspx.

Josephs, Jeremy. 2013. "Green Light for Red-Dead Sea Pipeline Project." *Water World*, December 1. Accessed June 1, 2015, http://www.waterworld.com/articles/wwi/print/volume-28/issue-6/technology-case-studies/water-provision/green-light-for-red-dead-sea-pipeline-project.html.

Marx, Leo, and Merritt Roe Smith. 1994. *Does Technology Drive History?: The Dilemma of Technological Determinism*, Edited by Leo Marx and Merritt Roe Smith. Cambridge, MA: MIT Press.

Matsura, Masahiro, and Todd Schenk. 2016. *Joint Fact Finding in Urban Planning and Environmental Disputes*. New York: Routledge.

Meisen, Peter, and Jenna Tatum. 2011 "The Water-Energy Nexus in the Jordan River Basin: The Potential for Building Peace through Sustainability." *Global Energy Network Institute*. Accessed June 1, 2015, http://www.geni.org/globalenergy/research/water-energy-nexus-in-the-jordan-river-basin/the-jordan-river-basin-final-report.pdf.

Murthy, Sharmilla. 2013. "The Human Right(s) to Water and Sanitation: History, Meaning and the Controversy over Privatization." *Berkeley Journal of International Law* 31 (1): 89–148.

Nagel, Stuart S. 2001. *Handbook of Public Policy Evaluation*. Thousand Oaks, CA: SAGE.

Namrouqa, Hana. 2013. "Red-Dead Feasibility Study Complete." *Jordan Times*, December 9.

Proctor, Keith. 2014. "Water Scarcity and the Syrian Refugee Crisis." *Mercy Corps*, March 9. Accessed on June 2, 2015, https://www.mercycorps.org/articles/jordan/water-scarcity-and-syrian-refugee-crisis.

Putnam, Robert D. 1988. "Diplomacy and Domestic Politics: The Logic of Two-Level Games." *International Organization* 42 (3): 427–460.

Salman, Salman M. A., and Daniel D. Bradlow. 2006. *Regulatory Frameworks for Water Resources Management*. Washington, DC: World Bank.

Schulman, Alexis. "Bridging the Divide: Incorporating Local Ecological Knowledge into U.S. Natural Resources Management." 2007. Master's thesis, Massachusetts Institute of Technology.

Shamir, Uri. 1998. "Water Agreements between Israel and Its Neighbors: Middle Eastern Natural Environments." *Transformations of Middle Eastern Natural Environments* 103: 274–296.

Susskind, Lawrence. 2014. *Good for You, Great for Me: Finding the Trading Zone and Winning at Win-Win Negotiation.* New York: Public Affairs.

Susskind, Lawrence, Alejandro Camacho and Todd Schenk. 2012. "A Critical Assessment of Collaborative Adaptive Management in Practice." *Journal of Applied Ecology* 49 (1): 47–51, http://web.mit.edu/publicdisputes/projarea/pdf/indigenous_peoples.pdf.

Susskind, Lawrence, and Isabelle Anguelovski. 2008. "Addressing the Land Claims of Indigenous Peoples." *MIT Program on Human Rights and Justice.* Accessed June 1, 2015.

Susskind, Lawrence, and Jeffrey Cruikshank. 1989. *Breaking the Impasse: Consensual Approaches to Resolving Public Disputes.* New York: Basic Books.

Susskind, Lawrence, and Larry Crump. 2008. *Multiparty Negotiation.* Thousand Oaks, CA: SAGE.

Susskind, Lawrence, and Shafqul Islam. 2012. "Water Diplomacy: Creating Value and Building Trust in Transboundary Water Negotiations." *Science & Diplomacy* 1 (3), http://www.sciencediplomacy.org/files/water_diplomacy_science__diplomacy.pdf.

UNESCO–International Hydrological Programme (IHP), World Water Assessment Programme (WWAP) & Network of Asian River Basin Organizations (NARBO). 2009. *IWRM Guidelines at River Basin Level—Part 2-1: The Guidelines for IWRM Coordination.* Geneva: United Nations Educational, Scientific and Cultural Organization. Accessed June 2, 2015. http://unesdoc.unesco.org/images/0018/001864/186418e.pdf.

US Army Corps of Engineers. 2014. *Building Strong Collaborative Relationships for a Sustainable Water Future: Understanding Integrated Water Resources Management (IWRM).* Washington, DC: US Army Corps of Engineers, http://www.building-collaboration-for-water.org/Documents/IWRMReportJAN2014.pdf.

Wikipedia, The Free Encyclopedia. s.v. "Water Supply and Sanitation in the Palestinian Territories." Accessed June 1, 2015, http://en.wikipedia.org/wiki/Water_supply_and_sanitation_in_the_Palestinian_territories.

Zeitoun, Mark. 2011. *Power and Water in the Middle East: The Hidden Politics or the Palestinian and Israeli Water Conflict.* New York: I. B. Tauris.

CONTRIBUTORS

Albrecht, Tamee is currently a doctoral student at the University of Arizona School of Geography and Development. She received her M.S. in Hydrology from the Colorado School of Mines and worked for several years on remediation efforts for contaminated groundwater in the western United States. She has extensive experience in GIS and other types of modeling of contaminant transport. She has a particular interest in increasing the use of scientific data analyses in policymaking and water management using innovative data visualization and communication methods.

Amery, Hussein A. is associate director of the Division of Liberal Arts and International Studies at the Colorado School of Mines. Trained as a geographer, he teaches courses on water politics and management in the Middle East, especially Lebanon and Gulf Cooperation Council countries. He is coeditor, with Aaron T. Wolf, of *Water in the Middle East: A Geography of Peace*, and has published numerous articles on Islamic water management. He has also served as consultant to the United States and Canadian governments.

Cahan, Jean Axelrad is senior lecturer in philosophy and director of the Norman and Bernice Harris Center for Judaic Studies at the University of Nebraska. She has published articles on modern Jewish thought and philosophy and on religious fundamentalism. She previously coedited a volume on the environment in the history of Jewish thought and *Returning to Babel: Jewish Latin-American Experiences, Representations, and Identity*.

Forsythe, David P. is Charles J. Mach Distinguished Professor Emeritus, Department of Political Science, University of Nebraska. He is widely regarded as having helped establish the study of international human rights within the fields of political science and international relations. Editor of the award-winning *Human Rights Encyclopedia*, he has published over one hundred articles on different aspects of international human rights, American foreign policy, and international law and organizations.

Kehl, Jenny R. is Uilein Endowed Chair at the Water Institute and School of Freshwater Sciences and director of the Center for Water Policy, University of Wisconsin-Milwaukee. She specializes in international political economy and comparative development. She has worked in Africa and Asia on water resource allocation issues. Her research focuses on transboundary water systems, governmental negotiations with foreign investors in water, and water and food security.

Lenton, Roberto L. is professor of biological systems engineering and was until recently founding executive director of the University of Nebraska's Robert B. Daugherty Water for Food Institute. He specializes in water resources and sustainable development and, among other posts, has served as director of the Sustainable Energy and Environment Division of the United Nations Development Programme, director general of the International Water Management Institute in Sri Lanka and senior adviser at Columbia University's Earth Institute. He is coauthor of *Applied Water Resources Systems, coeditor of Integrated Water Resources Management* and lead author of the final report of the United Nations Millennium Project Task Force on Water and Sanitation, *Health, Dignity and Development: What Will It Take?*

Lipchin, Clive is director of the Center for Transboundary Water Management, Arava Institute for Environmental Studies, Israel. He oversees research, conferences and workshops that focus on transboundary water and environmental problems facing Israel, Jordan and Palestine. He is currently coordinating a project funded by the European Union's International Research Staff Exchange: the project brings together Middle Eastern and European researchers to study conflict and cooperation in river basin management. He is also coordinating a USAID-funded project on mitigating wastewater conflicts between Israel and Palestine. He has coedited *Integrated Water Resources Management in the Middle East* and *The Jordan River and Dead Sea Basin: Cooperation and Conflict.*

McMahon, Patrice C. is associate professor of political science, University of Nebraska. Her research specialty is the role of nonstate actors in international relations, governance and security in comparative politics, and the interactions between global norms and local realities. She is the author of *Taming Ethnic Hatred: Ethnic Cooperation and Transnational Networks in Eastern Europe* and coeditor of several volumes, including *State Responses to Human Security: At Home and Abroad.*

Susskind, Lawrence E. is Ford Professor of Urban and Environmental Planning, Massachusetts Institute of Technology, and chief knowledge officer of the Consensus Building Institute in Cambridge, Massachusetts. He helped found the Program on Negotiation at Harvard Law School, and is director of the MIT-Harvard Public Disputes Program. He has worked on land claims of First Nations in Canada, Australia, New Zealand and the United States, as well as Bedouin land claims in southern Israel. He is the author of 16 books, and coauthor of *Water Diplomacy: A Negotiated Approach to Managing Complex Water Networks*.

Tal, Alon is professor in the Mitrani Department of Desert Ecology, Jacob Blaustein Institute of Desert Research at the Ben-Gurion University-Sde Boqer. He has represented Israel at the United Nations Convention to Combat Desertification and participated in the negotiations that led to the environmental and water provisions of the Oslo Accords in 1995. He is the recipient of a lifetime achievement award from Israel's Ministry of Environmental Protection. His research focuses on water management and policy, especially joint Israeli-Palestinian projects. He is the author and coeditor of several books, including *Water Wisdom*.

Zawahri, Neda A. is associate professor of political science, Cleveland State University. She has published extensively on hydropolitics in the Middle East and South Asia. Her main areas of research interest and publication are conflict and cooperation over international rivers, design and effectiveness of river basin commissions, and impacts of treaties governing international rivers and climate change. She has been invited to speak on the Arab uprisings at Case Western Reserve University, governing Middle Eastern waters at the University of Michigan Law School and cooperation vs. conflict on the Euphrates and Tigris Rivers at Princeton University.

INDEX

www.ingramcontent.com/pod-product-compliance
Lightning Source LLC
Chambersburg PA
CBHW022355280326
41935CB00007B/196